P9-ASD-079

THIS IS BROYHILL

This Is Broyhill

The Family
The Company
The Community

Paul H. Broyhill

KELLER PUBLISHING
Marco Island, Florida

ISBN: 978-1-934002-14-8

Designed and composed in Kepler Std
at Hobblebush Books (www.hobblebush.com)

Printed in the United States of America

Published by
KELLER PUBLISHING
590 Fieldstone Dr.
Marco Island, FL 34145

KellerPublishing.com
800-631-1952

To my late wife, Faye, and to my present wife, Karen. I was first attracted to each by physical beauty but soon found such a depth of human compassion and love that our spirits have resonated beyond measure.

To my children, Caron, Claire, and Hunt, and the extraordinary grandchildren they have given me.

And finally to all the employees of Broyhill whose loyalty, dedication, and competence were critical factors in making Broyhill the great success that it became.

Acknowledgments

IT HAS LONG been my desire to write down some of my memories. It took a little push from Wade Keller at Keller Publishing, Inc. to get me started. He helped with organizing the overall project and the publishing. My thanks to Wade and his staff.

I want to thank Sheila Triplett-Brady, my administrative assistant and the director of our foundation, who transcribed the dictations and edited them. Without her expertise and encouragement I would not have persevered to the finish.

I appreciate my family for their support, my niece Ann Hsu for providing many of the family pictures, my niece Becca Elliott for her input, and my former Broyhill Furniture colleagues for taking their time to reminisce with me. I enjoyed our walk down memory lane.

SHEILA TRIPLETT-BRADY AND PAUL

PAUL WITH WADE KELLER

Contents

Part 5 Perspectives from Family Members

Part 6 Perspectives from Business Associates

Appendices

Illustrations

Preface

"THE BUILDER" IS what I want as my epitaph. I just love to design and build. I'm fairly creative, and throughout the years I spent a large portion of my time in the design aspect of the furniture business. That experience helped develop my creativity in other areas. I literally designed, with a lot of help of course, the structure of my companies, their organization, and their expansions.

During my tenure, or as military people say "on my watch," Broyhill Furniture grew until ultimately we had five case goods plants making bedroom and dining room suites; three occasional furniture plants making occasional tables, decorative pieces, and wall systems; a chair plant making dining room chairs; two frame plants making the interior wood parts for upholstery; and three upholstery plants making sofas, loveseats, and chairs. We had three veneer plants and a particleboard plant for a total of 18 plants and a trucking division. (See Appendix A, page 309.)

More than just building business, I like to think that we built people. After the end of World War II, we increased the workforce about ten-fold from roughly 750 people to 7,500 people, recognizing that an organization is only as great as its people and their loyalty to it. I enjoyed not only building the workforce, but also maximizing the talents of the individuals who comprised it. The organization grew larger and stronger every year. Today I'm proud to see so many successful people who got their start at Broyhill. Many of them are scattered throughout the industry.

Our people were dedicated, almost as if I was their general. If I said to swerve to the left or go right or charge, they would execute promptly. Of course, we failed in some things, but we succeeded in a lot more. When I made a leadership choice and it didn't work, we reevaluated and moved on. I was a good salesman, merchandiser, and a pretty good production man. Having this wide perspective made me a good executive officer.

I loved my job and stayed at it for 38 years. That kind of continuity allowed me to build the company on the foundation my dad had laid. In my day we grew from about $15 million in sales to beyond $300 million. After I left the company, the same basic organization and number of plants continued to climb to over $700 million in sales. The business mushroomed in the '90s. It would have been fun to have been there when it was doing $700 million. Maybe I sold out too early. I wish I'd had that peak experience.

Over the past ten years much of the furniture manufacturing has gone overseas. It saddens me to see that today the factories are almost all closed and many fine people have become displaced. My dad and I built and built for sixty-eight years, and it's nearly all gone.

From time to time when I've told some tales from the past, various people have suggested that I write them down so that those memories will not be lost. My standard reply was always, "I plan to do that in my old age."

While I still consider myself young, I'm finding that my recollections are rapidly disappearing, and I now need a little help from the memories of my friends. Therefore, I think it is time that I write down some of those recollections.

It is not my purpose to do this to enhance my ego, but to pass on some awareness of the family history to young people who come after me and to give some appreciation to all the people who traveled the road to success alongside me.

The Bridge Builder

by Will Allen Dromgoole

An old man, going a lone highway,
Came, at the evening, cold and gray,
To a chasm, vast, and deep, and wide,
Through which was flowing a sullen tide.

The old man crossed in the twilight dim;
The sullen stream had no fears for him;
But he turned, when safe on the other side,
And built a bridge to span the tide.

"Old man," said a fellow pilgrim, near,
"You are wasting strength with building here;
Your journey will end with the ending day;
You never again must pass this way;
You have crossed the chasm, deep and wide-
Why build you a bridge at the eventide?"

The builder lifted his old gray head:
"Good friend, in the path I have come," he said,
"There followeth after me today,
A youth, whose feet must pass this way.

This chasm, that has been naught to me,
To that fair-haired youth may a pitfall be.
He, too, must cross in the twilight dim;
Good friend, I am building the bridge for him."

Part 1

Building the Foundation

1

The Beginning of Broyhill Furniture

MY BROTHER-IN-LAW William Stevens thoroughly covered the origins of the family furniture company in his book *Anvil of Adversity*. I will give just a short review of some of the important milestones in early company history.

In 1889, the remote Caldwell County town of Lenoir, North Carolina, had a population of fewer than 500 people. The town's namesake was Revolutionary War figure General William Lenoir, an early North Carolina statesman who had lived in the area. Caldwell County's natural resources included an abundance of timberland and ambitious workers with visions for a bright future. The citizens understood that establishing local industries was critical to future advancement in the area.

In my father's family were six boys and two girls. The eldest brother, James Thomas (Tom), was a father figure to the rest of the siblings in those early days. My father, James Edgar (Ed) Broyhill, was the youngest, 18 years younger than Tom. Dad always said that the most valuable assets to a farm family were the livestock: mules, cows, pigs, chickens, and having a lot of boys to do the work.

In the early days after working the farm into the fall season, my Uncle Tom bought up timber rights on neighboring tracks of land and used the mules, his brothers, and a portable sawmill to get into the timber business. While his largest product was railroad crossties, he also cut lumber for the fledgling furniture industry in nearby towns.

North Carolina was already home to approximately six furniture

PAUL'S FATHER, JAMES EDGAR BROYHILL ON THE FARM

factories at various locations around the state. Lenoir city leaders decided that their best interests would be served by building a furniture woodworking factory in Lenoir. They founded Lenoir Furniture Corporation and named J. M. Bernhardt as president.

The young company began operations in February of 1890 but was insolvent from the beginning. At the directors' meeting in April of that year, the president authorized borrowing an additional $1,000 at 8% interest. To satisfy creditors, the board of directors executed a deed of trust for the property belonging to Lenoir Furniture Corporation in order to secure debts amounting to $5,000. G.W.F. Harper was the acting trustee.

J. L. Nelson took over as president of the floundering company from J. M. Bernhardt after a stockholders' meeting on January 8, 1891; but, the one-year-old company was unable to survive. The factory sat idle until June 1892 when G.W.F. Harper and his son George leased the Lenoir furniture factory for one year at $1,000 and made $100 in improvements. At the annual stockholders meeting in January 1893,

Harper and son offered to continue their lease until the company could be sold. The consensus was that the company would be hard to sell due to Lenoir's remote location.

There were several attempts to sell the floundering Lenoir Furniture Corporation, but to no avail. In December 1898, the local paper, The *Lenoir Topic*, advertised that the company was going up for auction. One month after the advertisement appeared, George Lynn Bernhardt successfully bid $3,600 at auction on behalf of the Harper and Bernhardt interests.

After sitting idle for another year, the factory began production in March 1900 under the new name of Harper Furniture Company. It was under the management of past employee Frank Kritz, who had headed the mechanical department, and G. F. Harper, the new business manager. For the next few years the company struggled to stay alive. During that same period several other furniture woodworking operations appeared in the area.

My uncle, Tom Broyhill, had become a successful lumber operator in North Carolina by the turn of the century. He ran two small sawmill operations and was highly respected in the community of Lenoir. Tom supplied lumber from his sawmills to the new furniture factories in the area, which eventually opened the door to his own entry into the furniture business.

In 1905 Kent Furniture and Coffin Company was short of cash. In exchange for the timber they needed, they paid Uncle Tom $1,000 in stock instead of cash, which immediately gave him four percent ownership of the company. Over a number of years Tom continued to acquire stock. By the end of 1912, he held the majority ownership and renamed the company Lenoir Furniture Company. From that period forward, the company prospered and made a nice profit, so that by the early 1920s Tom was perceived to be relatively wealthy.

Being the youngest of the children, my father looked up to my Uncle Tom. None of the boys received much education except in the one-room school that they attended a few months of the year. In August of 1913 at age 21, my father entered the seventh grade and began a four-year curriculum at Watauga Academy, now known as Appalachian State University in Boone, North Carolina. In September of 1917, after finishing the tenth grade, Dad was drafted into service for the "Great War to End All Wars." Because he came down with influenza, which was an epidemic and killed literally millions of people, he was hospitalized for a time, during which he learned to type. Because of his illness, Dad did not go overseas. He attained the rank of sergeant and served stateside until he was discharged in December of 1918.

IN SEPTEMBER 1917, PAUL'S FATHER, J. E. BROYHILL, WAS DRAFTED INTO THE GREAT WAR.

In *Anvil of Adversity* Bill Stevens chronicled Dad's homecoming:

> *... in December of 1918, Ed Broyhill took his discharge papers and boarded the train for home. He was then 26 years old. He had been a farm boy, a student and a soldier. If he were ever to accomplish something in his life, now was the time to begin. Other men had gotten ahead. He had some catching up to do.*

He did not go directly to the farm in Wilkes County, however. Instead, he got off the train in Greensboro and walked over to the campus of the North Carolina College for Women. His purpose was to pay a call on Satie Hunt, a former Boone student, who was by then attending the college. It struck the young and impressionable Miss Hunt that Ed Broyhill's coming to see her first, before going home, had a certain significance.

Dad went to work for his brother Tom in 1919 and married my mother, Satie, in 1921. His typing skills enabled him to perform basic office duties, and he also worked as a bookkeeper. However, he quickly gravitated toward sales, as he had a natural sales talent.

PAUL'S PARENTS, J. E. "ED" AND SATIE HUNT BROYHILL, WERE MARRIED IN 1921.

In 1927, after Dad had been in the furniture business for about eight years, a fire occurred at Bernhardt Furniture Company. Up to that point, Bernhardt had been supplying Uncle Tom's company with dining room chairs, as Tom's plant did not make chairs.

My dad saw this as an opportunity and decided to go into the chair business and to supply the chairs Tom needed. He formed a new company called Lenoir Chair Company. Dad had saved up a little money, he borrowed money on his house, and Uncle Tom loaned him some money. Not limiting himself to dining chairs, my father quickly expanded the business into a line of upholstered chairs as well.

THE EARLY DAYS OF THE ORIGINAL LENOIR CHAIR COMPANY

LENOIR CHAIR COMPANY

MANUFACTURERS

Overstuffed and Cane Back Palor Suits - Boudoir Chair
Occasional Chairs and Bed Room Chairs

LENOIR, N. C.

STATEMENT of ASSETTS & LIABILITIES DEC 31, 1927

ASSETTES	
Cash in Banks	$ 8.30
Buildings	15,000.00
Machinery	13,882.36
Motor Vehicles	500.00
Office Furniture	519.02
Real Estate	3,260.84
Accounts Receivable	46,187.58
J. E. Broyhill	2,972.32
Lumber & Supplies	22,849.35
	$ 105,179.77

LIABILITIES	
Capital Stock	$ 14,150.00
Bills Payable	40,042.78
Accounts "	1,642.55
Depreciation Reserve	1,636.78
Mutual B. & L. Assn.	7,087.50
Discount Accrued	4,228.82
Invoices Payable	20,585.97
Profit for Year	15,805.37
	$ 105,179.77

LENOIR CHAIR COMPANY'S ASSETS AND LIABILITIES AT THE END OF 1927

In a relatively short time Dad had accumulated approximately $100,000 in assets, but most of that was owed in debt. He made money right from the beginning, even during the tough years of the '30s. He never finished a year that was not profitable.

In the mid '30s, Dad's company and Uncle Tom's company bought a majority interest in the previously mentioned Harper Furniture Company. At that point they had three plants: Lenoir Furniture, Lenoir Chair, and Harper Furniture. The third partner in Harper was Jimmy Marshall. Eventually, Dad and Tom purchased his interest as well.

PAUL'S UNCLE THOMAS H. BROYHILL

In 1936, Dad and Uncle Tom bought a defunct bedroom case goods plant in Newton, North Carolina, about thirty miles southeast of Lenoir. (The phrase "case goods" is a furniture industry term describing furnishings that provide interior storage space or a group of non-upholstered pieces sold as sets). However, Uncle Tom did not want to start production because economic conditions were slow at that time. My dad purchased Uncle Tom's interest and started up the plant in spite of the slow conditions. Costing about $15,000, the plant was situated on nearly 25 acres and had 100,000 square feet of floor space full of equipment. It is hard to realize how low prices were in the '30s. Starting up in those days was not easy, but the plant was profitable, continued to thrive, and became very successful as the years went on. Dad gave much credit for such a successful start up to Ab Clark, his plant manager.

In 1940 my dad bought another defunct plant, this one in Conover near Newton. Less than a year later he purchased yet another non-functioning plant in Marion, North Carolina, about forty miles west of Lenoir. Dad capitalized both of those plants with credit from his and Uncle Tom's businesses.

At the time I entered the business in January 1948, those six plants located within a forty-mile radius constituted the foundation of Broyhill.

LENOIR CHAIR COMPANY CIRCA 1940

2

Early Childhood Memories

SOON AFTER WORLD War I when Mother and Dad were first married, there was no such thing as an apartment building in Lenoir, and Dad could not afford to buy a house. Therefore, he rented two upstairs rooms in a big Victorian house owned by Mr. and Mrs. Hy Covington. The home was in Lenoir on the corner of West College

ED AND SATIE'S FIRST HOME ON COLLEGE AVENUE IN LENOIR, NORTH CAROLINA

PAUL BROYHILL AS A BABY

Avenue, diagonally across the street from Lenoir High School. Many years later the Catholic Church bought that property and erected a church building there, but the original house still stands on the church property. The location was walking distance to Lenoir Furniture Company where Dad worked for Uncle Tom. My parents lived there when my sister Allene was born.

In 1923 my father bought his first home at 218 East College Avenue. Previously, the residence had been a parsonage for the First Baptist Church. All of my childhood memories go back to that house.

Most babies in Lenoir were born at home attended by a midwife because there were only a few doctors in town and no hospital nearby. However, both my sister Allene and I were born in a hospital in Lincolnton, North Carolina. Allene was born April 24, 1922, and I was born two years later on April 5, 1924. Since my dad was born on May 5, he enjoyed telling my mom that all great men were born on the 5th.

Each year on my birthday my mother told me the story about the Crowell Hospital in Lincolnton and about Doctor Crowell: how kind he was and how crisply and efficiently he ran the hospital. Later, my Uncle Tom Broyhill was instrumental in building the first hospital in Lenoir, where my younger brother, James, was born August 19, 1927, and my sister, Bettie, on March 3, 1929.

PAUL, BETTIE, ALLENE AND JIM IN 1929

Uncle Tom was also instrumental in bringing the first surgeon to Lenoir, Dr. Rudisill. I remember quite well having my tonsils taken out by him. In those days tonsillectomies were standard procedure for children. I was quite uncomfortable for several days, but I was allowed to eat all the ice cream I wanted, as it was soothing to my throat.

ALLENE AND PAUL

JIM AND BETTIE

My siblings and I were raised in a relatively modest fashion. We felt no class-consciousness and certainly did not consider ourselves wealthy or any different from the other kids. Located in the downtown area of Lenoir, our home was a large, white frame house with ample front and back porches. On the first level were the living room, dining room, and kitchen. Four bedrooms and one bath were upstairs.

One upstairs bedroom was vacant. I wanted that spare room, but for some reason, my parents kept Jim and me in the same room. From an early age I had difficulty sleeping in the same room with someone who snored. That sensitivity has lasted until this day. One night Jim accused me of trying to kill him because he woke up and I had a pillow pressed over his face. He had been snoring and I was just trying to shut him up. When he complained to my mother, she finally allowed me to move into the empty spare bedroom.

On the back porch of our house we had a double-door icebox. There was a place on either side to store the ice. With an ice pick that hung nearby, we could pick off a little bit of ice, as we needed it. On the front porch hung a white, triangular sign with designations of five, ten, or fifteen pounds to indicate to the deliveryman how many pounds of ice we wanted that day. A single horse drew the ice wagon down the street. The iceman used large tongs to pick up the desired poundage, carry it through the house to the back porch, and put it in the icebox.

A long tree trunk supported the bed of the ice truck. The tree trunk stuck out sufficiently in the rear for two kids to jump up and ride on it. We often vied with each other to see who got to ride on the back of the ice truck. Eventually, Dad bought an electric refrigerator. About the same size as the icebox, it had double doors and a circular crown-looking affair on top. It was so reliable and did such a fine job that we kept it as long as we lived in that house.

Our first heating system was coal fired. The same company that sold ice also sold coal and delivered it by a horse-drawn truck, too. When we bought a gas stove, we all were frightened a little because you first turned on the gas and then lit the stove with a match. There was a “whoof,” and all the eyelets lit up. If they didn’t light, the gas continued to escape and could be dangerous.

The radio was a central piece of life in those days. We listened regularly to several of our favorite shows, such as *The Lone Ranger* and *Amos and Andy*. After dinner Dad listened to newscasts by Lowell Thomas and, of course, Franklin Roosevelt's *Fireside Chats*.

Almost every Saturday we went to the picture show. We had two movie theatres in town: the State and the Avon. My mother would give me 25-cents, which would get me two shows at 10-cents each and a 5-cent bag of popcorn. The first picture started at one o'clock in the afternoon and the second ended around five o'clock. Of course, we walked downtown with never any thought about security or concern about safety.

In those days when you misbehaved, parents threatened to spank you. My dad had a leather razor strap, which he used to sharpen a straight razor. Though he threatened to take his razor strap to me, I do not recall his ever actually using it.

When Jim was about 10 years old, he became very sick with rheumatic fever. At that time the disease was often fatal and most people who survived were left in a permanently weakened condition. The doctors actually told my parents that there was very little hope for Jim. Doctor Caroline McNairy was a friend of the family and one of the few doctors in Lenoir. She and a new young doctor named Dr. Hedrick had heard of a new miracle sulfa drug, and they arranged to have it flown into Charlotte, the closest large city. That was the first time anyone in this area had heard of sulfa drugs. Back then, having a drug flown in was nearly a miracle in itself. The doctor administered the drug to Jim just in time to save his life. Rheumatic fever is said to weaken the heart. Though Jim was exempt from military service because of his health history, today he is in his 80s and is still going strong. He and his wife, Louise, keep a fast pace and he is a favored speaker at many public events.

For several years in high school, the two classes above me, which included Allene's class and the class below hers, would get together on the spur of the moment, usually on weekends, and have an informal party at someone's house. No invitations were necessary; everyone just passed the word. We called those get-togethers "shindigs." I was probably the only member of my class to join in, because back then, I enjoyed going with older girls. The group took up a little collection to buy records and a record player, and Jimmy Todd kept track of them. We gathered at someone's house, pushed back the furniture, rolled up the rugs, put on the music, and danced. There might have been some light refreshments, but I don't recall even a bit of drinking in those days. Certain couples were "going together," but during the dance, everyone freely cut in on one another. Girls could break-in on boys as well as boys breaking in on girls. Neither Allene nor I was very good at fast jitterbugging, so when the jitterbug dance was too

ALLENE WITH HER HUSBAND BILL STEVENS

fast, I danced with my sister. I remember those shindig occasions clearly. Everyone had a great, informal time. Through those shindigs we developed a wonderful circle of friends.

Allene had a beautiful voice. She actually was serious enough that she not only studied voice in college, but also went on to study it in New York after college. After returning from New York in December 1944, Allene married her childhood sweetheart, Bill Stevens. Bill was good-looking, made good grades in school, played first-chair clarinet

JIM WITH HIS WIFE, LOUISE

in the band, and went on to become an officer in the Navy during the war.

My brother, Jim, also was quite interested in the band and followed my example by choosing to play the flute. In addition, he became the drum major of the Lenoir High marching band, a position he enjoyed.

Bettie was the youngest, and by being the baby in the family was petted a little bit. We always felt that Jim was petted because of his sickness, and I always felt that my sister Allene was petted because she was the oldest. From my perspective that left me catching the blame in most instances, whether I deserved it or not.

Bettie played the viola in the regular band and the glockenspiel in the marching band. Both she and my sister Allene went to Converse College, which was noted for its musical training. Bettie became a proficient organist, and Allene was an outstanding vocalist.

During her senior year in college, Bettie married a local boy, Mast Dickson, and dropped out of school. Needless to say, my parents were not very happy about that. Unfortunately, that marriage was not successful and they divorced. Wanting to get away from all the memories, Bettie moved to Clearwater, Florida, more or less on her own. My dad's brother John, his wife, and their daughter, Virginia, had spent some time in Clearwater in the wintertime. Bettie was close to Virginia, so that may have been a factor in her decision to move there.

While playing the organ in a Clearwater church, Bettie met her future husband, Will Gortner. Will was a stockbroker who was personable and had a zest for life. My wife, Faye, said she loved Will because he showed the Broyhills how to spend a little money. Will and Bettie later relocated to Naples, Florida, and that is why Faye and I ended up eventually having a home in Naples. Bettie and Will had a good marriage, and they lived happily together. They were involved in many local activities. They enjoyed travel and Will sometimes organized small tour groups of close friends.

Unfortunately, Will developed Lou Gehrig's disease at almost the same time Bettie was diagnosed with cancer. They died almost simultaneously. As the youngest of the family, Bettie's early death in 2000 came as a shock to all of us.

BETTIE WITH HER HUSBAND WILL GORTNER

THE BROYHILL CLAN: FAYE AND PAUL, ALLENE AND BILL, SATIE AND J.E., WILL AND BETTIE, AND JIM AND LOUISE

3

Ed and Satie Broyhill

MY DAD WAS somewhat of a paradox. On a personal level he seemed mild mannered, but in business he was very aggressive. Back in the '30s he had to be tough at times in order to survive. I saw that tough side of Dad on various occasions in business, but never saw that side of him at home.

James Edgar Broyhill, or "Mr. J.E." as many knew him, worked hard and struggled financially in those early days. Certainly, he did not have excess money for luxuries. I remember that on Sunday mornings my dad and I would go to the post office before we went to Sunday school. We would open all the envelopes addressed to his business looking for checks. He needed those checks desperately to cover bills and expenses the next week, especially payroll.

The only significant difference that I recall between us and other families was our car. Dad bought his first Cadillac in 1932 and always drove a Cadillac after that. Dad traveled extensively and largely by car in those days. Sometimes he traded cars twice a year because he put so much mileage on them. He worked night and day and traveled upwards of a hundred thousand miles a year. He needed a good car for that kind of hard driving. By about 1938, Dad decided to get a chauffeur. He hired one of his former truck drivers named Talmadge Biddix. Talmadge drove regularly for Dad, and also drove the family from time to time.

Early on, my dad personally sold his furniture line in the nearby regions of Charlotte, Asheville, and Greenville-Spartanburg. Later, he

PAUL'S FATHER, "MR. J. E." BROYHILL

PAUL'S MOTHER, SATIE HUNT BROYHILL

You may enjoy

some of my memories

about the good old days.

I appreciate your friendship.

Paul

Paul Broyhill

paul@broyhillasset.com

branched out to Atlanta and Baltimore-Washington, and then to New York, Chicago, and New Orleans. He developed close friends in all of those regions. I have many childhood memories of taking business trips with my parents to Charlotte. My mother used the opportunity to shop, mostly at Belk's and Ivey's department stores, while Dad attended to the necessary business. During most of those trips, we ate our meals at the S & W Cafeteria.

My mother said that when she and Dad traveled before I was born, their car did not have a radio or even a heater. She recalled how cold she often felt on those trips. Once, when she was expecting me, she was so cold that she took some of Dad's fabric samples from the back seat and tucked them all around her legs and body to keep herself warm.

Dad eventually bought a car that had both a heater and a radio, which certainly made trips more enjoyable. On one particular occasion he was listening to the Grand Ole Opry broadcast from Nashville, Tennessee. The announcer kept saying that he wanted to know how far away people were receiving the signal. As Dad was going through the town of Newton, he stopped at the telegraph station. He actually sent a telegram to the radio station that read, "Receiving you loud and clear in Newton, North Carolina, signed Ed Broyhill." As he continued his trip, the announcer read his telegram over the radio and gave his name. That gave Dad and Mom quite a thrill.

I remember my mother's interactions with us as kids. She was loving but firm. Because she realized that Dad dealt with problems all day at work, she tried to have things running smoothly when he came home. After we were all in school, she kept the house, grew and arranged flowers, pursued her music interests, belonged to two or three civic clubs, and helped with church work. She didn't do much performing, but she could sit down at the piano and play fairly well. At church, Mother sang in the choir. Her interest in music certainly influenced all four children.

Mother really was quite energetic. Highly regarded by people who knew her, she enjoyed visiting the sick and taking little gifts and flowers to shut-ins. She loved being involved in public service clubs such as the Lenoir Woman's Club. My sister Allene inherited those qualities and does a great deal of public service today.

SATIE AND J. E.

Satie Broyhill: A role model for all women

The following tribute was composed and presented by Dr. Sharon Smith Pennell before the presentation earlier this month of the Satie Hunt Broyhill Lifetime Achievement Award to Dorothy Simon.

The "First Lady of Appalachian" always will be remembered as that vivacious, spirited young woman who won the heart of Mr. J.E. Broyhill.

Former ASU Chancellor John Thomas called Satie Hunt Broyhill, "The First Lady of Appalachian" and she wore that title very well. Miss Satie has meant so much to Appalachian through the years. An unusual and little known fact is that she was born the same day a charter was granted for what was then known as Appalachian Training School. She began attending Appalachian Training School when she was only 15. That is when she met Mr. J.E Broyhill, who was 22 at the time, and also attending Appalachian.

The story goes that J.E. knew Satie's father, Hartley Hunt. "Thinking to take advantage of his acquaintance with Satie's father, he introduced himself with, 'I'm Ed Broyhill. I think I have heard of you somewhere before.'"

Young Satie looked him up and down very coolly and replied, "Well, I've never heard of you."

That rather lukewarm meeting did not deter J.E. He was determined to win her heart. As one source said, "She was 15, lovely, robust, and round-faced, his ideal of a 'girlie' to be kidded, courted and captured."

One of J.E.'s instructors recalled that, "Ed got along very well as a student until he met Satie; he found her to be more interesting than Greek and Roman history."

Mr. Broyhill confirmed his instructor's observation. He said, "In my second year at Boone a little 15-year-old started to work on me. She had me so confused I didn't know what I was in school for."

He did survive his confused state and by the time he left to serve in World War I, he and Satie considered themselves a couple. The Appalachian community tells the story that Mr. Ed ultimately proposed to Miss Satie "under the pine trees that now stand in front of our Administration Building ... at least that is the story. We're not sure if it was those EXACT trees ... but that's the way the story goes, and that's the way Miss Satie remembered it."

In a 1977 interview with "Nation's Business.," J.E. Broyhill said, "... I like to kid people, and Satie is one of my kidding favorites. Whenever people ask how we met, I say I found her under a pine tree at Appalachian Training School, and she gets indignant ..."

Since that long ago courtship, Miss Satie and the Broyhill family have been very special to Appalachian State University. They have given generously to programs, scholarship initiatives and other worthy causes at the University. Miss Satie always was loyal to her alma mater, and gave so much of her time. She served on the Board of Trustees at ASU for six years, and was involved with many cultural arts and humanitarian activities. In 1983, the Satie Hunt Broyhill Music Center was dedicated in her honor, and she supported the activities of the Broyhill Hill Inn and Conference Center.

There is an extensive, display at the Broyhill Inn dedicated to Satie's memory. The display includes some wonderful photographs, including one of Satie in 1914 arriving in Boone on her horse, Maude. Those pictures tell the story of her growth from a college student to the leader in education and civic activities she became as the years passed.

The tiara she wore in 1974 when she was honorary Homecoming Queen is on display, along with other awards given to her by A.S.U.

The letter Governor Martin wrote to her when she was chosen as the very first recipient of the Appalachian Medallion, the "highest honor ASU can give to an individual for ... outstanding contributions to the University," is in the display, along with the newspaper article published when she received the first Appalachian Summer Pendant, presented to the founders and spouses of "An Appalachian Summer," a program that continues to be invaluable to ASU.

Because of her many civic and personal contributions, and because of her unceasing generosity and goodness of soul, it is most appropriate for the Caldwell County Council of Women to name its lifetime achievement award for Satie Hunt Broyhill. The women nominated for this award each year will have the honor of representing the image and character of Miss Satie. She helped to pave the way for successful women everywhere.

Miss Satie and the entire Broyhill family always have believed in giving back to the community and to education. The "First Lady of Appalachian" always will be remembered as that vivacious, spirited young woman who won the heart of Mr. J.E. Broyhill. As her daughter, Allene, said, "She was a remarkable woman, and her influence will be felt for a long time to come."

Dr. Sharon Smith Pennell is an associate professor at Appalachian State University's Department of Communication and is chairman, the Caldwell County Board of Education. The Appalachian State University Office of Public Affairs contributed information for this story.

Comments are welcome

The News-Topic invites readers to comment on editorials, columns, letters and cartoons expressed on this page. Write your comments: To the editor, News-Topic, P.O. Box 1110, Lenoir, NC 28645. Or e-mail letters to: ntnews@newstopic.net

SATIE BROYHILL: A ROLE MODEL FOR ALL WOMEN. EXCERPT FROM THE *LENOIR NEWS-TOPIC.*

On December 26, 1997, I lost a friend, Satie Hunt Broyhill. I'm sure she rode into heaven on a red carpet, not riding on a horse, or on egg crates, but on the wings of an angel...

–Helen Maynard Hunter

A reception celebrating the grand opening of the Satie Hunt Broyhill Outpatient Rehabilitation Center at Blowing Rock Hospital and Dr. Charles Davant Extended Care Facility will take place this Tuesday, the 14th of July.

This celebration and dedication will be an appropriate honor for Satie as she had always had a keen interest in the progress of the hospital and was a benefactor in many other institutions and programs as well.

I will not write about these contributions; I will write about Satie as my friend. Through the years I never lost contact with her. Even after I married and left my hometown of Lenoir, I would return for visits with her. She had logged a lot of golden memories and led me down the path of remembering happenings of my family and Lenoir landmarks. When she and Ed were married in 1921, they lived in the Covington house, next door to my home-place on West College Avenue. The Covington home was later turned into a Catholic Church. She told me she was keeping a keen eye on my mother rocking on our front porch, always with a baby in her arms. She identified with my mother then, as she was pregnant with Allene, her first child.

She told me my mother had such pretty babies. Wasn't this a fun thing to hear after all these years.

Shortly after Allene was born, they moved to what had been the Baptist parsonage at 218 East College Avenue; they simply moved from West College Avenue to East College Avenue. The other three children, Paul, James, and Bettie, were born while residing there. Later they moved to what I called, "The Big House", in East Lenoir. She chuckled when she told me of all her church friends asking why they moved so far out of town, thinking they would never get to see her!

My mother and Satie were among the charter members of the Eastern Star Chapter which her husband, J.E., started in Lenoir. Mother played the piano for the meetings and when mother couldn't attend, Satie took her place. Satie always had a deeply embedded interest in music. She loved her Mozart Music Club and often spoke of it.

Since Satie had lost most of her sight in her later years, it was difficult to communicate though letters. I've always had an affinity for recording audio tapes. I perceived the idea of putting my letters to her on tapes; this I did for m any years. I would give her all the news in which I thought she would be interested.

When I visited Lenoir from Charlotte, I would even come back home and describe to her, via tapes, all of the things I did in Lenoir and tell her of my friends and their family happenings. She was interested in the whereabouts of all these people. It gave her a way of keeping up with "the world" of Lenoir. No one was too unimportant, no story was too trivial, for her to be uninterested.

I would tell her of changes made here in Charlotte. She was familiar with many of these places as she and Ed frequently made trips here.

Her daughter, Bettie, told me of her love for Lawrence Welk music. I told Satie of an experience I had dancing with Lawrence Welk in California. I finished out her tape with some of his best recordings. She also loved the stories I recorded for her by Garrison Keillor. She remembered every little detail of these stories. She had a very sharp mind; little or big things, she remembered them all.

Another interesting thing about Satie was, she was a very witty person. Once we were discussing aerobics of this fast moving world. She said, "Ugh, I didn't need aerobics - try walking a mile over a hill and carrying back a gallon of buttermilk! I did this many times. I guess that was the aerobics of my day."

Allene was telling me of a trip they were preparing to make to the mountains. To make her comfortable, she had placed on her car seat a sponge-like pad that resembled egg crates. While riding up the mountains she made the remark: "I used to ride up the mountains on a horse and now I'm riding up on egg crates!' As I said, she was a very witty person.

A friend of mine, Liza White Plaster, was associated with Satie through the Caldwell Arts Council. I will quote her: "Mrs. Satie was benevolent, caring, compassionate, and unlimited in her generosity."

For 55 years, the Broyhill family has had an American Elm tree hovering over their home. With its forceful limbs it is very impressive. While standing under this tree. I looked up and thought how much this mighty elm was like Satie, hovering over her family with her protective arms.

On December 26, 1997, I lost a friend, Satie Hunt Broyhill. I'm sure she road into heaven on a red carpet, not riding on a horse, or on egg crates, but on the wings of an Angel.

–Helen Maynard Hunter, Charlotte, N.C.

A SPECIAL TRIBUTE TO SATIE'S LIFE FROM HELEN MAYNARD HUNTER

Of course everyone inherits family traits, and everyone is a product of the environment in which he or she grew up. My siblings and I were blessed with parents who had many admirable qualities. They held high expectations for us, and we all had a desire to emulate them. Both of our parents took seriously their responsibility to lead by example but also to remain humble and appreciative.

When I asked Dad what he felt to be the secret of success, he most often answered: *Determination*. He would say, "You have to be determined to do it. You have to be determined to do the job." Those words describe him. There was no particular brilliance other than just what I call *pushing, pushing, and pushing*. He was always pushing himself, pushing other people, and pushing the business. I think that if I inherited anything directly from him, it would be that characteristic.

The Charlotte Observer

For and about

WOMEN

Page 1 Sunday, April 21, 1963 Section F

Observer Photos by James Denning

Furniture manufacturer J. Edgar Broyhill and wife pause outside their stately Lenoir home built on a hill and surrounded by gardens.

THE *CHARLOTTE OBSERVER* ARTICLE FROM 1963

FILLED WITH LAUGHTER AND MUSIC

Broyhill Home Caters To Grandchildren

Grandmother reads to Caron (left), Claire Broyhill.

By BARBARA McADEN
Assistant Women's Editor

LENOIR — The spacious home that Mr. and Mrs. James Edgar Broyhill built 24 years ago for their children to enjoy is still filled with youthful laughter and fun.

Their 15 grandchildren romp through the expansive basement recreation area, swim in the large outdoor pool and join Mrs. Broyhill around the piano in the music room as her own children did.

"My piano has always meant a lot to me," said Mrs. Broyhill as she sat at the bleached mahogany piano in the wormy cypress paneled room.

"Music was my major. All my children are musical. My daughters (Mrs. W. E. Stevens Jr. and Mrs. Mast Dickson) play, one the organ and one the violin. My sons Paul and James T., U.S. congressman) were in the high school band.

"I could accompany them on the piano when they practiced," she recalled.

Her smallest grandchildren adore singing nursery rhymes with a perpetual "play it again" request for their grandmother.

The Broyhill sons and sons-in-law, all connected with the family furniture business, have homes in Lenoir, so there are frequent visits from the grandchildren.

★ ★ ★

THE BASEMENT recreation area is always the site for a holiday family gathering. "There are 25 of us when the family gets together," Mrs. Broyhill said.

A massive pine-paneled den has a large fireplace, two Broyhill-made Early American loveseats upholstered in a red provincial print, tall cane bottom chairs and a harvest table. The family Christmas tree is put up in the room.

"This has never been a decorative place. It's a place for our children, grandchildren and their friends. My little grandchildren have had their Sunday school class parties here."

Next to the den is a kitchenette and a larger room where one granddaughter teaches ballet to her friends.

"Our own children used this area for their friends. When Lenoir didn't have a woman's club, groups sometimes met here. We could have 40 women in for a buffet," Mrs. Broyhill recalled.

The outdoor swimming pool was built at the same time the large house was constructed, The pool is heated in spring and early fall and is framed by dogwoods.

More dogwoods add a landscaped look around the house. "The dogwoods are natural. People think we planted them where they are, but we didn't," Mrs. Broyhill said.

"We live in Blowing Rock in the summer, and we hire a lifeguard for the pool so that our grandchildren can use it while we're away," Mrs. Broyhill said.

"I have a lot of memories of people who've visited us and been around that pool . . . Sen. Bob Taft . . . Sen. Kenneth Waring . . . " mused Mr. Broyhill, who's been national Republican committeeman from North Carolina for about 16 years.

★ ★ ★

LOCATED on a hill facing Hibriten Mountain and surrounded by well-cultivated gardens, the stately Broyhill house has classic, high columns. Mr. Broyhill's own putting green, located at the side of the house, helps keep his golf strokes in practice.

An elevator, installed when the house was built, whisks passengers quickly from the basement to the main floor and the upstairs bedrooms.

Most of the furniture is traditional and was selected before the Broyhill furniture firms expanded production of upholstered furniture. The family's home in Blowing Rock is furnished predominately with Broyhill furniture.

★ ★ ★

YELLOW, one of Mrs. Broyhill's favorite colors, appears often in the house. A sunny sitting room off the master bedroom is decorated in yellow. The room overlooks the swimming pool, and Mrs. Broyhill recalled with a smile, "I did a lot of chaperoning while I sat there."

The dining room has yellow walls handpainted with spring flowers in an Oriental mood by a Baltimore artist. Green brocade draperies lined with Chinese red fabric are used with an attractive inlaid Chippendale hunt board and dining furniture.

Figurines in Meissen and other fine china, ones that Mrs. Broyhill has collected in trips abroad, are used throughout the house. She also has decorative trays from Mexico and South American countries.

Most of the items she's collected are functional as well as attractive. "I believe in puttting to use whatever I have," said the genial grandmother.

AN ARTICLE FROM THE *LENOIR NEWS TOPIC* ABOUT THE BROYHILL FAMILY HOME. THE HOUSE IN THE BACKGROUND IS THE HOUSE I LIVED IN FROM AGE SIX TO 20 WHEN I JOINED THE SERVICE.

History of the Broyhill House

by Allene B. Heilman

Construction of the Broyhill home began in 1939. The pool was completed first and was in use during the summer of 1940 but the house was not finished until December of that year. The architect was Clarence Coffey of Lenoir, the landscape architect was Aiji Tashiro of Hickory and the builder, Herman Sipe Company of Conover. The interior designer was the H. Chambers Company of Baltimore.

During the ensuing war years the Broyhills allowed the pool to be used by the Lenoir Recreation Department, which provided lifeguards and supervision for young people during the summers. Later, after public pools were available in the city, the pool was made available to office employees of Broyhill Industries and their families. When she was in her 90s, Mrs. Broyhill would often recount that she rarely went to the grocery store that someone didn't stop her and say, "I learned to swim in your swimming pool."

Since the house was the home of four lively teenagers, it soon became a popular gathering spot for young people. There are many people in Lenoir today who can still recall picnics, Cora's cookies, and dancing to the records of Glen Miller and Tommy Dorsey.

The house has also extended hospitality to many distinguished adults including former President Gerald Ford and presidential candidates Robert Taft, Harold Stassen, Thomas Dewey and Robert Dole. North Carolina governors who were entertained here include Gov. James E. Holshouser, Jr., Gov. James Martin and Gov. James Hunt.

Through the years the house has welcomed many different groups-garden clubs, music clubs, church groups, political rallies, family reunions, Arts Council affairs, wedding and funeral get-togethers, birthdays and the list goes on. One of the musical highlights of the house's history was a recital given here by Dorothy Kirsten, star of the Metropolitan Opera.

Continuing in the tradition established by the Broyhills so many years ago, their home is still being used today for the enrichment of the community and the people they loved.

4

Grandparents

ON MOST SUNDAYS after church, the family piled into one car and went to my father's parents' house for Sunday dinner. Grandpa and Grandma Broyhill lived in Boomer, a township between Lenoir and Wilkesboro, about 18 miles away. They had a large farm and had raised six boys and two girls to help with the work. Grandpa Broyhill's home had several outhouses: a well house, an icehouse, a chicken house, and a barn. We children delighted in playing around the farm on a Sunday afternoon while our parents and grandparents visited with various family members who popped in.

THE BROYHILL HOMESTEAD IN BOOMER, NC

J.E.'S PARENTS, MARGARET AND ISAAC BROYHILL

Grandpa Broyhill was a rather frail man, and by the time I was around him he did little farm work, but he certainly had other things to do. He had a small grain mill on a creek not far from his house. After harvest he would spend much of his time grinding the corn from neighboring farms, as well as from his own land. In a little cup he measured a certain amount of grain that he kept as payment for the milling. He also had a group of beehives. Grandpa specialized in sourwood honey. Sourwood is a local tree with a very white bloom. According to our family, honey from the sourwood tree tastes the best of any kind.

GRANDPA BROYHILL GATHERING SOME OF HIS FAMOUS SOURWOOD HONEY FROM HIS BEE HIVE

After visiting at Grandma and Grandpa Broyhill's for a while, we would ride about fifteen miles to Grandin where my mother's family lived. That was one of my favorite destinations. My Grandpa Hunt was sent down to Western North Carolina from Pennsylvania in 1913 by W. J. Grandin to help purchase and supervise a large lumber operation. In that era, Grandin was on its way to becoming a boomtown as a railroad connected it to Wilkesboro and was projected to go on to Boone.

Unfortunately, two heavy floods came along close together in 1916 and in 1918. The water washed away the railroad so thoroughly that it could not be rebuilt. Because of the destruction caused by the flood, Mr. Grandin closed down the entire lumber operation and retained Grandpa Hunt to liquidate the property and the land, which consisted of more than 60,000 acres. Grandpa Hunt stayed in the area to supervise the land for the rest of his life. He worked to sell off bits and pieces over the years, and by the time of his death, he had managed to sell all of it. Interestingly, the land Grandpa Hunt originally sold for a few dollars an acre has "been discovered" as scenic home sites. Today developers spend thousands of dollars an acre to get a piece of it.

GRANDPA HARTLEY HUNT WITH DORIS, SATIE, ALICE AND GRANDMA NELLIE

The REA (Rural Electrification Administration) in 1935 was one of the best programs to come out of the Roosevelt New Deal as it helped tremendously in the late '30s and early '40s to bring electricity throughout the area. When I was a boy, I can remember many times spending the night at Grandpa and Grandma Hunt's house. They had installed toilets and running water but still had no electric lights. It was quite an experience to eat and go to bed by lamplight.

5

My Tom Sawyer Days

I WENT TO school in Lenoir from 1930 to 1941 during the depths of the Depression years. Lenoir was not a wealthy city, but our schools were good. Our teachers were capable, and the students were attentive. Everyone obeyed the teacher, though we may have cut up a little bit when the teacher was out of the room. Throwing blackboard erasers was a serious offense. If a person had to be severely punished, he was sent to the principal's office for a stern lecture, and that usually did the trick.

For the first six years of school my siblings, the neighborhood kids, and I attended East Harper School on East Harper Avenue. It was only about a half to three-quarters of a mile from our home, and nearly all the kids walked to and from school. We actually made four one-way trips each day because we went home for lunch. Each grade had two classes with about twenty children in each class.

I still can recall the names of several of my elementary schoolteachers. First grade, Mrs. Tuttle; second grade, Mrs. Howard; third grade, Mrs. Marley; fourth grade, Mrs. Gaston; and in fifth grade, Mrs. Grimes. Every one of those teachers thoroughly taught the basics of their subjects, and I received an excellent foundation at East Harper School. I had an equally good experience with my teachers at Lenoir High School.

Back then the boys all dressed similarly. Typically, we wore corduroy knickers and three-quarter-length boots. On the side of one boot was a little pocket to hold a small knife.

PAUL AS A YOUNG SCHOOL BOY

In the mornings, everyone filed out to the playground for a fifteen-minute recess. Some people headed straight to the swings. The girls often played hopscotch, jump rope, and crack the whip, where several people would hang on in a fast moving, serpentine line. The person at the end of the line would end up getting "cracked."

Because time was short we boys couldn't really organize a baseball game, so we tossed a ball back and forth. We carried marbles in our pockets for an impromptu, competitive game. We would draw a circle on the ground, and each boy would place one marble inside it. The object of the game was to hit the center marbles with a shooter. You won the marbles you knocked out of the ring, as long as your shooter stayed inside the circle. We played marbles "for keeps," which meant that each of us could win the other guy's marbles or lose our own.

After finishing the sixth grade at East Harper School, I went to the seventh grade, which was located at the Lenoir High School building. I joined the junior band and played the flute. I particularly remember seventh grade graduation because seventh grade was a passing from grammar school to high school. Back in those days, high school was eighth grade through eleventh with no twelfth grade, so graduation was a big deal.

One of the greatest events of the school year was the celebration of May Day. We had a maypole and a Queen of the May. All the girls dressed like little princesses and danced around the maypole. The boys wore white shirts and white pants, and we hung back shyly from dancing. My sister Allene was the May Queen one year.

My list of "wants" started when I was a young boy. As we go through life, our desire for various "things" starts in a small way and never seems to end. It seems that we, men particularly, always want more toys. My first "want" was roller skates. Back in those days, all the young boys became proficient on roller skates. As we got a little older, we played roller skate hockey. We used a tin can as the puck and a sawed-off broomstick to swat it. Hibriten Street, above our house, was a lightly traveled road, and we played hockey there. The people in the area knew to drive slowly past our games to keep from hitting any players.

I considered myself an expert roller skater and ice skater and thought those were skills I would never forget. That idea changed one day many years later when I took my kids to a roller skating rink in Boone. I thought I could show them how well I could skate. I put on the skates and tore forth onto the floor, immediately and ungracefully falling on my bottom. Needless to say, that was quite an embarrassing incident. I hurt my pride as much as my bottom.

After roller skates I wanted an electric train. One Christmas I received a Lionel train with tracks and all the accessories. I was thrilled. However, even that fascination lasted only a limited time. Then I had a new idea; quite an unusual one, I might add. As a matter

Girls 1 Died age 2. - Victoria

Mary. old maid

Myrtle marr[illegible] William McColery

John was Tom.

Brother to Ed

Tom B — 1 — 6 - Ed -

Gordan. 2 -

John 3 -

Will 4.

Jeff 5

of fact, this next "want" I almost hesitate to mention, because I doubt if many people had a similar childhood desire. Roller skates and trains are common, but this one was a little different.

I wanted a little cart and a billy goat to pull it. Somewhere along the way, I actually got that billy goat and cart. I built a little house for the goat in the rear of our property. I harnessed the goat to the cart and would drive up and down the street. I had lots of fun and thought I was pretty hot stuff. However, the fun didn't last long. My sister Bettie always tried to love on the goat. One day she hugged the goat around the neck, which the goat didn't particularly like, and it proceeded to butt her. She fell down and was hurt just a bit. When my dad heard about the incident, he promptly got rid of the goat. We had dogs, cats, and even rabbits, but no more billy goat.

Next door to our home was a wooded area that seemed large at the time. Several boys lived at the other end of the woods. We called them the "Robbins Gang." Our nearest neighbor on our side of the woods was Reverend Lackey, and our closest friends were his sons, Boston and Bob Lackey. "Our Gang" consisted of about a half-dozen boys that included the Lackeys and me. We were constantly plotting against the Robbins boys. I don't remember any actual altercations or fisticuffs, but we had a few rubber gunfights. A rubber gun was a homemade device with a rubber band or garter attached to the front of a clothespin and hooked in the back. When the shooter released the clothespin, the rubber band would fly off the front of the gun. The projectile would travel for a few feet (depending on how tightly it had been pulled) and strike the target. But as we got older, we all had cap pistols in holsters on our hips. We preferred them because when we shot at each other, they were loud and smelled like sulfur.

When I got a little older, I wanted to build a tree house. That was my first experience in building, and I have loved to build ever since. My dad sent over lumber from the factory lumberyard, and my friends and I nailed 2x4 boards to four trees that were in proximity to one another. Then we added a floor, overlapping boards on the sides to support the walls, and a slanted roof, which we covered with a little bit of tin. It became the location where the boys gathered and held our secret meetings. Sometimes the girls would come up and have tea parties.

My most memorable experience occurred one day as I was climbing the ladder. My sister Allene and her friends were having a tea party and she didn't want me to interfere. Therefore, as I neared the top, Allene threw the ladder to the side. I fell to the ground and broke my arm. I was rushed to the hospital.

My mother and dad had been in Charlotte that day. When they came home that night and saw me lying on the sofa with my arm in a sling, they asked excitedly, "What happened? What happened?" Cora, our maid, replied, "Nothin' happened 'cept Miss Allene threw Mister Paul out' the tree house and broke his arm."

Allene always hates to hear me tell that story.

I also recall that we dug quite an extensive cave. I look back and cannot imagine that our parents allowed us to dig such a cave considering the potential danger of a cave-in. However, we had it braced with wood and worked diligently digging into a bank. We lit the cave with candles. As you might expect, we would come home covered with dirt and soot following another adventurous day.

When I was nine I really wanted a bicycle; however, my dream didn't come true quickly or automatically. Then in 1933, my dad decided to take the entire family along with his unmarried sister, Mary, to the Chicago furniture market in July. That year the market dates coincided with the Chicago World's Fair. My dad had purchased his first Cadillac the year before, so all seven of us piled into that big car for the trip. That time we stayed at the Seneca Hotel, though later Dad always stayed at the Drake. While I attended the fair and have vague memories of it, my primary memory is of working in Dad's Chicago showroom.

There was no air conditioning, just large fans, and July in Chicago can be quite hot. Smoking was a widespread habit and walking into our showroom was like walking into a sweltering fog. While the rest of the family enjoyed the fair, Dad expected me to clean up all the ashtrays and debris from the heavy smoking. He also had me pick up and restore order to the numerous fabric samples, which were often left lying around in disarray.

At the end of the market, to reward me for my work, Dad took me upstairs to a showroom full of bicycles. I picked out a beautiful blue model and we took it down to our showroom space. One of our Broyhill trucks picked it up and took it home for me.

It wasn't long before my neighbor Boston Lackey and I got into a bit of trouble. It happened one Saturday when were riding our bicycles down the road towards Hickory, a town about 15 miles south of Lenoir. On a whim we decided to go all the way to Hickory for lunch. I had a small amount of money in my pocket, enough to buy each of us a sandwich at the drugstore. Without a care in the world, we rode to Hickory, ate lunch, then turned around and came back.

We reached Lenoir in late afternoon. As we approached home, we noticed quite a few people yelling at us from the sidewalk. Until we arrived at my house, we really did not understand the commotion. We learned that my Dad had become very worried, had called the police, and literally had put out a search for us. That happened only a year after the 1932 Lindbergh kidnapping, and I was only nine years old. Our families were so glad to see us that we were not punished immediately. However, my dad quietly said that the bicycle had to go into the attic for a period of sixty days. I remember going into the attic, rubbing the bicycle with a cloth, and longing for the sixty days to end. In retrospect, that was a very wise punishment. During those sixty days I had to deal with delayed gratification and plan for a future reward.

My first memory of going away from home alone was when I was ten years old. For many years a fine girls' camp called Yonahlosse was located on Shull's Mill Road near the resort town of Blowing Rock. Allene went there two summers for an eight-week stay each time. They also held a four-week camp for boys. I attended that camp twice during the summers when I was ten and eleven. At the camp, a dam created a small lake. I still recall swimming in the cold water. They also offered canoeing, riflery, horseback riding, and archery. I remember a little bit of hazing; some of the boys sent me from place to place to ask for some striped paint and a left-handed screwdriver.

It was at camp that I developed my love of horses. Each year at the well-known Blowing Rock horse show, the camp put on an exhibition and even at that young age, I rode in it. Naturally, the next "want" on my list was a horse. I really enjoyed getting some training on horses at Yonahlosse and having the opportunity to ride from time to time. I recall going to Blowing Rock, renting a horse at the Blowing Rock stables, and riding through the Moses Cone Estate Park.

The summer I was 12 years old I went to a camp in the mountains of Georgia on Lake Burton. On the way to camp my father took me to Atlanta to visit the Havertys of Haverty Furniture. We were a little early for camp, so Dad left me in Atlanta with Mr. Witherspoon, Haverty's general merchandise manager. At that time I got to know for the first time Rawson Haverty and his father, Clarence. After my visit with them, I took a bus from Atlanta to the camp.

At Camp Burton I won a horseshoe pitching contest, so when my dad came to visit at a midpoint during my camp stay, I asked him if he knew how to play horseshoes. We went out and played a bit, and my dad beat me. He later apologized and said that he should not have beaten me, but that he had played a lot of horseshoes when he was a boy.

PAUL, 12, WITH HIS FATHER AT CAMP BURTON

When I was about 14, my dad allowed me to buy a horse on the condition that I look after and feed it. I dubbed my horse "Chief" and kept him in a barn behind the house of a neighbor, Milton Shearer. Shearer was an elderly gentleman, but he was agile for his age. He was Justice of the Peace, and he walked back and forth to his office uptown at the courthouse. He never owned a car. I remember from time to time young people coming to his house at night or on the weekends to get married. We children would watch and sometimes even sing a little song for them. Mr. Shearer's granddaughter was Elizabeth Blair from Thomasville, one of Allene's best friends through the years.

PAUL AND HIS HORSE, CHIEF

With the help from some men at our plants, we refurbished Mr. Shearer's barn, built a fence, and made a pasture for the horse to run. Every morning I had to feed the horse before I fed myself. In the afternoons I had to clean the horse. A horse is like a lot of things: the time it takes to maintain it is a lot more than the time spent using it. I did not belong to a horse club or horse association, but it was nice that I had a way to get out of town, primarily on dirt roads, to ride alone through the countryside.

PAUL'S GRANDFATHER HARTLEY HUNT

My favorite destination in the summer was my Grandpa Hunt's house in Grandin, about 15 miles away. People waved as I went by; everyone was friendly. Some people invited me in for a drink of lemonade or a cookie. I am not sure that today we would let a young boy go riding alone, but back in those days there was less concern about security.

I was 13 when I attended Camp Mount Mitchell in Western North Carolina close to Burnsville, not far from Asheville. There was a nine-hole golf course nearby. I'm not sure when I started playing golf, but I know that I was playing by then. I recall my first set of clubs.

My dad had a salesman in New York by the name of Billy Sussman. Oftentimes, the salesmen made as much or more money than the owners, and Sussman was considered to be a high-powered type. He and Dad played quite a bit of golf together.

One day while golfing, Billy had Dad three holes down with four to go. Dad told Billy that he was going to beat him on all four holes. Billy in his cockiness said, "Mr. J. E., if you do that, I'm going to give up golf, and give Paul my clubs." Dad proceeded to beat him the four holes. That night Dad walked into our living room and presented Billy's bag and clubs to me. I think that was my first set of clubs. As you might expect, Billy bought another set of clubs. He came to me rather sheepishly, asking if I would mind giving back his favorite putter, which, of course, I did.

Originally, my dad wouldn't gamble; eventually, instead of playing for the customary dollar, he began to play for golf balls. Somehow, he didn't think that was the same as playing for money. Dad had a small closet in his office and when World War II started he had won enough golf balls to fill up a large part of that closet. Due to the war effort and rationing, they no longer made golf balls out of real rubber, and the "new" ones weren't nearly as good. Dad, however, had his stash and always played with pre-war balls. He occasionally gave a sleeve of those balls as a gift. Any golfer considered it a real privilege to play with those pre-war golf balls.

6

High School

MY ENTIRE FAMILY was musical. My mother sang and played the piano. I played flute in the band and was serious about it from the seventh through eleventh grades. My brother Jim also played the flute and was the drum major of the band. Allene was a vocalist, and Bettie played the organ.

For a short while I took piano lessons, but I never was able to get good enough to maintain my interest. I also took voice lessons for a couple of years and sang in the high school glee club and the church choir. One year I sang baritone in the state music contest where I received a "one" rating. However, it was the band instruments that I started with in the seventh grade that I really enjoyed. The school system furnished instruments to most of the kids. When I took up the flute and piccolo, I very quickly became so absorbed that I wanted my own.

My dad bought me a silver Haynes flute, which was one of the best at the time. I started playing in the junior band in the seventh grade and practiced sufficiently that I was promoted to the senior band by the end of the year. In 1938, my eighth grade year, a new band building was constructed and opened. There was literally nothing like it in public schools anywhere in the country. The building consisted of practice rooms, a rehearsal hall, and various offices. It was a great facility for Lenoir.

Boston Lackey, my close friend and neighbor on our side of the woods, was first chair flutist that year and I was second chair. When he graduated, I moved to first chair and retained my seating for the next three years, grades nine through eleven.

PAUL PLAYED THE PICCOLO AND WAS THE TOP FLUTIST IN THE LENOIR HIGH SCHOOL BAND.

The Lenoir High School Band became quite famous. James Harper, an ex-World War I infantry captain, had inherited a considerable amount of money. He was of the same family who had sold us the Harper plant. He devoted his life and some of his fortune to building up the high school band to be one of the finest in the entire country. Perhaps, he may have wanted to emulate John Philip Sousa.

As a former captain in the Great War, Harper had a militaristic approach and established a strict regimen. He expected us to practice individually and in sectionals every day and to practice twice a week with the entire band. During the fall season, we had marching drill for an hour starting at 7:30 in the morning, before school started at 8:30. Despite the rigorous expectations, Captain Harper had such charisma that he inspired us to become a proficient marching band as well as an outstanding concert band that was recognized far and wide.

I played piccolo in the marching band and flute in the concert band. We went to state and national contests each year and performed both as a band and as individuals. All that practice paid off. Our band always walked away with first place top honors.

For five years I practiced three hours a day on the flute: one hour on slow tones, which built muscles in my lips, one hour on technique by playing scales, and one hour on music. In addition, I went to music summer camp for two years.

Captain Harper did not approve of any activity that competed with our music, but I insisted on taking time occasionally for my love of horses. For three years, I was one of the best flute players both statewide and nationally. I was almost as good as a professional flutist, and I received first place honors for three consecutive years.

Our band made a number of trips during the season, going to college ball games, other events, and to the state contest. The band had two large trailer-type band buses and a truck to haul the instruments. I particularly remember the 1940 New York World's Fair trip and the West Palm Beach trip.

In New York we stayed out on Staten Island, such a distance from the fair that we had to take a ferry from Staten Island to Wall Street and then catch buses from there to the fairgrounds. Built on a grander scale than anything of its kind before it, the fair inspired Walt Disney to build Disneyland. Standing prominently were an architectural spire (the Trylon) and beside it a round ball (the Perisphere). Both structures were white to contrast with the frenzy of color of the rest of the exhibits and buildings. "The Iconology of Hope," as they were called, together symbolized the theme of the fair: "Today in Preparation for Tomorrow."

While the World's Fair made quite an impression on me, so did my outing with Jean Phillips Carpenter. One night during that trip I took her all the way to Bronx, New York, where we listened to Cab Calloway and his orchestra.

When our band took the trip to West Palm Beach, I had just turned 16 and had my driver's license. Mother agreed to let me drive her new 1939 LaSalle and take some of my friends. I had heard about the speedway at Daytona Beach and how the Daytona races had begun with cars racing on the beach. So, as we approached Daytona, I thought it would be a fun idea to take the LaSalle down on the beach and go for a little run. Unfortunately, the tide was rising and the car sank in the sand. In my mind's eye, I could visualize my mother's new LaSalle covered with salt water. My friends and I were desperate.

Some old beachcombers came along and for five dollars offered to get us out of the sand. I quickly and gratefully gave them the money. All they did was to leak nearly all the air out of the tires. Because of the deflated tires, we were able to drive off the beach, go to the nearest filling station, and refill the air. We were a little poorer, but a little wiser.

Mr. Harper did his best to discourage the band members from going out for football, but I wanted to give it a try just for the experience. In spite of his objections, I went out for the team. I had never been a good athlete, and this attempt was no exception. I played second-string tackle, and for practice we scrimmaged against the first team. My job was to lower my head and charge at the opposing tackle. In those scrimmages the first-string tackle was Clark Pennell, who was much larger and much stronger than I. He easily could have pushed me aside with the brush of one hand. Had he been so inclined, he could have pounded me into the ground. However, Clark went out of his way to teach me and to look after me, never deliberately hurting me in any way. I have remembered him for that kindness for the rest of my life. Some of the other members of the team that year were George Reighard, U. D. Pitts, Bruce Chester, and Eddie Cruz.

The summer I was 14, I went to music camp on the campus of the University of North Carolina at Chapel Hill. At the same time my sister Allene was there attending a drama camp. That provided me an opportunity to get acquainted with Chapel Hill, where I ultimately graduated. The following summer I attended a music camp at Davidson College that was organized and led by James Christian Pfohl. Later, Pfohl moved the summer music program to Brevard College in the mountains of North Carolina. It still exists today. The Broyhill Foundation has supported it through the years, funding numerous scholarships.

At the Davidson music camp I managed to get into a little trouble along with my close friend Jim MacGill. Jim talked me into climbing out the window one night and going into town. We did nothing at all, other than flirt with some girls and drink some beer, but the escapade came to light. Dr. Pfohl reprimanded and threatened us with dismissal, so we learned our lesson.

During that summer, I progressed well at playing the flute. In spite of my previous escapade, and likely because of my proficiency, I developed a good reputation with Dr. Pfohl. That was to my advantage when a small band from Lancaster, South Carolina, under the direction of one of Dr. Pfohl's friends, was invited to Pueblo, Colorado. The band was asked to participate in the town's centennial celebration. His friend asked Dr. Pfohl to choose three experienced players from the summer camp to reinforce his band. He "borrowed" a trumpet player, an oboe/bassoon player, and me, a flute and piccolo player. We were obviously considered somewhat superior to the other musicians in the band, so it was easy for me to become quite popular with a couple of the girls. The band director even let me assist a little with directing. The train trip was long, the seats were hard, and there were no berths, so I had ample time to flirt with the girls. Recently, I met someone who said he had lived for a time in Pueblo, and I boasted that I had the distinction of having marched down the main street of Pueblo for their 100th anniversary in 1938.

7

Baptist Heritage

I WAS BORN and raised a Southern Baptist. Customarily, my family attended four Sunday services at the First Baptist Church of Lenoir: Sunday school, morning worship, BYPU (Baptist Young People's Union), and evening worship. We returned to church during the week for various activities, including a mid-week Bible study on Wednesdays. About once a year our church held a revival event led by a visiting minister. That meant church every night for a week. Some of those long-winded revival preachers kept on preaching and singing until they could entice several people to walk down the aisle to the altar and either join the church or ask for prayer.

LENOIR FIRST BAPTIST CHURCH

Our church struggled financially. At least once a year there would be "Pledge Sunday." We still have an annual Pledge Sunday, but in those days Pledge Sundays were like this: ushers shut the doors of the church and placed a blackboard at the front of the sanctuary so that our pastor, the Reverend Richard Hardaway, could record pledges on it as alternately each member stood at his seat to state his pledge amount. Uncle Tom, who was the wealthiest man in our congregation, typically started off. Tom would make his pledge, then my dad would follow. After Tom and Dad, the procedure progressed with decreasing amounts to the most common pledge of a dollar a week. However, some people could not afford even that much, and they pledged ten to twenty-five dollars per year.

As you might imagine, over time this practice made Reverend Hardaway open to criticism and it created division in the church. When I was about 15 years old, there was a faction that supported our minister, and a smaller faction that was against him. A rift like I have seen many times since occurred at our church. A congregational contention demanded a vote as to whether or not to retain the minister. While the vote was very much in his favor, the conflict took such an emotional toll on the minister that he moved on to another church soon after that.

Because I have witnessed such contention, I am appalled at church people who end up in controversy. All we have to do is to look at history and to see examples of how people, such as the Crusaders of the Middle Ages, have killed others over religious differences and of how people still are killing each other in some parts of the world. To me such misguidance seems ridiculous, but some people feel as if they receive their orders directly from God and that anyone who disagrees with them disagrees with God.

When I was a young adult, I taught Sunday school for quite a number of years. At one time I instructed high school boys, and then I taught a group of older men. I helped to organize a "young marrieds" class and led it for a number of years. Though the members aged, for quite a while it was still dubbed, the "young marrieds."

I think that teaching Sunday school helped me, not only from the standpoint of defining my personal moral and religious philosophy, but also from a practical standpoint. Teaching Sunday school helped me become comfortable with public speaking, and that skill was invaluable in the business world.

At Lenoir First Baptist I was chairman of the Board of Deacons for two terms. I served on two building committees and on two pulpit committees that were responsible for the hiring of a new minister. Unfortunately, I also was involved in the firing of two preachers. I hold the position of Life Deacon there. I have served on boards at other Baptist institutions including Wake Forest University, Baptist Children's Home, and Gardner-Webb University. In 1996 the Baptist Foundation honored me as Philanthropist of the Year.

These days I am quite ecumenical. In Naples, my wife and I attend Naples United Church of Christ; in Charlotte, Meyers Park Methodist; in Lenoir, First Baptist; and in Linville, Wee Kirk Presbyterian. I'm hoping one of those denominations will let me in when I get to the pearly gates.

High Point Enterprise, Wednesday, May 15, 1996

Broyhill, Whitaker win awards from Baptists

FROM STAFF REPORTS

Awards were presented Tuesday to two Baptists, one described as an actor, the other as a gourmet cook.

When Michael Blackwell presented the philanthropist of the year award to Paul H. Broyhill, he called Broyhill "an actor - I don't mean a Hollywood-type movie star, I mean a man who acts. Paul Broyhill is a man of action."

High Point

Blackwell is president of Baptist Children's Homes of North Carolina Inc.

Broyhill, former chairman of the board of Broyhill Furniture Industries, was honored by the North Carolina Association of Baptist Development officers. Cited were the millions of dollars that Broyhill and his family have made in Baptist causes in "just the past five years" to Baptist Children's Homes, Baptists Committee, Baptist Theological Seminary in Richmond, Bowman Gray School of Medicine, Brenner Children's Hospital, Friends of Missions, Gardner-Webb University, Hawaii Baptist Academy, Mars Hill College, Meredith College, N.C. Baptist Foundation, N.C. Baptist Pastoral Care Foundation, Wake Forest University, Wingate University and Woman's Missionary Union.

Blackwell also described Broyhill as "friend, mentor, investor, fellow churchman and Baptist philanthropist of the year."

Evans P. Whitaker, vice president of development at Wingate University, was recognized as fund-raiser of the year. Edwin S. Coates, executive director of North Carolina Baptist Foundation, called Whitaker "a gourmet cook, a connoisseur of North Carolina barbecue - the Cleveland County variety - and a quality manager of people."

This is the fifth year that the awards have been presented.

Paul Broyhill

■ **Born:** 1924, Lincolnton.
■ **Family:** Wife, Faye Arnold Broyhill; children, Caron Broyhill Wilson (High Point), Claire Broyhill Davis, Hunt Broyhill.
■ **Interests:** Chairman, The BMC Fund Inc., Broyhill Investments Inc.; Broyhill Realty Inc., Broyhill Nurseries and the Broyhill Family Foundation Inc.
■ **Education:** University of North Carolina at Chapel Hill.
■ **Career:** Worked odd jobs in father's plant, then started with Broyhill Furniture Industries in sales, took charge of product development, styling and pricing the line, scheduling production, organizing and developing a strong sales force; became Broyhill president in 1959; was chairman of the board when he retired in 1985.

Evans Whitaker

■ **Born:** Shelby.
■ **Occupation:** Vice president of development, Wingate University; currently directing $35 million capital campaign.
■ **Career:** Service in several capacities at Gardner-Webb University; director of trust and development at North Carolina Baptist Foundation.

PAUL WAS NAMED BAPTIST PHILANTHROPIST OF THE YEAR FOR 1996.

8

Leaving Home—Culver and UNC

LENOIR HIGH SCHOOL ended with the eleventh grade. After graduating in June 1941, I began planning my future. I wanted further education and thought that military training would be a good idea. Captain Harper, as band director at Lenoir, was an influential mentor. He had connections with the band at Culver Military Academy in Indiana. Culver had the reputation for being the finest military school in the country. It was, in fact, the only secondary military school where a student could graduate and receive an Army second lieutenant commission.

Bill Stevens, who was two years ahead of me in school and who ultimately married my sister Allene, had attended Culver on a band scholarship for his eleventh and twelfth years. He came home at Christmas of his senior year and brought his roommate and friend, Bob Heilman. They were in their uniforms and cut quite a figure with the girls. Both told tales about Culver, making it sound heroic and fun. I took it all in. I decided that I wanted to go to Culver, but not on a music scholarship. Because of my love for horses, I wanted to be in the famous Black Horse Troop. It was a Cavalry regiment that reminded me of John Wayne movies with bugles blowing, flags flying, and swords flashing. So, impetuously, I applied and was accepted. I went to Culver for twelfth grade.

At Culver I was an oddball. Because all new entrants had to spend their first year as a plebe, I was hazed just like the freshmen, even though I was a senior. I had been naïve in thinking I would be treated

PAUL WAS A CADET AT CULVER MILITARY ACADEMY DURING HIS TWELFTH GRADE YEAR.

differently. I had no contact with people my own age, and very little contact with the people in the ninth grade. I led a lonely life. I had started there somewhat behind academically, but since I had nothing more to do than work hard, I caught up fairly quickly and made excellent grades. I credit my experience at Culver with fortifying my character and preparing me for higher education. When I took my entrance exams at Carolina, I did quite well.

On Sunday, December 7, 1941, we were shocked to hear over the radio about the bombing of Pearl Harbor. The next morning the entire Cadet Corps marched into the auditorium where we listened to President Roosevelt's radio speech as he declared war on Japan. One could not help but look around that room and realize that a lot of those young men soon would be in active combat and that many would lose their lives.

I went home from Culver for Christmas vacation and my mother came to see me at Easter. These were the only contacts I had with friends or family for those nine months of my life. The rest of the time I was treated as if I were some kind of untouchable. Every night at a certain hour a train went by, and that train whistle was one of the loneliest sounds I have ever heard.

I did not get a diploma from Culver because you have to go two years in order to receive a diploma. Perhaps, I should have gone another year and come out of Culver as a second lieutenant. However, during the war, second lieutenants were highly expendable. I applied to Virginia Polytechnic Institute in Virginia, a men's military college.

At VPI, I was a plebe again from September through December. I don't know why in the world I thought that I wanted to be a plebe for another year. Apparently, I was thinking that the military school experience would help me when I got to the Army. However, without a commission, the Army didn't give a darn about whether you had been in military school or not. Regardless, I made excellent grades, and I obviously knew how to handle myself with the military. I got along fine.

That winter when I started home for Christmas, I was "bumming" my way. In other words I was standing on the side of the road and sticking out my thumb to catch a ride. My dad had suggested that I take the bus, but I thought that bumming was quicker. I got a ride to Mt. Airy, North Carolina, a town about two hours from home. The weather was severely cold, and when we stopped, I went into a small café/filling station to get warm. Would you believe, sitting there inside the café, looking around for me, was my dad's chauffeur, Talmadge Biddix? Dad had sent him out on the road to look for me. What a coincidence that he actually found me!

The same scenario happened at a later time in my life. I was on my way for a visit home from where I was stationed in the Army at Camp Maxey in Paris, Texas. The crowded train I was riding had no vacant seats and I actually sat in the aisle on the floor part of the way. Somewhere in western Tennessee I got off the train and again started bumming. I had gotten one ride, but then got hung up somewhere. I finally hitched a ride on the back of a truck and rode for about an hour. When I could no longer stand the cold, I banged on the rear window and waved for the driver to let me off. He dropped me at the next town. Would you believe I walked into a similar café/filling station and there again sat Talmadge Biddix with my dad's Cadillac waiting for me? Can anyone explain to me how I happened to walk into the same kind of establishment two separate times and find Biddix there? Was that coincidence, or was someone looking after me?

When I went home from VPI for Christmas, my friend Rooster Bush and I double dated. Rooster entertained me with stories of the good times he was having at the University of North Carolina at Chapel Hill. He told me all about the parties and the wonderful girls at the two colleges in the neighboring town of Greensboro. The Woman's College of the University of North Carolina (WC) and Greensboro College (GC) provided plenty of opportunities for two college boys. Rooster convinced me I ought to be at Chapel Hill.

On the spur of the moment, during Christmas break, Rooster drove me to Blacksburg, Virginia, where all the VPI buildings were closed and locked. Of course we had no keys. Not to be foiled, we broke into my dorm room. Actually, Rooster pushed me up into a transom. I fell into the dorm room, was able to get the door open, packed my personal things in Rooster's car, and away we went to Chapel Hill, stopping first in Bassett, Virginia.

I don't remember how we met them, but we hooked up with a couple of nice girls there in Bassett before heading back to Chapel Hill. The father of one of the girls was very cordial to me when we first met. To him we were just a couple of nice boys dating his daughter. But, when he learned that my name was Broyhill, you would have thought that I had leprosy. The man worked at Bassett Furniture. Back then, our family was very competitive with Bassett, and that girl's father didn't want to make a bad impression with his bosses by saying that his daughter was dating a Broyhill. So, Rooster and I took the hint and left for Chapel Hill.

When my dad heard about our escapade and my "escape" from VPI, he was furious. I can't blame him for not approving of the way I left, but it turned out to be a good decision for me. I was able to establish myself at Carolina, and join the Phi Delta Theta fraternity. That gave me a good foundation for when I returned after the war.

9

Sergeant Broyhill

AT THE END of my first school year at Chapel Hill, I applied to the Army Air Corps and to the Naval ROTC. However, because I had slight color blindness, I could not read the color charts sufficiently. That condition immediately disqualified me from entering either program, but it did not exempt me from the draft. Fortunately, my color blindness turned out to be a mild condition, and after the war I was able to pass a sight test well enough to obtain my private pilot's license.

During the summer of 1943, three months after my 19th birthday, I was called for active duty along with a large contingent of local boys. Two buses pulled into the square in Lenoir, loaded us up, and carried us to Fort Jackson in Columbia, South Carolina. We spent about a week there at Fort Jackson, subjected to typical hazing and harassment by some officious corporals and sergeants. The military seems to think that hazing is necessary to shape up recruits. Ultimately, I was sent to Camp Croft in Spartanburg, South Carolina, for sixteen weeks of intensive basic training.

At Camp Croft we were trained to handle an M-1 rifle with expert precision. For six days each week, we marched constantly. Generally, we had a ten-minute break every hour, and literally, we would fall down in our tracks to rest for the ten minutes, unmindful of weather conditions. I can remember overnight maneuvers when we dug latrines or slept in foxholes in the rain. Sometimes in later years when I had uncomfortable hotel accommodations, I would remember sleeping in a wet foxhole. The memory made me more tolerant.

Equally unpleasant is the memory of crawling on my belly with my rifle cradled on my arms, pulling myself along with my elbows. We learned to stay down because about a foot over our heads, someone with a machine gun was firing live ammunition. That is a good reinforcement for learning to keep down.

The firing range was set up so that two people were on the firing range and two were at the target. As one person fired the gun, another person with binoculars kept score. At the same time, out at the target area in a trench, one person pulled the target up and down while the other person pasted a repair patch over the bullet holes. Since neither pulling up and down nor repairing was all that difficult, one person could easily do both. Therefore, we could take turns sloughing off and going to sleep. I remember how I could sleep like a baby with guns firing overhead and bullets popping into the target just a foot away.

A benefit to life at Camp Croft was that on weekends we actually got some time off, usually Saturday night and Sunday. My sister Allene attended nearby Converse College and set me up with dates. I fondly remember some of the girls at Converse College, those carefree days, and the good times we had.

I asked my dad for a car while I was still at Chapel Hill, but he refused. However, he agreed to get me one when I went into the service. True to his word, while I was stationed at Camp Croft, Dad gave me a used 1938 maroon, four-door convertible Packard Touring Sedan with the convertible top going over both seats and the spare tires mounted on the sides. That was undoubtedly the most outstanding classic car that I ever owned. It would be worth a fortune on the market today.

Trainees were not supposed to have cars on post, but through my sister I met a military police sergeant who was also dating some of the girls at Converse. He and I became friends and he gave me an officer's sticker, which I placed prominently on my car. I would pull up to the gatehouse with my officer's sticker, get a salute, return it fancily, then hide the car in the woods until the next Saturday, thinking that no one would be the wiser.

One Saturday my platoon sergeant called me into his office. I froze in fright as he said, "Broyhill, you think you're pretty smart, but you're not kidding me. I know you've got a car hidden out down there in the woods." I figured I was in big-time trouble. However, he continued, "Okay, Broyhill, from now on we don't have a problem, as long as you take me with you into town on Saturdays and bring me back on Sunday night." I agreed and from then on, I had it made.

At the end of my Camp Croft training, it was time for me to ship out. They were shipping all the boys for immediate transfer overseas. For some reason, I was detained for a short while. I used the time to my advantage by dating three different girls at Converse. I gave each of them my sad story that it wouldn't be long before I'd be going off to war. I was trying to get their sympathy and a little loving besides. The last night, the girls ganged up on me, and together they confronted me. They made it perfectly clear that it would be safer for me to go to war than to face their wrath.

As my training buddies were shipping out, an interesting thing happened to me and that fortuitous event probably saved my life. In my initial paperwork that I had filled out when I joined the Army, I had indicated that I had typing skills. When I was younger and working in my dad's office, the secretaries taught me to touch type properly by covering up the keyboard with cardboard tabs.

As the orders were being made, I was singled out, categorized as a clerk-typist, and transferred into administration. My first assignment was at Camp Maxey in Paris, Texas, about a hundred miles east of Dallas. There I learned the rudiments of administration. About a year later, I was assigned to Camp Hood, about a hundred miles south of Dallas, not too far from Austin.

At Camp Hood, I began progressing up the ranks and went from corporal to buck sergeant, which is three stripes, then eventually earned two more stripes and ended up being a technical sergeant, which is three stripes above and two stripes below.

Temple, Texas, was not far from Camp Hood. In those days civilians held soldiers in high esteem, so various people at the First Baptist Church of Temple would invite me to have lunch with them and their families. That turned out to be a great way to meet girls.

One night in the suburbs of Austin, Texas, one of my buddies and I were parked at a drive-in eatery. We were in my convertible, and looked pretty good, when a couple of cute girls drove up in another convertible with the top down. We started flirting with them and before long, one of them invited us to follow her home.

We followed her to a huge mansion. It turned out to be the Texas governor's mansion. The girl I had picked up at that drive-in was the daughter of Buford Jester, the governor of the great state of Texas. What a surprise! A number of years later, I received an invitation to her wedding.

While visiting in the governor's mansion I met a gentleman who told me that he was the head of the railroad commission. The title didn't sound all that important to me, but I learned later that the railroad commission regulated all the oil wells in Texas as well as all the railroads. The commissioner controlled the amount of oil that could be produced. After the governor, he was probably the most powerful man in the state.

When I first transferred to Camp Hood, I lived in a barracks with a lot of men. As my rank increased I was given a small, private room in one corner of the barracks. I felt a connection to home when I noticed that some of the beds in the barracks were stamped "Lenoir Furniture Corporation" and were made in one of our plants. At the office I was in charge of 30 or 40 people. On one occasion, an administrative problem arose regarding the reorganization, and reassignment of thousands of people. The colonel thought the process would be quite complicated, that we were going to have to account for all persons and list their names. I came up with a simple, easy way to do it administratively. I tried to explain my method to my colonel, but he never could understand what I was trying to do.

Finally, the colonel said, "Sergeant, do you know what you're doing?"

"Yes, Sir!" I replied.

"Then go ahead; but if it doesn't work, God help you."

We went ahead and did it my way. I thought I was real smart until a few days later when a captain way down the ranks called my office, saying he was in company so-and-so, and could not figure out where he belonged in the chain of command. I started looking him up, and lo and behold, I had left him out! Needless to say, I quickly and quietly fixed that problem so that my colonel never found out about it. So, I know all about cover-ups.

As a tech sergeant, I was proud of my stripes, but I wanted the next rank: master sergeant. I had been pushing for that, but my boss, a major, was making me wait the customary amount of time. While I waited, I came to know another major down the ranks who needed a sergeant major for a particular job. He was impressed with what I had done with the reorganization and reassignment job.

"Sergeant," he said. "Come work for me and I will give you another stripe right away."

I went back to my own major and said, "Major, I quit. I've got a better offer."

Talk about blowing up! My major demanded, "Sergeant Broyhill, you SOB, who the hell do you think you are? This is the Army; you can't just come in here and tell me you quit!" Obviously, I settled back into my old job.

During those days I saw a familiar name from Lenoir, North Carolina, come across my desk: Private Harper Beall, Jr., whose family was also in the furniture business in Lenoir. Curious, I immediately researched and found that Harper was in Texas for training. He had permission to live off base. He and his wife were living in primitive quarters in Colleen, Texas, a small boomtown that had sprung up next to camp and that still had dirt roads. I took the Bealls out to dinner a few times. Harper always seemed to be appreciative that I gave him attention at a time when they were far away from home and were so lonesome.

After Texas, I transferred to Fort Meade, Maryland, where I was stationed for about a year. It was an embarkation depot, not a training camp, and was used as a place to process persons going overseas. It was from there, in December 1945, that I received orders for my discharge, just in time to go home for Christmas.

While I was thrilled at the prospect of going home, I also felt pride at having served my country. A sense of duty is an honorable trait. My parents instilled that sentiment in my siblings and me. After having served in the United States Army, I am convinced that a one-to two-year enlistment should be compulsory. Military service changes a person's perspective and promotes loyalty and dedication to the country, to the family, and to self. While it is not a panacea for every personal problem, many misdirected young people could learn to focus and to work together as a team to make a better life for everyone.

10

Academics and the Battleground

MY FATHER WAS successful in the business world without the benefit of a college education. He was convinced that a degree was not essential to success, and he was also quite anxious for me to come into the business with him. Though he financially had helped a lot of young people go to college, he thought that my business experience under him might be more valuable than a college education and he tried to convince me. On an occasion after my discharge from the Army, Senator Kenneth Wherry from Nebraska, one of my dad's closest friends, was visiting with us. The senator overheard some of our conversation. Senator Wherry called me aside and said, "Paul, I love your dad, but in this instance he is wrong. You must go back to college." With that encouragement, I returned to the University of North Carolina at Chapel Hill in January of 1946.

During my first two quarters at Carolina, I lived in the fraternity house. Because it was difficult to study there, I rented a room in town with a roommate and I rode a bicycle to class. I took my meals at the fraternity house and had a lot of camaraderie there; yet, I had a place where I could get away and have quiet study time. I had a routine of studying from seven until eleven every night and had occasional study halls during the day.

I found I could get a student membership to the Hope Valley Country Club in Durham for a nominal fee. Few people had heard of a college student having access to that prestigious club. However, I was able to get away and play some golf from time to time.

SENATOR KENNETH WHERRY, ONE OF J. E.'S CLOSEST FRIENDS, WITH MAJORIE WHERRY, SATIE AND J. E.

I dated a girl from Charlotte named Helen Hunter. Her father was an editor for the *Charlotte Observer.* One day as Helen and I were playing golf in Charlotte, I stood behind her to instruct, as I usually liked to do. Unexpectedly, she drew the club back, struck me in the face, and literally laid my nose off to one side. I fell unconscious to the ground. An ambulance rushed me to the hospital where my nose had to be sewn back on. When I returned to the fraternity house and my brothers heard the story, they dummied up something to look like a newspaper headline and posted it on the bulletin board. It read "Masher hit by Mashie." A Mashie used to be the name of a golf club in the 1930s.

Since then I have had nose problems and have had two nose operations. Despite that painful experience, I still instruct pretty girls in golf at every opportunity. My friends in Naples, Florida, call me "Doctor Golf."

Back at Chapel Hill, on weekends my friend Rooster Bush and I took off to date the Greensboro girls. We went over on Saturday, went out with the girls on Saturday night and Sunday, then went back to Chapel Hill late Sunday.

For only a few dollars a night Rooster and I stayed at the YMCA close to the girls' dorms. Our normal routine was to take the girls to dinner, then go to the favorite parking place for young people, the battlegrounds at the Guilford Courthouse National Military Park. We spent as much time at the Battlegrounds as possible. I can tell you in great detail about General Greene's battle with General Cornwallis at the site of the Guilford Courthouse.

We drove in Rooster's 1936 Plymouth. The steering wheel was very loose on that car, but he had a steering knob on it, which we called a "chunking knob." The knob made it easy to drive with one hand. The Plymouth ran very smoothly because the valves were completely worn out. It blew a tremendous amount of smoke out of the tailpipe because oil flowed through the valves almost as fast as it burned gas. Most filling stations in those days stored their used oil in a large drum to be hauled off. We would stop at a station, fill up small containers from those drums, and put them in the trunk of the car. We would have to pour in the oil just about as fast as we poured in gasoline, but that car sure did run loose as a goose.

After college, Rooster returned to Lenoir and went to work for the post office because his dad had worked there. Later, his dad worked in the lumber business and, on occasion, our company bought some lumber from him. While retaining his job at the post office, Rooster started a used car lot and started selling cars on weekends. After a few years of success, he agonized over whether or not to go into the car business full time. He was having a tough time making a decision about giving up post office security and retirement benefits. I strongly encouraged him to make the move. As things turned out, his sideline grew from an unpaved car lot under some trees to one of the largest car dealerships in Western North Carolina.

PAUL, NC CONGRESSMAN CHARLES TAYLOR, AND ROOSTER BUSH MANY YEARS AFTER PAUL AND ROOSTER'S ANTICS AT CHAPEL HILL

In my second year at Carolina my brother, Jim, came to Chapel Hill and pledged my fraternity, so he and I were there together for a year. After the war my dad bought each of us a two-door Plymouth, one green and one red. My sisters called them the "Green Bean" and the "Red Ted." One weekend my car was in the shop, and I borrowed my brother's "Green Bean" for my usual weekend trip to Greensboro.

In those days we drove about seventy miles an hour on the two-lane road between Chapel Hill and Greensboro. One evening I was cruising along and had pulled out to pass the car in front of me when the driver suddenly swerved. Something was lying in the road ahead, and he tried to dodge it. Apparently, he didn't realize that I was parallel with him. When he swerved, I had no alternative but to go off the left side of the road, at seventy miles an hour. The car rolled over onto its left side, came upright, and then rolled over and landed on its right side. Somewhere in the process, my door came open, and I was thrown into a field. The impact knocked me a little woozy. When I came to, I was bleeding from scratches and cuts. Though I was sore, I didn't seem to have any serious injuries. I walked back to the car.

My two passengers were still inside the car. Both boys were beat up and bleeding a bit, but miraculously, none of us was seriously hurt.

Together the three of us pushed the car upright. The right side fender was smashed, but the engine seemed to run just fine. In spite of our wounds, we went on into town, stopped at the YMCA, and cleaned up a little. Then we went to pick up the girls, had dinner, and went to our usual place, the Greensboro Battlegrounds. Only after taking the girls home did we go to the hospital emergency room to get bandaged. First things first.

After that incident, when I got back to Chapel Hill, I parked Jim's car with the damaged side against a wall. Jim came to pick it up but didn't notice anything wrong. When he finally saw the damage, he thought someone had hit it in a parking lot. I kept really quiet, but after a period of time the truth finally came out. Fortunately for me, Jim had calmed down by then.

At least a couple of times a year, big name bands came to the campus. Generally, they played an afternoon concert to a full auditorium and then played for a dance at night. After listening to music in the afternoon, we'd dress up for the dance, stay late, and then we would all go to a Carolina football game the next day.

For boys, usual ballgame attire included a coat, or at least a sweater, and a tie. Oftentimes we wore hats. For the dances, the men wore tuxedos or tails, but tails were prevalent. As a college student, I owned both a standard tux and one with tails. A little later, I added a white dinner jacket to my wardrobe. Girls wore suits and hats to the games and long evening gowns to the dances. They arrived from Greensboro on a Greyhound bus, and we'd put them back on the bus late Sunday.

Several very attractive girls drew my attention during those years. I still get Christmas cards from some of them along with pictures of their children and grandchildren. I have many fond memories of those years. Long after I graduated, I continued to go back to Women's College, until one night when I took a young girl back to the dorm and she politely thanked me by saying, "Goodnight, Mr. Broyhill, I certainly had a good time." By calling me "Mr. Broyhill," she made me realize that I might be getting a little too old for the students. Therefore, not to be discouraged, I took up with a housemother and dated her for some time. She was a little older, in her mid-twenties. For a while, it was as if I was an associate housefather to the students in one of the dorms at WC.

On one occasion my dad called and said he wanted Jim and me to meet him and Mother in New York City at the annual meeting of the National Association of Furniture Manufacturers at the Waldorf Astoria. Jim and I drove to the Greensboro railroad station, but when I went to buy our tickets, Jim said, "I'm sorry, except for a five dollar bill, I don't have any money." I had to buy his ticket.

When we got to New York, Mother was upset because Jim brought no coat, so she bought him a nice, dress overcoat. After two days in New York, when we were nearly home Jim said, "Ha, ha, ha. I've been to New York, I have a brand new coat, and I've still got my five dollars!" That was typical Jim. He has always been frugal and watched his money. Later when he served in Washington, he watched the taxpayer's money as closely as he did his own.

During my last week at Chapel Hill, I was talking to my friend Marion Stewart. Marion had been in one of my classes and quite impressed me. I asked him what he planned to do now that school was over. He told me that he had no idea. I invited him to come by and talk with us about the furniture business. I had a similar conversation with a hard-working young man, Tommy Culbreth, who was working part time behind the counter at the Carolina Inn. Both young men came by later, and we hired them. They became wonderful salesmen and worked for Broyhill for many years. After he finished college my brother, Jim, also came into the business and worked for twelve years in administration, personnel, and public relations.

I finished school at Chapel Hill in December 1947, having attended during the calendar years of 1946 and 1947: three quarters prior to the war and eight quarters afterward. I finished school in 11 quarters rather than the normal 12 or more because I was anxious to get out and go to work. I didn't even attend the formal graduation ceremonies. Similarly, I had not attended a formal graduation from high school. I received my University of North Carolina diploma by mail, and much to my surprise, I received memberships in Phi Beta Kappa, the nation's oldest academic honor society, and in Beta Gamma Sigma, a national honorary business society.

Part 2

Building Broyhill

11

Joining Dad in the Business

FROM AN EARLY age, during summer vacations from school and whenever I was free, I spent time at the office doing odd jobs such as sealing envelopes, affixing stamps, and refurbishing Dictaphone records. The records were made of hard rubber and were like a phonograph record, but cylindrical in shape. After use, we would stick the cylinder into a device that had a sharp blade, and it would shave off a thin layer, making the record reusable. A more important job was running the telephone switchboard. One person could operate the board. It involved sticking a cord-like device into a receptacle when a light indicated an incoming call, then taking an adjacent cord and plugging it into the receptacle designated for the intended recipient.

When I got older, I worked part time in the plants, mostly around the lumberyard and machine room. I pushed factory trucks from station to station, and when I was older, I unloaded lumber from trucks and boxcars. We piled it into hacks suitable for going into the dry kiln. Sticks had to be placed between every layer. We handled every board one at a time. Later, those tasks became completely mechanized.

As a boy, I went with my father when he bought a small, red brick building on Oak Street in Lenoir. Previously a grocery warehouse, it became his office building and showroom. Lenoir Chair Company, his original factory, stood on adjoining property. Dad converted the warehouse so that it had a large, open first floor for the showroom and a second floor mezzanine consisting of eight or ten offices.

After the war, one of my first building projects was an expansion and remodeling of that office building. We extended the building to more than double its original size and put a modern facade on it. We also installed air-conditioning. Up until that time, we only had open windows and oscillating fans. Very quickly the office staff grew from about 25 people to more than 50.

When I entered the business in January 1948, we had six small plants and employed between 700 and 800 workers. They included Uncle Tom and Dad's original plants, Lenoir Furniture Company and Lenoir Chair Company, the Newton company that we called Lenoir Chair 2, the Conover plant, the Harper plant, and the Marion plant.

BROYHILL'S OUTPUT CONTINUED TO ESCALATE AS SEEN HERE IN AN UPHOLSTERY PRODUCTION FACILITY.

With the combined output from those six plants, we became one of the largest furniture manufacturers in the industry. Our annual sales at that time were approximately $15 million. All of the operations were fairly profitable. The overall business was making five or six percent pre-tax, which ended up being three or four percent after tax. Because taxes had been so high during the war years, our net worth was small. The bank debt we had incurred was within reasonable limits relative to our sales, profits, and net worth. I admired our competitors, Drexel and Basset, both of which were highly profitable. Because they had been established much earlier than our company, they each had built considerably more net worth than we. I set a goal to catch up with them.

Upon my homecoming from college, my dad immediately sent me to the Chicago furniture market. That market was held twice a year in January and July in a furniture exposition building at 666 North Lakeshore Drive. During the war, a governmental agency had commandeered our showroom space. When I arrived in Chicago, though we had our space back, we had been unable to refurbish our showroom in time for the January furniture market. So, we adapted. We didn't actually show furniture, but we entertained our customers in an office area and handed out quotas to our dealers based on their past buying history.

Dealers accepted anything that we could give them, and we were careful to be fair with our small dealers as well as with our large ones. In addition, immediately after the war, we gave a small allotment to every returning serviceman who owned a store.

From the start of the war through 1948 there had been shortages of nearly every kind of manufactured goods, including furniture. We concentrated our efforts on building production. Our total shipments for 1946 were approximately $12 million, but for 1948 shipments jumped to approximately $15 million. The increase was due to our ability to obtain more supplies, and also to our being able to hire additional men who were returning from the war. During the war years manufacturers had hired women to work in the plants for the first time. At Broyhill, we continued to use women from that time on.

Dad believed that when I came on board, I would join the manufacturing part of Broyhill and that Jim was more suited for sales. When he first came home from school, Jim worked a local territory but gravitated towards administration and personnel work in the plants. With the help of Corporate Personnel Manager Beef Johnson, Jim organized an effective personnel department in each plant that involved the hiring and training of supervisors. He also became the general office manager and was in charge of company benefits and local community affairs.

JIM, J. E. AND PAUL

I jumped full force into selling, but it became readily apparent to me that the areas where I was needed most were design and merchandising. Before I joined the company, Dad and a consultant friend, Jack Garrett, had handled merchandising. When I took over, I had my work cut out for me creating a new product line. Competition in the industry was growing as customers, hungry for change, were looking for new, contemporary designs. When I took over the marketing of our product line, our most popular style was contemporary bedroom furniture. We also produced a small line of traditional bedroom and dining room furniture, a line of upholstered occasional and lounge chairs, and a line of kneehole desks and secretaries.

I was able to take charge at a young age because the workforce had been depleted during the war years, and there simply was no one else there to do the job. While we were on quotas, building staff had been unnecessary. As we added to our plants and to our employee organization, we constantly added to our product line. In just a few years, we needed a 20,000 square foot showroom and a little later, a

40,000 square foot showroom. Gradually, we expanded the styles in our lineup to include contemporary, English, European traditional, and American colonial.

In 1949 the country had a recession that didn't last long, but it was severe. Prior to the recession we could sell everything that we made. All of a sudden, it was like turning off the lights. Business just quit. We had a stockpile of inventory and nobody wanted any furniture. It seemed that everyone was canceling orders. My dad and the production people had worked steadily to increase production by enlarging the plants. After the war, good people had come back to work, and production had grown rapidly over a very short time. When the recession hit, we neither wanted to cut back production nor to cut employees' time. We were proud of giving our people full-time work.

As a result of that substantial economic readjustment, we rapidly transitioned from having our customers beg us for furniture and our begging for supplies to a more competitive market situation. As inventory began to accumulate, it wasn't long before production had to be curtailed. That was a shock to the entire organization. We were confronted with an inventory crisis and were forced to develop some new styles to stimulate business.

As furniture piled up in the warehouses we soon saw obsolescence in the old merchandise. Resolving that dilemma became my responsibility. We were faced with a slow down at the plants and a lot of excess furniture to move.

Until that time we had no need to emphasize sales or sales managers. We had one sales manager, Mr. Bowman "Bo" Crisp who was experienced and knowledgeable, but due to health reasons was unable to travel. I personally took charge of moving the inventory. I called on our major accounts, but my thrust was to work through the sales force. Every evening I called salesmen and assigned them 12 suites of this, 20 suites of that, 15 suites of the other, and I allowed them to offer the dealers a discounted price. I asked them to call me back when they had sold all their assigned merchandise. When they called, I marked whatever they had sold off the master inventory list and gave them another assignment.

During that period, I received a real baptism by fire, learning how to negotiate prices and how to handle overbearing customers. Many of them had been trained during the old guard days of the '30s, and they knew how to wheedle and intimidate to get their way.

I learned quickly that the lifeblood of any organization is sales. We started an aggressive program to expand our sales force, we developed a professional sales training program, and we implemented a non-traditional method of compensation for the new salesmen.

When I came into the business, we had 20 sales people selling $500,000 to $1,250,000 each. Customarily, the industry had paid salesmen a straight 5% commission and they paid their own expenses. Those were good jobs. As the industry grew, many salesmen started making a lot of money; in some cases, they made more money than the company executives. We decided to pay salary, bonus, expenses, and to provide a car for each salesman. Our starting salesmen were earning $50 a week, plus expenses.

It is certainly hard for young people today to understand the difference in the dollar value and the conditions of that day. I went to work in my dad's plant in 1939 for 25 cents an hour, and in 1940 my salary increased to 30 cents. I worked 40 hours a week to receive $10 minus withholdings. Times were different in those days; people appreciated a good job.

Our sales manager, Bowman Crisp, had been the prior owner of the Marion plant. He stayed with us when we bought the plant after it had gone defunct. Bo had a tremendous amount of experience dating back into the '30s and he had a lot of good contacts within the industry. He was a wonderful mentor. He was an ideal person to help train the young salespeople as he did not resent their being hired and moving upward in the company.

My brother in law, Bill Stevens, jumped into the sales arena along with Bo Crisp and me. Bill was a great teacher, and with excellent writing skills, he created superb training manuals. He wrote *Anvil of Adversity*, an historical book about Dad and the evolution of Dad's business. Bill's greatest achievement was the hiring, training, and developing of our new sales force and our plant supervisors. We did not fire any old time salesmen. They continued working right along, side by side with the new, young sales people. Obviously, we constantly had to reduce territories to make room for the additions.

However, that was in pace with our increase in volume, so our old salesmen did not lose out, and most of them stayed with us until their retirement.

From approximately 20 salesmen in 1948 we built a sales force of more than 300. We were called "Broyhill U" in the industry because of the quality of training we gave our salesmen. Many competitors in the industry constantly combed our sales force to solicit them. We lost a number of salesmen to those companies and some we lost because they were not doing a good job, but we retained enough of the good ones that we consistently were able to grow our business. With our innovative salary structure, we could put new men to work rapidly. Our decision to retain the former salesmen on the old commission basis saved us from a mass exodus.

Originally, I shared the sales responsibilities with Bo Crisp and Bill Stevens, but as we added salesmen, we organized regional and divisional sales managers. I tried to assign most sales to others but found that the top customers always wanted to deal with the boss. I personally remained involved with key account sales. However, the largest portion of my time was spent in merchandising.

BROYHILL BUILT A SALES FORCE GREATER THAN 300 FROM A FOUNDATION OF 20 SALESMEN IN 1948.

Merchandising included the product development, advertising, and display. We had two periods a year when we introduced new patterns. That meant that we were constantly looking for saleable ideas and were building new designs for market introductions every six months. It was more complicated than just coming up with isolated good-selling patterns. In order to make money, the patterns had to conform to plant production capabilities. With that in mind, we developed a merchandising formula for each factory that fit the potential of that particular factory.

A certain amount of friction always existed between the merchandising people and the production people. The production people subscribed to Henry Ford's concept that "the customer could have anything he wanted as long as it was a black, four-door sedan." The sales people wanted a variety of products that were all new and different. Clarence Beach, our production manager, drummed into me at an early age what the plants could and could not do. One reason I was successful was that I had the ability to blend the capabilities of plants with the needs of the sales department.

Furniture industry sales are built around a market cycle. We had many markets, far too many for efficiency. Some of the major markets were held in Grand Rapids, Chicago, New York, High Point, Atlanta, Dallas, Los Angeles, and San Francisco. In the early years the market cycle began in Chicago the first week in January and the first week after the Fourth of July. High Point, New York, and then the West Coast markets followed Chicago. Later, Atlanta and Dallas were added.

In the mid '50s, the cycle began to change. The big dealers wanted to have a pre-market look at the new merchandise, and they started coming south in April and October to get a jump on their competition. In the beginning that was an informal time when we manufacturers showed mock ups and sketches without any elaborate presentation, and we also played a little golf with our customers.

As the number of people who came to those pre-markets began to grow, we made more and more preparations and began to show complete suites. It wasn't long until we set up showrooms. With each market the showrooms tended to expand and to become more elaborate until the April and October dates became more important

DEALERS VISIT THE WAREHOUSE FOR A PRE-MARKET VIEW TO TRY TO GET AHEAD OF THEIR COMPETITION.

than January and July. Actually, we were marketing every ninety days, but we brought out most of our new merchandise at the April and October markets.

During this heyday of markets, a man by the name of Trammel Crow from Dallas, Texas, came to visit me. He came into my office looking like a country bumpkin just off the farm. Trammel presented himself as a real estate developer. He said that he had started in business by building industrial warehouses and had conceived the idea of constructing a furniture market building in Dallas. At that time, Dallas area manufacturers had been showing their products twice a year at the local fairgrounds. It was quite an ordeal because they brought in the merchandise overnight, set it up, showed it, and then took it down again. Trammel wanted to build a beautiful, permanent building, but he had trouble securing tenants. The national manufacturers complained that there were too many markets already and covertly boycotted him. Trammel offered me a sweetheart deal: free rent for the first five years, and low rent for the next five. I had nothing to lose, so I signed on. Our participation in Trammel's venture broke the ice. The industry followed, and the rest is history as the Dallas market became successful.

Trammel went on to develop a tremendous Dallas market complex, starting with the furniture building and adding other facilities that catered to more than 30 different industries. He was fortunate to have hired Bill Cooper as manager of the Dallas complex. Bill was a man who had a natural flair for both sales and management. He and Trammel held trade shows throughout the year and Trammel continued to build on a large scale until ultimately he became one of the largest developers in the world. He has remained a lifelong friend to me. I served on the Dallas market board of advisors, so Bill and I became close friends. Later, he served on my Broyhill Management Corporation board until his death in 2008.

PAUL AND FAYE WITH BILL AND SUE COOPER,
LONG TIME ASSOCIATES AND FRIENDS

Market Week A Busy One

J. Edgar Broyhill, like many other Tar Heel furniture manufacturers, will concentrate on furnishing other people's homes this week during the Southern Furniture Market.

Buyers from all over the nation and some foreign countries will visit many North Carolina companies to buy furniture for their stores.

Eleven Broyhill furniture plants are located within a 40-mile radius of Lenoir.

Furniture manufacturing is a family enterprise for the Broyhills. Both of his sons and his two sons-in-law are associated with the business. (Son James T. is inactive, however, since his election as Ninth District Congressman.)

The growth of the Broyhill Industries is beyond the youthful dreams of J. E. Broyhill, who grew up on a Wilkes County farm. "I left the farm when I was 21 and went to Appalachian Training School. I started in the seventh grade at the age of 21. You have to want an education a lot to do that," he recalled.

He attended the school four years, but missed his high school diploma when he went into the Army.

After his discharge, in 1919, he went to work with his brother, the late T. H. Broyhill, who had started a furniture company.

"He was the oldest of six boys and I was the youngest. I didn't know anything about furniture, but I wanted to get away from the farm.

"I never dreamed of building a business like this," he said candidly.

Spacious basement den is favorite locale for family.

Mr. Broyhill has his putting green at home.

MARKET WEEK A BUSY ONE, FROM THE *LENOIR NEWS TOPIC*

My dad went to every Chicago market for 50 years, from 1924–1974. At each market he rented a suite at the Drake Hotel. My mother and Dad's secretary, Iris Laney, accompanied him. Dad entertained every night. First, customers would come to his room where he would serve drinks and play gin rummy. Then he would take them all to dinner and sometimes to a show in the Camelia Room of the hotel.

I sometimes joined my father, but after a few markets, being young and independent, I moved from the Drake Hotel to the Ambassador East Hotel where the action was in the famous Pump Room. I, too, entertained key accounts almost every night, though some nights I slipped off and dated some of the local young ladies. Late nights never prevented me from being one of the first people in the showroom space the next morning.

As the April and October markets developed, manufacturers' showrooms spread across North Carolina from High Point to Thomasville, Lexington, Hickory, and Lenoir. We owned the Green Park Hotel in Blowing Rock, a resort town about twenty minutes up the mountain from Lenoir. We used it to accommodate and entertain our dealers. Each night during market we hosted a cocktail party, served an elaborate buffet dinner, and provided live band music. We certainly had no problem drawing a crowd. Over the course of my career, I interacted with literally hundreds and hundreds of dealers who felt that they personally knew the Broyhill family and me. Most American cities had at least one Broyhill dealer who felt close to us.

Between markets, we constantly looked for design ideas and, of course, were constantly looking for business. I spent quite a bit of time visiting dealers across the country, walking their floors, and questioning them for business improvement and styling ideas. I did not pay much attention to the accounting aspect of the business, except the cost accounting that we used in pricing. Accounting was really the last thing my dad kept under his personal control. The cost sheets on each pattern gave us some theoretical knowledge as to whether or not we were making money and on which products.

In the early days, my father was always very secretive about divulging the business accounting records to anyone. If we made money, he didn't want anyone to know. If we didn't make money, he would have been embarrassed, and wouldn't have wanted anyone to know that either. We had an old time accountant who quietly took me to a safe. He showed me where books were kept that showed the profits from each individual plant and he gave me the combination to that safe. I literally went down to the office at night, and by the light of a flashlight, opened the safe and got out those accounting books to find out whether we were making any money, and at which plants.

Later, when I took over the accounting, I held monthly and quarterly meetings with vice presidents and plant managers, projecting charts and figures on a screen with full disclosure. We set goals and objectives, along with the strategies to accomplish those plans. Over a period of years, we literally doubled the profit margins. That was a great lesson in the power of professional management, which involved everyone in the process.

12

Selling to Major Accounts

IN THE EARLY 1950s, we had a large customer base of more than 10,000 accounts made up mostly of independent furniture stores. We also were doing substantial business with Sears and Montgomery Ward. I personally handled the Sears and Ward accounts and certainly got an education from them during my early years in the business. I made money on them for some years, but the more business they gave me, the more demands they made. When it got to the point that they were too hard-nosed and we were making little profit, I decided we should reduce our volume with them. I gradually began cutting back. I was able to develop business elsewhere while Sears actually broke several fine furniture companies.

Broyhill had been doing only a small amount of sales volume with other major department stores, although at that time they represented a sizeable factor in overall industry sales. Business was slow, and we had developed two new groupings, one fairly low priced and one more upscale. I decided to try to sell those groups to some department stores. I had samples shipped to New York and set up in a New York hotel suite. I called on a holding company called Allied Stores that owned a sizeable number of major department stores throughout the country. I introduced myself to Leonard Smith and his boss, Sig Schlesinger. In the years following, Leo and Sig came to be among my very best friends. Initially, they were impressed with my enthusiasm and the fact that I had a display set up to show them. When they went to the hotel for a look, I think they liked what they saw, but they did not want to make a commitment to a new, unproven resource. They shrugged me off with what I later found out was a standard method of getting rid of someone.

Smith and Schlesinger said I might show my line to Jordan Marsh, one of their department stores in Boston, and that if Jordan Marsh liked it, I could come back. Immediately, I had the merchandise loaded onto the back of a U-Haul truck. My New York salesman, David Barlow, drove the truck the following day and night to Boston. We had the merchandise set up in a Boston hotel similar to our New York display. Then we knocked on the door of Jordan Marsh. We told their people that the New York office had sent us and had requested that they take a look at what we had. The upshot was that we sold Jordan Marsh two railroad cars of merchandise.

We put the suites back on the U-Haul, drove back to New York, and were back in Allied offices just a few days later with the orders in hand from Jordan Marsh. Our quick response so impressed the Allied office that they bought approximately a thousand suites. Other than Sears and Montgomery Ward, that was by far the largest order that I had ever written. That sale gave us an entrée into the department store business. From that first sale, over the course of our relationship, I ended up getting many millions of dollars in sales from all of the Allied stores. I still can recall their New York phone number: Oregon 9-0800.

The Allied people were a substantial influence on me and taught me much. They took a personal interest in me and loved to kid me about being a country yokel. They claimed that they had to make me over and get me out of my two-toned shoes, broad lapelled suits, and loud flowered ties. I wasn't quite that bad, but I played along and let them have their fun. They were good friends and made an impact on my life.

Another major department store relationship was with Goldblatt's in Chicago. I became good friends with Louis Goldblatt, one of the owners. He was a bachelor in his early 40s, and I was in my early 30s. He was a dynamic guy and taught me a lot about business. A master of the "good guy/bad guy" routine, he showered my family and me with attention, while at the same time his executive vice president of merchandising could really chop me up when bargaining for a deal.

Always Close To His Employees

He earned the devotion of his customers, his competitors, his employees and his family.

Why I love Ed Broyhill? Here are only a few of the many reasons:

From the very first time I met him at my late brother Nathan Goldblatt's home in the early 1930s, he made an impression upon me as being the kind of man I would like to know personally, and with whom I would like to do business.

In 1945, directly after World War II, I accompanied my buyers on many furniture-buying trips to the southern market. None of the manufacturers had any goods available at that time; and, for that matter, neither did the Broyhill company. However, there was something about the way Ed Broyhill said "No" and turned you down: There was hope of getting a "Yes" in the near future.

He would rather turn down an order than make an inferior piece of furniture in order to be competitive. He not only thinks in terms of quality standards but exercises stringent controls for quality. He always deals with his accounts on an equal basis.

Ed and his wife, Satie, have always been known to many as Mom and Dad. There is an aura of hospitality around them that makes you feel like a member of their family.

When his son, Paul, was just out of school, I remember Ed taking him around with him while visiting the various accounts they did business with — of teaching and exposing him to the world, and eventually giving him his head and also full reins.

To the best of my knowledge, Ed and Satie never missed a furniture show in Chicago for 50 consecutive years. He was always close to his employees and to the trade; he was always on hand to welcome his many friends.

He earns devotion from all — his customers (like Goldblatt's), his competitors, his employees, and his family.

I am sure that everyone fortunate enough to have met Mr. Ed Broyhill loves him as I do.

Louis Goldblatt

LOUIS GOLDBLATT
President
GOLDBLATT

LOUIS GOLDBLATT, PRESIDENT OF GOLDBLATT'S FURNITURE

Another business relationship that stands out in my memory is my association with Sig Hahn and his son, Stanley, of Hahn Furniture Company in Pittsburg. Sig had been a good friend to my father for years. Both he and Stanley became a significant influence on me. Sig was a master of ingratiation. He could use his winning personality to get his way. I remember his gifts of silk stockings and perfume for the ladies at a time when it was almost impossible to get them and our giving him a greater merchandise allotment. Whenever I really needed business, I could always go to Stan Hahn and get a substantial order to clean up certain discontinued merchandise, all at a deep discount, of course.

Probably my father's oldest friends were the Havertys of Atlanta. I recall first meeting them when I was twelve years old on my way to Camp Burton in Georgia. I met Mr. J.J. Haverty, the patriarch, when he came to visit my father in Blowing Rock in the early '30s. I knew his son, Clarence, and his grandson, Rawson, who was my contemporary, and most recently, his great-grandson, Clarence Haverty Smith. The Havertys were always loyal, but they could be just as tough as any of our other larger accounts. Not only did Rawson Haverty himself have tremendous influence on me, but also various key people in the Haverty organization such as Frank McGahee, Jay Slater, Deacon Witherspoon, and Hamp Slater. Clarence Smith supported my nomination for the Furniture Hall of Fame in 2004.

One of my best friends in the retail business became Louis Rippner of Watkins Furniture in Cleveland, Ohio. Lou worked closely with me to develop retail-oriented programs. He often tested them in his stores, then he helped me to implement them with other accounts. I eventually bought Watkins and will explain that relationship in a future chapter.

Another of my early industry friends was Bill Breuner with Breuner Furniture Company of San Francisco. Even for me, it is difficult to conceive that my first three trips to the West Coast were by railroad. That was before I started flying. On my first trip to San Francisco, Bill Breuner met my train at 6:00 in the morning. Obviously, for the head of a company to meet anyone at 6:00 a.m. was unusual. From that time on, Bill and I stayed close friends and did a lot of business together.

Ed Broyhill—Thoughtful Fair—Humble

A Furniture Industry Pioneer

As a third generation member of furniture merchants serving the South, I was bound to know the Broyhill family.

My father, Clarence Haverty, and "Deacon" Witherspoon were long time friends of Ed Broyhill; and as they took me with them on their market trips, they talked of the past. How Tom Broyhill had been in the sawmill business, and how his younger brother Ed joined with him in pioneering the development of the furniture industry in North Carolina.

My earliest memories of the Chicago markets always included a visit with Ed Broyhill. Broyhill was an important furniture source for us, but we always tried to make it one of our last stops in the market.

Ed Broyhill was friendly with everyone — merchants and retailers. He knew the manufacturing and retailing businesses. He was familiar with the markets and how they worked. After the first few days of the market he had visited with people throughout the country and had gathered a wide range of information. When we talked to Mr. Ed we came away with a good "feel" of the market. We had absorbed worthwhile information, and the visit was always pleasant. He was a delightful person to be with.

In the spring and fall, driving through the Carolinas on those market trips, a stop at Lenoir and the Broyhill factories would frequently include a late afternoon visit with Mr. Ed and Mrs. Broyhill, together with the children at their beautiful home in Lenoir.

In recounting the earlier years and my acquaintance with Mr. Ed, I cannot disassociate the names Bo Crisp, Harry Dews, and Lawton Cater. These men were magnificent sales representatives. They always made us feel as if they were a part of our team. Harry Dews still works with us, and makes us feel he is a part of the Haverty organization. I am sure that the ability of these men has made them valuable members of the Broyhill organization.

As my father turned more responsibility for the operation of our business over to me, Mr. Ed was, likewise, turning the operation of the Broyhill Industries over to his son Paul. For a while the two brothers, Paul and Jim, worked together. Both had wonderful personalities, were natural salesmen, and represented their company well. Jim turned to politics, and represents the State of North Carolina in the Congress of the United States — and apparently with great success, for he continues to be reelected each term. Paul progressively assumed the direction and leadership of the Broyhill factories and has built them into one of the world's largest furniture manufacturing institutions.

As Paul and I grew in our respective businesses we bumped into each other on many occasions and became good friends, with a close relation both in business, as supplier and retailer, and on a personal level.

Mr. Ed, although he has turned over the operation of the Broyhill Industries, will throughout his lifetime be "Mr. Broyhill." I am sure that in the days when he was "putting it all together" he must have exhibited an exeptional drive, a verve and enthusiasm that dominated those around him, for so very much was done.

Yet, over the years, I have known him only as the gentlest of men who commanded the greatest respect of his associates. He always spoke with a soft voice, exhibited great thoughtfulness, total fairness, and an unusual humility; and, his associates that I knew went out of their way to do what Mr. Ed liked to have done, because, I think, they loved him.

RAWSON HAVERTY
President
HAVERTY'S

RAWSON HAVERTY, PRESIDENT OF HAVERTY'S FURNITURE

A Remarkable Man

Ed Broyhill's leadership contributed to the development of the furniture industry.

The Golden Anniversary of Broyhill Industries is an accomplishment which adds luster to the entire furniture industry. It is a particularly enjoyable occasion for those of us who have personally known and admired J. E. Broyhill, builder of an outstanding firm from modest beginnings so long ago. His accomplishment is doubly remarkable, because it was performed under one-family control. The reins of management are now ably held by Mr. J. E.'s son, Paul.

The Broyhill company has been the lifework of this extraordinary man with a keen sense and zest for living. Providing dedicated leadership through personal example, Mr. J. E. molded the corporate character and style which has brought the Broyhill firm so successfully through the vicissitudes of the past half-century. A vigorous entrepreneur, he contributed the critical business attributes: forceful and imaginative organization, efficient manufacturing operations, innovative design and marketing policies. His astute leadership has also contributed to the development of our industry. It is especially gratifying that he participates in the celebration.

Mr. J. E. might have followed other careers just as successfully. His charisma could have been directed into a distinguished political career, and it seems to follow naturally that his son, James, has been a Congressman from North Carolina for 13 years. To his many, many friends and golfing companions and the thousands of acquaintances who have met him through SFMA markets, his hospitality has been proverbial. Mr. J. E. epitomizes the South.

As one of his "victims," I should also like to reflect on another career Mr. J. E. might have followed quite happily and undoubtedly with great success: that of riverboat gambler. I can visualize him out of a scene by Mark Twain, with planter's hat and mint julep — only he is playing gin rummy. In this connection I recall painfully that several years ago I accepted Mr. J. E.'s gracious invitation to join him on his Lear jet from California to the market at High Point. When we landed, as a result of his superior luck and unquestioned skill, I was down more than the price of a transcontinental airfare. He refused my check, but with a twinkle in his eye demanded an IOU — and ever since, time and time again, he has returned my checks. I heard that at one time he had that IOU prominently displayed on the wall of his office, like the trophy head of a rhinoceros.

So now, Mr. J. E., after all these nice things I have written about you here, wouldn't you please let me redeem that IOU you earned on my "free" ride across the country?

William R. Breuner

WILLIAM BREUNER
President
BREUNER'S

WILLIAM BRUENER, PRESIDENT OF BREUNER'S FURNITURE

I first called on Louis Blumkin of Nebraska Furniture Mart in the early '50s. At that time he had a modest-sized store in downtown Omaha. He was always there and was generally out front, not back in an office. The day I met him, Louie made an exception to that practice and asked me to go with him out to his club to play golf. I had not brought clubs or golf clothes. He bought me a pair of shorts and loaned me a set of clubs.

Through the years, I got to know the Blumkin family well, including Louie's mother, Rose, who was a Russian immigrant. She migrated all the way across Russia, through Vladivostok and around the world, ending up in Omaha. In 1917, she started in business with used clothing and furniture. From that humble beginning grew the largest retail furniture operation in the country. She, too, was always in the store, usually in the carpet department, until she was over 100 years old. Over the years, I took all three of my children to hear Mrs. Blumkin tell the "money tree" story.

"You young kids don't know anything about hard work and making money," she said. "You think money grows on trees and that all you have to do is to shake the tree and pick up the money." I loved that story.

Rose's son, Louie, and her grandsons, Irv and Ron, followed closely in her footsteps and carried on her legacy. I visited the Blumkins at least twice a year and always received a warm welcome. Sometimes Louie and his wife, Fran, would have me to their home for dinner. I considered them my close friends. Irv recommended me for induction in the Furniture Hall of Fame. I will always appreciate his support.

When my son, Hunt, and I were on our second career and owned Custom Sofa Gallery, a best friend was Dan Kelley of Kelley Furniture in Paducah, Kentucky. He gave us valuable input as well as help with managing our stores. My wife, Karen, and I continue to see Dan and his wife, also named Karen, when they come in the winter to Naples, Florida, where they live on a boat.

Over the course of a year, I visited many of those major business accounts at least once. I learned how to be personable, aggressive, persistent, and above all not to accept the word "no." I learned that when anybody says "no" to you, you just turn back around and start again. Those people were all tough buyers. Although they were

PAUL WITH ROSE BLUMKIN OF NEBRASKA FURNITURE MART, CARON, AND JOHN COLLETT

friends, they wanted a good deal, so I had to learn how to sell tough people. Nevertheless, those guys were fair with me, and we developed personal as well as business relationships.

When I was the buyer, I believed in leaving a little bit on the table for the other guy. I tried to pass on the concept to our buyers that if the other guy is your friend, he can do things for you that oftentimes make the relationship more valuable than taking that last nickel.

Whether I was selling furniture or buying supplies and equipment, I really enjoyed working with someone who owned his own business. Generally, business owners seemed to value our relationship and were often more reasonable than a representative buyer for a big department or chain store. With the big guys you had to watch every move. Like being in a prizefight, you had to bob and weave. If you approach selling like a game and keep that in mind, you become a good player. If they are hitting and beating on you and you start getting mad or you get discouraged, you lose. I tried to teach that idea to my people.

Two of the best ways to become a successful salesman is to cultivate the relationship and to offer good service. I had salesmen who were not particularly aggressive but who became good friends with their clients and ended up being good salesmen. To handle big, tough guys, you had to be more than friends. Certain salesmen just had the knack. There were times when some big buying groups came in with six, eight, or ten people who started jabbering all at once. One got you out of balance and then the other came at you. A lot of times when I was the boss, I'd have a salesman and a sales manager with me. With three of us, we learned how to double team and handle those tough guys.

The final key to being liked as a salesperson is that you have to like the people. That was one of my main points about successful selling. Even though some customers were tough and hard, I truly learned to like and respect them.

13

Building Blocks of Broyhill

FAMILY BUSINESSES ARE often characterized as being inefficient and unprofessional. I had heard stories about how nepotism ruined many family businesses, so I took that idea as a challenge and committed myself to having a professional, hard-hitting organization.

CHAIRMAN J.E. AND PRESIDENT PAUL BROYHILL OF BROYHILL INDUSTRIES

Going from fewer than 750 employees to over 7,500 employees requires a lot of good management. I was determined that we were going to manage as competently as anyone in the furniture industry, or any other industry, for that matter. About ten years after I went into the business, my responsibilities included four major areas: organization development, production (plant efficiency), merchandising/sales, and administration.

Organization

I took training courses and read a lot of books on professional management. Then I sent our key people to training courses. I was impressed with American Management Association. They had many types of short-term courses lasting a week or just a weekend. From time to time, we hired consultants and used on-site motivational speakers to help implement our training programs. One consulting firm I particularly remember was Aubrey Daniels International. Daniels presented a course based on a book entitled *Behavior Modification* by B. F. Skinner. For our purposes, I changed the name to *Performance Management.* Daniels then integrated that name into his own programs. I later kidded him that he owed me a fee for the name.

One of Aubrey's primary precepts was what he called "utilizing at-a-boys." When someone or some department did a good job, we taught our supervisors to motivate using praise and various types of awards. We were big on giving service awards, and nearly half of our employees had five years or more tenure with the company.

As a way to keep employees informed and involved, we began publishing in-house organs: *The Broyhill Bugle, People Today at Broyhill,* and *Outlook.* Through those magazines we recognized people who had reached various performance milestones by featuring their pictures. We included articles about the company such as "Understanding your Profit-Sharing Plan," "The Design of the New Complex," and articles on production innovations. Those publications served to boost morale and to make all the segments feel part of the whole.

W.I.N. TEAMS AT WORK

DECLINING PRODUCTIVITY

Our nation has been faced with a problem of declining productivity as indicated by the chart below.

Change in output per hour of all workers

1948-1966	+3.2%
1966-1973	+2.1%
1973-1978	+1.0%
1978-1980	−1.0%

This reduced efficiency has contributed to the loss of large segments of business to foreign competition including automobiles, steel, television sets, and many other products.

Declining productivity has been blamed on lack of capital investment by management and a general "don't give a darn" attitude on the part of labor.

We are not letting this happen at Broyhill. The company has consistently invested capital back into the business to keep plant and equipment as modern as possible. Our employees have maintained a high degree of interest in doing the very best job possible.

THE WIN PROGRAM BEGINS

Recently, a company-wide program was initiated to enlist the aid of all our employees to effect improvements and beneficial changes. This program is completely voluntary, and a large majority of our people have offered to participate. Already, significant results have been attained.

Some teams are still in the organizational process. This 2nd shift Pacemaker team is meeting for the first time. At this first meeting they are being introduced to the program and its objectives.

Particular emphasis is being placed in the following areas of our work:

1. **Quality of Product**

   How can we turn out a product that we are proud to bear our name, in both materials and workmanship.

2. **Quality of the Environment**

   How can we make the job more safe, more comfortable, and more enjoyable.

3. **Quality in Productivity**

   How can we be more efficient so as to reduce the cost of manufacture.

THE COMING YEAR

As we enter 1982 we feel certain that our W.I.N. teams will make meaningful contributions in all of these areas. Their suggestions will play an important role in the continuing increase in our productivity — a factor which makes Broyhill a leader in the industry.

Other teams have had numerous meetings. These Corporation team members are reviewing a list of suggestions covering a number of different topics.

Teams such as this one at the Rutherford Plant are working hard to improve the daily operation of our company. Their contributions will play a significant role in the continuing growth and prosperity of Broyhill Furniture Industries.

4

A SAMPLE PAGE FROM *PEOPLE TODAY AT BROYHILL* (CONTINUED NEXT PAGE)

Health Insurance Can Provide Protection And Peace Of Mind For You . . . And Your Family.

"There has been an accident . . . He's pretty sick. We had better admit him at least for a couple of days." The admitting desk asks, "Who will be paying the medical bill . . . do you have insurance?"

Most people seldom think about their insurance coverage until someone they know or they themselves have been injured or are ill. Then comes the worry over bills and insurance coverage.

If you are insured through the Broyhill Employee Benefit Plan, you can have peace of mind knowing that your insurance plan is among the best in the industry. Furthermore, our insurance is a "good buy" providing protection at a cost much lower than that obtained through outside insurance agencies.

When reading through our insurance booklet the "before mentioned", "coordinator of", "coverage with respect to", and other legal sounding phrases are difficult to understand. They are necessary to precisely define our insurance policy, but to most people they sound confusing. Let's set these terms aside and briefly examine some of the main points of our policy.

When a person comes to Broyhill on a full time basis, he or she can immediately sign up for insurance. The cost currently is $2.00 per week for an individual policy or $6.00 per week for a family policy. It is always best to sign up right away, because if you wait longer than 31 days, you must fill out additional paperwork. Insurance coverage will begin on the first day of the month which follows your first month of employment. For example, if a person begins work on September 15, and takes out insurance on that date, his coverage will begin on November 1.

The schedule of benefits is contained on page 17 of your "Employee Benefit Plan" booklet. This chart lists the major categories of benefits:

(1) $50 weekly disability benefit which you will receive if you are sick or disabled and under a doctor's care (he verifies your period of disability);

(2) $85 per day for room and board; - charges such as X-Rays, laboratory work, anesthesia, use of the operating room and etc. 80% up to $500;

(3) Major Medical is $100 deductible per cause which must be accumulated within a consecutive 3 month period and pays 80% up to $100,000.

A detailed explanation of the "Schedule of Benefits" can be obtained either by consulting the "Employee Benefit Plan" booklet or by asking for details from your plant personnel manager.

One of the most important rules to keep in mind in order to obtain the maximum possible benefit for which a person is entitled, is that all accidents or other claims should be promptly reported. Our policy is designed to provide coverage for a host of problems and the claim filing process is not complicated. These are the steps to follow:

I. Report the accident or illness.
   A. Be careful to turn in all insurance information to the hospital or doctor.
   B. Contact your personnel manager if you receive any bills from the doctor's office which you feel have not been filed on insurance.

II. Save all receipts for medicine being sure that they list the prescription number and date.

III. Bring all bills to your plant personnel office.
   (Most bills will be sent directly to Broyhill if the hospital or doctor has complete insurance information.)

After Pilot Life has received all of your bills, they will carefully review each one and calculate the correct amount to be paid toward each bill. Pilot Life will then develop a work sheet listing all the bills which they have received and the payment which they have sent out to the doctor and the hospital. Broyhill will receive two copies of this worksheet, check them carefully and send a copy to the employee who made the claim.

After the insurance has paid all that it can, the employee will normally be notified by the doctor or hospital of any remaining charges.

Since some expenses which are not covered by insurance are tax deductible, you should keep accurate records of all bills which are paid. These will be used to document medical deductions on your income tax return.

This is a very brief explanation of our insurance plan. If you have additional questions concerning a specific aspect of the policy, please consult your handbook or speak to your plant personnel manager. He or she will be able to provide answers to almost any question you may have concerning your coverage under the Broyhill Employee Benefit Plan.

SAMPLE PAGE (CONTINUED)

For Oldest And Largest, A Key Step

VENEER ROOM—The veneer room is one of the departments at Corporation where a more thorough scheduling and production control system already has been installed. Numerous improvements have been achieved as a result of the changes.

The oldest and largest plant in the Broyhill organization is also the first to undertake establishment of a more thorough scheduling and production control system.

Lenoir Furniture Corporation, founded in 1905 and bought by T. H. Broyhill in 1913, has undergone many changes through the years but the latest is regarded as the most important.

Henry Medlock, superintendent of Corporation, outlines the purposes of the scheduling and production control system in this manner:

—To schedule sufficient lead times on specific items that require more than the average work.

—To see that workloads are properly balanced throughout the plant.

—To be able to measure the work that is being done in each department and to follow up to see that it is done in sufficient quality and quantity.

Initial steps in the system were taken 20 months ago. George Murphy, formerly plant personnel manager, was selected to be the coordinator of scheduling and production control.

The changeover is now 60 per cent complete and the tentative target date for completion has been set for October.

—6—

PRODUCTION INNOVATIONS AT LENOIR FURNITURE CORPORATION HIGHTLIGHTED IN THE BROYHILL *OUTLOOK*, 1967 (CONTINUED NEXT PAGE)

DANIELSON

BEACH

MCGEE

AUSTIN

JARVIS

MURPHY

TUNSTALL

MEDLOCK

WALKER

HARTLEY

KIZER

CHESTER

TOLBERT

CLAY

In commenting on the results to date, Superintendent Medlock had this to say: "In the departments where the system has been installed, the flow of materials has been improved, working conditions are improved, storage space is properly maintained, and there is a better-balanced workload for employees."

Since 1913, when T. H. Broyhill acquired the plant, Corporation has moved from a state of virtual bankruptcy to become one of the largest and most modern case goods plants in the country.

Following the death of T. H. Broyhill in 1955, J. E. Broyhill and his family purchased most of the company stocks owned by the T. H. Broyhill family, including those of Corporation.

Today the plant has 436,000 square feet of floor space and over 700 employees who combine their talents to turn out dining room and bedroom furniture in the Premier case goods line.

Frank Barlow and Vance Craig are vivid examples of the loyalty of Corporation employees. Both of these men have been on the plant payroll for 49 years, sticking to the job through successful as well as lean years.

And virtually every plant supervisor is a veteran member of the Broyhill organization, with their combined service totaling 391 years.

Superintendent Medlock has been with the company 17 years, being promoted to his present post in 1961 after serving as general manager of Lenoir Veneer Co.

Joe Tunstall, who joined Broyhill 10 years ago, has been assistant superintendent at Corporation since 1959. He previously served as cabinet room foreman at the Marion plant.

Other plant supervisors and their years of service to the company include:

George Murphy, scheduling and production control coordinator, 16 years.
Charles Jarvis, personnel manager, 11 years.
Jack Austin, construction engineer, 20 years.
Pat McGee, quality control, 39 years.
William O. Beach, chip core, 16 years.
J. E. Danielson, lumber yard, 19 years.
Clarence Walker, rough mill, 35 years.
Harry Hartley, finish machine, 18 years.
David Kizer, assistant in finish machine, 35 years.
Bill Chester, glue room, 3 years.
Paul Tolbert, veneer room, 8 years.
James Clay, sanding, 20 years.

VETERANS—Both Vance Craig, left, and Frank Barlow have been on the Corporation payroll for 49 years. They're shown here carrying out duties in the cabinet room.

Cecil Crump, cabinet room, line No. 1, 19 years.
Archie Triplett, cabinet room, line No. 2, 11 years.
Junior Ford, cabinet room, line No. 3, 9 years.
Haywood Puett, finishing, 17 years.
Bobby West, bleach, 10 years.
Ed Caudill, rub and pack, 16 years.
Stanley Rash, shipping, 31 years.
John Livingston, maintenance, 11 years.

CRUMP

TRIPLETT

FORD

PUETT

WEST

CAUDILL

RASH

LIVINGSTON

—7—

PRODUCTION INNOVATIONS (CONTINUED)

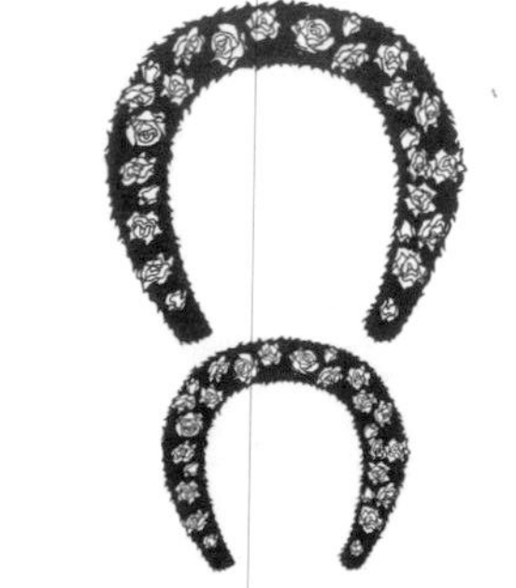

KEY ACCOUNT INTENSIFICATION PROGRAM

Saleable Products

Broyhill will design, produce, and ship the most saleable line of basically designed, good quality, reasonably priced merchandise available on the market today. While it will always be possible to cherry pick the market and beat us on a given suite, it is impossible for you to get an across-the-board line-up from one manufacturer that can compete with what we have to offer.

Efficient Service

Broyhill has the best trained and most conscientious sales service and traffic department in the industry. Our traffic specialists will work with you on an individual basis to administrate orders and to keep merchandise rolling on a consistent basis and at the lowest possible freight costs.

Sales Training

Broyhill has the best trained sales force in the industry. Their emphasis this year will be to help you move Broyhill merchandise through your store on to the ultimate consumer.

To achieve this goal we have produced a full library of product oriented audio/visual sales training programs. In the spring of 1980 Broyhill will be introducing a comprehensive five part audio/visual retail sales training program complete with printed support material. This program will be offered to you first!

Sensible Distribution

Key dealers deserve discretion in the handling of distribution. While Broyhill needs multiple placements in more trading areas, the most business we can get from key dealers, the less business we have to get elsewhere.

Brand Awareness

Broyhill has one of the best known brand names in the industry. We enjoy this position by having pioneered our brand name in national magazines and television. In effect, we have created an umbrella for our entire dealer network.

We are committed to build an even greater consumer organization by intensifying our "brand name" advertising. Such a commitment can only be achieved through the mass medium of television.

THE PRICE IS RIGHT

Promotions

During the coming year we plan to develop in-line promotions on a continuing basis sufficient to keep ours and your business coming in at a normal rate. The biggest promotion of the year will be the Broyhill Factory Authorized Sale. Other promotions will be developed on a continuous basis at various times during the year by each Broyhill division. All these promotions will be offered to Broyhill key dealers first.

Broyhill Factory Authorized Sale

Key Dealer Trip Award

In order to get a chance to personally visit with our key dealers on a more intimate and personal basis, Broyhill is inaugurating a key dealer trip award. Winners will be the top 100 accounts out of approximately 500 qualifying key dealers. So, there will be a high percentage of winners. The top 100 will be chosen on the basis of percentage increase over the previous year in total Broyhill volume, so that each dealer has just as good a chance as another. The top 100 will be entertained at a well known resort area and the trip will be given free to the winner and wife.

THIS BROCHURE EXPLAINED HOW BROYHILL WOULD HELP INTENSIFY SALES.

The problem with teaching effective professional management, we theorized, was that the responsibility usually fell upon the personnel department. The bosses rarely became involved. I, however, determined it was going to be learned and taught from the top down. Bill Stevens and I developed a set of courses called *The Cascading Principle of Professional Management* that he and I taught to about 50 managers. After completing the course, the managers had the responsibility of teaching the management principles to the layer below them. When you teach something yourself, you learn it better. Through that approach, we fostered among our managers a tremendous desire for efficiency, professionalism, and for the pride of a job well done.

The American Management Association's *Management by Objectives* identified four components of effective leadership: planning, organizing, motivating, and controlling. We worked with every manager to analyze his own area of responsibility under each of those four headings. From that, each wrote down his specific management objectives.

BILL STEVENS TEACHES *MANAGEMENT BY OBJECTIVES* TO BROYHILL MANAGERS.

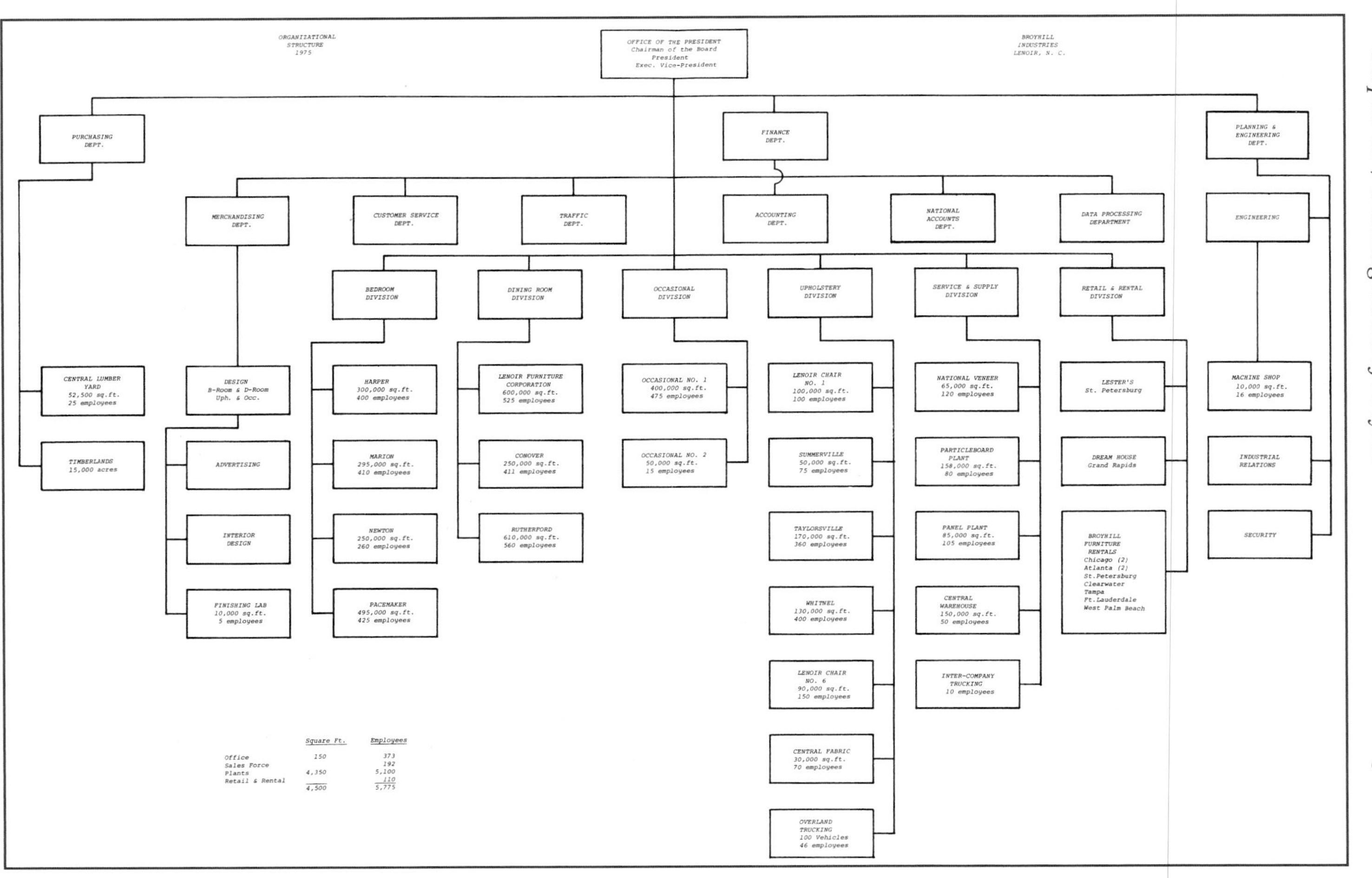

BROYHILL FURNITURE ORGANIZATIONAL CHART

We also implemented a technique called short interval scheduling. Previously, we measured efficiency through broad numerical objectives by plant and by department. Under short interval scheduling, we established objectives at every production terminal. It is amazing how something that simple increased output.

I previously mentioned that my dad had been secretive about financial information. Under my administration, we did just the opposite. We set goals for more than 50 profit centers. Each quarter we held a meeting with key people and put all the facts and figures on a screen. Each manager reported on his operation and I summarized. Through all our efforts, gradually our results improved until by the early '60s our overall operations had become highly profitable. We were finally equal to Bassett and Drexel, my long held objective.

Historically we had been unable to hire many engineering graduates into the plants. They came in at a higher pay scale, requiring as much or more than our long-term employees, thus creating a potential morale problem. At that time, Appalachian State University was oriented toward teacher training and teachers were not making as much money as engineers. ASU did have a woodworking education program. Under Bill Stevens' direction, we began hiring 10–15 people a year from the Appalachian program. We put them through our plant training programs. That alleviated the pay differential problem by allowing us to bring in recruits at a more reasonable pay rate. Nevertheless, they were college graduates, they fit in well, and they progressed quickly into management positions.

With Broyhill Furniture Industries headquartered in Lenoir, when we added plants we concentrated on Western North Carolina, locating them in the nearby towns of Newton, Conover, Taylorsville, Marion, and Rutherfordton. That geographical proximity gave the company the flexibility to combine shipments from the various plants. That was a distinct advantage over manufacturers with scattered operations. Being localized, we could combine and ship, cost-effectively, to every nook and cranny throughout the United States, and even to some foreign countries.

LENOIR FURNITURE CORPORATION

THE PACEMAKER PLANT, PART OF THE COMPLEX

THE WHITNEL PLANT, AKA LENOIR #3

The company focused on a highly defined market. We had low-medium to high-medium priced residential furniture for living room, dining room, and bedroom settings. Our marketing strategy placed Broyhill at the center of a retail bell curve. If the retailers were high end, the Broyhill line would be their starting point. If the retailers were lower end, Broyhill would be their best.

As the company grew, we had to devise a way to break down the organization into smaller, more productive units. We ended up with four divisions: bedroom, dining room, occasional, and upholstery. Each had a division manager, a sales manager, and a production manager who was responsible for the operation and profits of specific plants.

Because I needed a simple but effective way to keep a close eye on every aspect of the business, I devised a system of weekly reports. I asked that all top executives including division managers, plant managers, sales managers, and department managers (about 50 people) write a concise, weekly report of less than a page in which they documented important decisions, problems, or suggestions. I could read all the reports in less than two hours on Saturday mornings. From those reports I kept an up-to-date grasp on the entire organization.

Production

We always believed in being on the cutting edge. As technologies changed, we were determined to change with them. One of our first major innovations was the hot plate press. Veneers had been used through the years, even back to ancient times. However, veneers are inclined to turn loose at the glue line and warp or twist. When I came into the business, there were new glues available, which through a chemical reaction from heat and pressure from a hot plate press, became firm and long lasting. Prior to the new, innovative presses, we had used what had been known as a cold press. That was a slow and ineffective process.

All through the early days we made our furniture using five-ply panels. The interior ply was lumber sandwiched between two plies of veneer. The outer layer or "face veneer" was the select wood such as walnut, cherry, maple, pecan, or oak. On a trip to Germany in the '40s my dad and Clarence Beach saw an innovative product called chip core made from ground wood chips mixed with resin and pressed into boards or panels of stock sizes and thicknesses. German manufacturers were using it in their products instead of lumber core. Dad and Clarence were so impressed with the product that they bought four of the machines and installed them in our various plants.

The reprocessed wood industry continued to develop in Germany, and by the mid '70s they were making a product called particleboard that was strong yet had a nice, smooth surface. Particleboard has no grain, so it virtually is free of splitting, checking, shrinking and warping. We at Broyhill first used it to make three-ply panels instead of five-ply. Later we were able to print a wood grain directly onto it and make certain portions of our construction using single-ply printed board.

When we bought the particleboard machine, it was by far the largest machinery purchase we had ever made, but it made us self-sufficient in that we could produce our own chip core and particleboard.

Our next big innovation was "conveyorized" finishing rooms. We used to haul cases into a hot box by hand and pull them out by hand. It was slow, tedious work. We began putting conveyors into all of our finishing rooms. The conveyor took the furniture in and out of the hot boxes and spray booths, saving time and labor costs. That equipment was expensive, and in those days we had to make a little money before we could spend the money. Over a period of about five years, we automated all our finishing rooms. That was a tremendous leap forward.

THE CONVEYORIZED FINISHING ROOM MADE THE TEDIOUS WORK GO MUCH SMOOTHER.

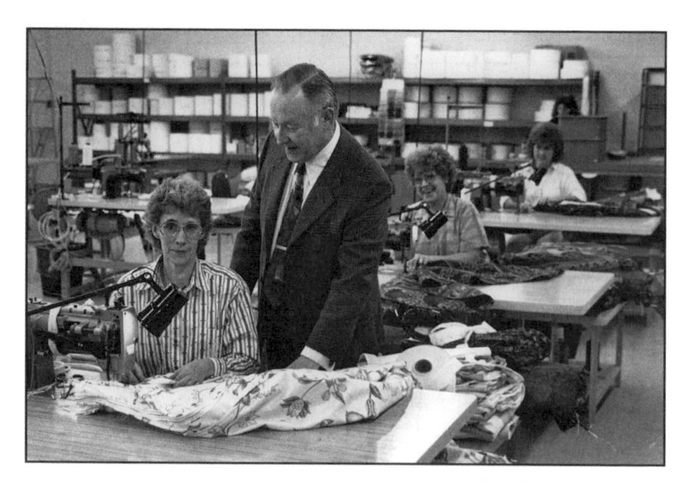

PAUL VIEWS PART OF THE UPHOLSTERY PROCESS IN THE SEWING ROOM.

The machine room also had been run completely with manual labor. Stock was put on the bed of a factory "truck," which was on wheels, and the stock literally was wheeled from one station to the next. We made changes first by automating the lumber cutting department. Then, instead of manhandling each board up to the machine, the boards were laid on a roller conveyor and automatically pushed along. Gradually, we added roller conveyors throughout the entire machine area and eliminated the need for factory trucks.

New automation in the assembly area transitioned the approach to a much more efficient process. Rather than one person doing most of the assembly on one piece at a time, now a system of moving conveyors with stations allowed each person to do a particular portion of the work. The piece continued moving through each station until it was completed.

Throughout the United States and the European woodworking industry, machinery was constantly being modernized. Our production people loved new machinery and would rather go to a machinery show than to a county fair. There was a large international show every two years in Hanover, Germany. Several times I took a contingent of six or eight engineers and plant managers to Europe. We split into various teams to work the show and came together each night to review notes. At the end of the week, we collectively made the final decisions right there on the spot. I authorized and placed millions of dollars worth of orders on those trips. While visiting the overseas shows, we also visited numerous plants and picked up production techniques that were not common in the United States. I managed to make a little time to take our country boys into a palace or chateau and give them a little history lesson.

Not only did we improve efficiency by "conveyorizing" our input and output, but as new machinery became available, each machine itself worked even faster. As time went on, the setting up of the machine became electronic rather than mechanical, saving even more time. Machines became multi-purpose, with one machine doing multiple tasks. Many of the machines were designed to operate in tandem.

There were similar innovations in almost every aspect of production. We constantly improved our capabilities through keeping abreast of the innovations and through implementing new ideas. We sought input by placing suggestion boxes around the plants so that employees from all levels could make suggestions to increase efficiency. We met regularly to discuss the submissions, and we gave awards for good ideas.

At every plant we had a wish list for capital expenditures. As money became available, we added more space or bought equipment. For a number of years, we even had our own construction crew. We had the ability, literally, to tear down a plant a little at a time and keep production going. We could not afford to let production stop, so we built roofs over tops of roofs, floors over tops of floors, moved machinery from one side to the other side, and somehow were able to keep the factories running and producing while we tore out the old roofs, walls, and floors all around them.

Fourth of July was the annual barbecue for our employees at all of our plants. After the Fourth, we completely shut down the plants for a vacation week with pay. For Thanksgiving, we worked on Thursday, but were off on Friday. On Thursday we had a big Thanksgiving dinner with turkey and all the trimmings at every plant. At Christmas we had another big dinner in each plant, and another paid vacation week. The management team of each plant and their spouses had a separate party at a local restaurant. We had a large office party for employees and spouses, which filled a club ballroom on two consecutive nights. I attended as many of the parties as possible, sometimes going to three in one night. At the end of the year we handed out bonuses and gave raises for the following year.

By the time Christmas was over, I was exhausted. Typically, the day after Christmas my family and I would jump in the plane, and go to Florida for a few days.

Merchandising/Sales

In the 1930s and '40s our product was known as the Lenoir Line because our two major companies were Lenoir Furniture Company and Lenoir Chair Company. During the early 1950s, we created a sales entity called Broyhill Furniture Industries through which we funneled the sales from all the plants. The dealers soon forgot the names of our individual plants and learned to know us as the Broyhill Line. That was the beginning of building up the Broyhill brand name.

Broyhill furniture had been known in the trade as promotional to medium-priced. In the early '60s we decided to create an upper-end division that would hit middle to high-middle price points. That strategy positioned us slightly under Drexel and Thomasville but above our existing price lines. We called the new line Broyhill Premier. With the advent of the Premier line, we ventured into national advertising. One of the first things we did was to hook up with *The Price is Right* on television. Broyhill has stayed with that show until this day, and has given away a tremendous amount of furniture to the game show's winners.

The most prominent magazines in the '60s were *Life* and *Look*, and we placed double page ads in them. No one in the industry had

BROYHILL BEDROOM ADVERTISEMENT

done that kind of multi-page advertising. We added to our magazine ads the very successful component of a dealer listing. When we sold a certain amount of product to a dealer, we listed him, free of charge in the magazine. That innovative advertising feature was a real hit with our dealers and caused them, in turn, to advertise *our* name in *their* local promotions. That strategy provided us a lot of momentum in building up our name.

By the early '80s our line was so broad and so strong that we were selling the idea that dealers should concentrate on fewer manufacturers. Of course, we wanted to be the dominant line on their floors. As that idea progressed, we came up with the Broyhill Gallery Program, an entirely new idea.

We went onto a dealer's floor with our interior designers and literally, structurally redesigned his space to accommodate a 5,000

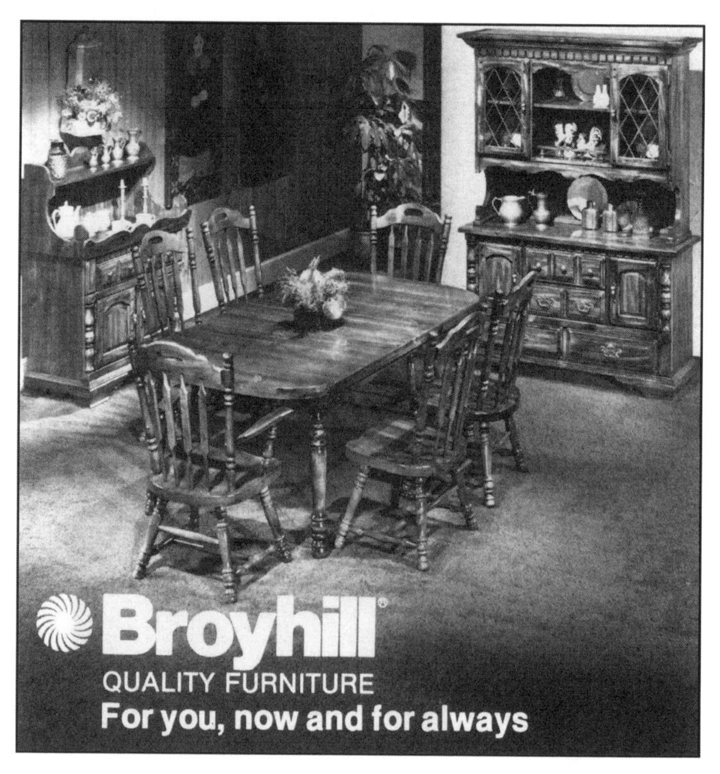

BROYHILL DINING ROOM ADVERTISEMENT

BROYHILL LIVING ROOM ADVERTISEMENT

square-foot Broyhill showcase gallery. Often, a dealer would give us much more floor space than the minimum we required because our showrooms tended to be substantially better looking than the average dealer showroom. In a short time, we were able to upgrade a dealer's existing store by creating well-merchandised and well-decorated settings. The Broyhill Gallery Program greatly increased our volume per dealer. Gradually, we were able to reduce the number of overall dealers, which eventually enabled the company to reduce the number of salesmen and still maintain our profit margins.

I put a lot of personal effort into the gallery program and went to many of the gallery openings. At those openings, the dealers would have arranged PR with local TV, radio stations, and celebrities. I enjoyed those events and look back at those times as dynamic ones for me as well as for the company.

In Broyhill Firm

Furniture Progress Evident

By JEANNE BARNES
Home Editor of The News

LENOIR, N.C.—The progress of the furniture industry is spelled out more clearly here in the new Broyhill showroom and offices than anywhere else visible.

Opening the new 138,000 square feet of space at the fall furniture market, the firm related its past 40 years, and particularly the past 40, to the vast changes in the way of living, of doing business and of technology most vividly.

DALLAS MORNING NEWS

Broyhill Industries An Empire Grows

HOME FURNISHINGS DAILY

40-Year Climb From 'Obscurity'

Broyhill Furniture Claims Spot As One of Industry's 'Big Four'

By Harold Ellison

WINSTON-SALEM JOURNAL AND SENTINEL

PARTHENON — When Broyhill Furniture Industries set out to build a new office building, said president Paul Broyhill, they thought not only of functional efficiency, but "beauty and timelessness" as well. Broyhill's management and design staff studied architecture of all types and all ages, and finally focused on ancient Greek architecture, which is about as timeless as you can get.

The interior is designed to expedite the work of a 250-member office force, includes such features as air-conditioning fed through a perforated ceiling, piped-in music, 180-seat dining room and kitchen, and 43,000 square feet of show room space which is entered via a marble-floored court.

Broyhill's new Parthenon - type building is a far cry (although located only 2 miles away) from the old blacksmith shop where J. E. Broyhill, now chairman of the board, went into business in 1926. In 40 years Broyhill has risen to the top four of the industry, now employs 5,000 persons in 13 plants covering over 3 million square feet of floor space.

STATE MAGAZINE

Growth In Furniture World

WHEN THE FALL furniture market across the middle of the Piedmont came to a close it brought forth a new story of the remarkable growth of this industry when the Broyhill Furniture Industries, headed up at Lenoir, opened their fine new general office and showroom building which was designed as a modern adaptation of the Parthenon at Athens which was constructed in 500 B.C.

buying a $2,000 interest in a plant, died in 1955. J. Ed Broyhill, who is fifteen years younger than his brother, came into the business later. In 1926 they owned one plant. J. E. Broyhill is now chairman of the board which operates fourteen plants with three million square feet of working space.

The Broyhill story is an inspiring one. However, Lexington and Thomasville, can just about match it. The big Dixie chain in Lexington and Asheboro and the United-Philpott plants here have each grown from small beginnings through local effort and Thomasville Furniture Industries can tell a like story through individual enterprise. And west of us Hickory, Morganton and Drexel can provide examples of the growth of the furniture industry through the efforts of home folks at the western end of North Carolina's great "furniture highway".

LEXINGTON DISPATCH

Broyhill Headquarters Modeled After Parthenon

Furniture Firm Unveils Showplace

DURHAM MORNING HERALD

Broyhill Furniture Industries' New Office Building And Showroom

Furniture Industry Now Has Its Own 'Parthenon'

By ROY COVINGTON

LENOIR — They're calling it the "Parthenon" of the furniture industry.

J. E. Broyhill, Chairman Of The Board

Paul Broyhill, President

The Charlotte Observer Business

CHARLOTTE OBSERVER

FROM BLACKSMITH SHOP TO FURNITURE INDUSTRY LEADER IN 40 YEARS

In October, 1926, J. E. Broyhill started making furniture in a blacksmith shop. In spite of the depression, his business grew. One of the reasons was his philosophy about his business. "We give more," he insisted.

FURNITURE WORLD

FURNITURE SOUTH

J. E. Broyhill, Board Chairman

FORTY-YEAR CLIMB of Broyhill Furniture Industries from "obscurity" to top prominence as one of the industry's "big four" is symbolized in this multi-million-dollar structure recently completed on a 40-acre tract north of Lenoir, N. C. Broyhill's new office building and showroom is a modern adaptation of the Parthenon, constructed in Athens, Greece, in 500 B.C. The building has 138,000 sq. ft. of floor space on three floors.

J. E. BROYHILL — PAUL BROYHILL

BROYHILL'S NEW HEADQUARTERS in Lenoir, N. C., is a modern adaptation of the Parthenon, built in Athens, Greece, in 500 B.C.

FURNITURE DESIGN & MANUFACTURING

FURNITURE DESIGN & MANUFACTURING/DECEMBER, 1966

IT WAS NO SECRET THAT BROYHILL WAS A MAJOR PLAYER IN THE FURNITURE INDUSTRY.

J. E. AND SATIE AT A GALLERY OPENING
DURING THE SEATTLE WORLD'S FAIR

PAUL AND TOM BROYHILL AT HUTSON FURNITURE
COMPANY GALLERY OPENING

PAUL WITH HERB, RALPH, AND MARLENE SCHOENFELD AT A GALLERY RIBBON CUTTING

DEALERS ARRANGED MANY TYPES OF PR, SUCH AS THIS LOCAL BAND THAT PLAYED FOR A BROYHILL GALLERY OPENING.

In the middle '70s I remember walking through our showrooms and seeing extensive amounts of plastic being used as embellishments on our case goods line. I theorized that soon the plastics trend would no longer be considered in good taste. In fact, I was actually ashamed of some of our merchandise. I called our production and sales people together for a meeting. I told them exactly what I thought: "In looking at our furniture, I'm no longer proud of it. I have decided that we are going to get back into the furniture business and replace plastic with wood."

The prouction people rose up and said, "This is going to hurt our production!"

I remember my exact reply: "Just call me Brer Rabbit and throw me back into the briar patch."

Because of that decision, we got a little ahead of the competition in getting away from plastic and back into wood furniture. We created a product line made from pine and oak. That suited us well with so much pine and oak wood growing in our area. The demand for European (English, French, and Spanish) styles stayed strong, along with contemporary. But the pine and oak availability created a surge in Early American and American Traditional, both heavy and light scale, which continued for at least the next ten years.

Administration

Until the early '50s, our administrative procedures had been archaic. As with other areas, we wanted to upgrade. We installed the latest office technology, the IBM punch card system. We did not use punch cards very long before the first viable computer came out: the IBM 1401. It was a miracle in its day, but I am told that the smallest handheld computer today is more powerful than that original large-scale model. As computers evolved, we constantly updated, continuing into the modern era with mini-computers and company networks replacing the old, giant mainframe.

The customer service people held the hands of dealers. I organized a system whereby specific persons in the office were responsible for the service needs of specific dealers. Our dealers came to love their Broyhill contact persons in the office. They always wanted to meet "their" service person and often sent cards and presents to them at Christmas. Large companies tend to centralize functions; we did just the opposite and constantly tried to decentralize.

As our enterprises grew, we often started a new corporation. We had only a small amount of personal money to put into a new company, so we borrowed capital through the established corporations. That process allowed us to include a number of our key personnel as stockholders in the new entities. At one point we had more than 30 companies, and having all those corporations made accounting extremely complicated. One corporation might own part of another, and that one would own part of another, and so on.

As we began to reorganize the administration, I realized that we had to change our corporate structure. I worked with Ed Beach, vice president of finance, to devise a plan to merge all the companies. He and I worked out the details through complicated algebraic equations. We decided the value of each company, how the consolidation should proceed, and the plan for a tax-free merger. Ed had to go to Washington to present the plan to the IRS. He took a planeload of financial statements to back up our desire for a modern, corporate structure. Ultimately, all the companies converged into Broyhill Furniture Industries.

During that time, as we were building facilities, building the organization, and building the product line, we were gradually building our profit margins. It was not until the mid '60s, however, that all our building began to pay off as highly profitable operations. My dad had borrowed money throughout his career. During my career I had a rule not to borrow more than 50% of our net worth, and then I backed it down as rapidly as possible.

In 1966 my dad and I went to Charlotte to play golf with the head of First Union Bank, Cliff Cameron, and his chief financial officer, W. J. Smith. W. J. was a great person and a competent banker. At the end of the day when we were paying off the few dollar bets in the locker room of the Charlotte Country Club, I pulled out a check for two million dollars, handed it to Cliff and said, "This pays off the last note that we have with your bank." As far as I know, that was the first time my dad had been completely out of debt since he went into business in 1927. Slightly stunned, Cliff said he'd never before done that much bank business in the locker room.

I hesitated to join outside organizations because I felt that I already was associated with so many of my own organizations, and I really did not have time for extra-curricular obligations. In spite of my usual reluctance, when I was 39 some friends convinced me to join YPO (Young Presidents Organization) while I still qualified. The stipulation for membership in the group of young businessmen was to achieve the position of company president prior to the age of 40. Members aged out at 50. I decided to join. YPO is a national organization, but we formed a special group of company presidents from the South. We called ourselves *The Rebel Chapter of YPO* and met four times a year for a weekend at a resort area. Gathering on a Thursday evening, we held three business sessions on Friday, Saturday, and Sunday mornings. Afternoons were free for games of tennis or golf. Faye and I attended those meetings for ten years, and through them I gleaned a lot of business information and made many friends throughout southeastern United States.

There was an interesting side effect of my membership in YPO. Until that time, I was technically a vice president. I had acted as general manager and had never used a title nor had a printed business card. The company had never held a board meeting or a stockholders' meeting. Once a year, I wrote up some minutes; then, as officers of the corporation, Dad, Ed Beach, and I signed them. When I was 39, in order for me to qualify for YPO, we wrote into the corporate minutes that I was elected president and that Dad was elevated to chairman. So, technically, I made myself president of the company.

THE 1967 MANAGEMENT TEAM.
SEATED L-R: PAUL BROYHILL, J.E. BROYHILL, AND BILL STEVENS. STANDING L-R: JIM MCCALL, CLARENCE BEACH, HUBERT THOMAS, AND CLARENCE HOLDEN.

14

Diversification

Plastics

LIKE ANY INDUSTRY, styles come and go in furniture. Contemporary was popular for a while, then traditional, and there was a period when Spanish took center stage. The Spanish style is somewhat more ornamental than contemporary or traditional. That ornamental furniture took quite a bit of hand carving to achieve the embellishments. The industry began to gravitate toward the idea of making simulated wood moldings out of plastic. Various kinds of plastics were used and were molded by numerous processes. The kind of molding that became most popular was called injection molding. That process used a huge machine that bore down on a jig with heat and pressure. Using the injection molding method we were able to take a piece of plastic carving, attach it to a piece of furniture, and make it look like wood carving.

We decided that rather than buying moldings from a supplier, we could make them ourselves. I always liked diversification. We bought a dozen or so of the injection molding machines in different sizes. Then I got carried away. We were diversified in furniture, and I thought how smart it would be to be diversified in plastics. We bought an extrusion machine, which was a wide machine that constantly extruded a stream of plastic that looked similar to a tabletop. A cutter would cut the plastic and would put it into another type of mold. Then we purchased a machine that produced a tremendous bubble of film that was almost like blowing up a balloon as tall as the room. The bubble was contained and formed into sheets. From the sheets we made, for instance, garbage bags and grocery bags. There were a number of uses for blown plastic and we were momentarily successful. However, because this was an entirely new business, we had to hire outside people from the plastics industry to help us. We hired and fired a number of people, ending up with only a moderately capable organization.

If that weren't enough, in 1973–74 we faced the oil crisis. In our plastics business we used primarily polystyrene and polypropylene as our basic raw materials, both of which were derivatives of oil. All of a sudden we had difficulty getting the raw material to keep the plastics plant running. Previously, anytime I had a major problem, I could dedicate my attention to it, and with hard work and drive, see it through. With that crisis in our plastics business, I personally went to six or eight of the largest suppliers. While I was able to get in to see vice presidents and presidents of companies, after a month or so of trying, I had secured only a miniscule amount of material. I remember working right up until Christmas on the West Coast. I recall landing in Denver, Colorado, in a blinding snowstorm, spending the night in Denver, and then coming home the next morning. So discouraging was that trip that I decided to sell the plastics business.

I had heard that Bassett Furniture Company, our strongest competitor for many, many years, had gone into the plastics business. I also heard that they had recently sold their business to Libby Owens Ford, a company out of Toledo, Ohio. Libby Owens Ford was originally in the glass business. Their background probably came out of some combination of Ford Motor Company and Libby Owens. I called the president of Libby Owens Ford and told him that I had a successful plastics company and that I liked the business, but that I couldn't get sufficient raw material. I knew he had contacts that enabled him to buy the raw material. I asked him if he could help me. He suggested that I come to Toledo and talk with him. I took with me Ed Beach, my right-hand man in finance, and Ken Kepley, the man who was running our plastics operation.

We traveled to Toledo in the company Learjet that I had purchased and learned to fly. We landed in icy conditions. My Lear did not have reversers, but it did have anti-skid brakes, similar to those later used on cars. If a plane starts to skid, the wheels will release for a slight moment. In a car you may not notice, but in a plane you can feel it happen. As we went down the runway in the plane, it went screech . . . screech . . . screech . . . as it was braking. I will never forget that icy runway and hitting those brakes and nothing happening. Even when idling, jet engines have a certain amount of thrust. As I touched down, I cut off both engines. In spite of having non-skid brakes, we slid off the edge of the runway. Fortunately, the runway and the ground around it were level for an adequate distance. We were lucky to be within that distance. I restarted the engines, whirled the plane around, and taxied back very slowly.

When we finally arrived in Toledo, we went to the company president's guesthouse in the country. We had dinner with several of the Libby Owens Ford executives there. During dinner I extolled the virtues of our plastics business. Quite frankly, we were sick of it. I was just doing a good sales job. As a rule, my friend Ed Beach did not drink much. However, that night he sat with a wine glass in his hand. Ed squeezed that glass so hard that all of a sudden he broke the damn thing. Fortunately, there was not much wine in it and Ed nervously mopped it up with his napkin. He later told me that the more I exaggerated, the harder he squeezed that glass.

We did make a deal. I had brought our financial information with me, and we sold the business that night. We more or less got our money out of it and were glad to bid farewell to the plastics business.

The building that housed the plastics plant was located in an area of several buildings that we called the Broyhill industrial complex. I was very proud of the complex and didn't really want to sell the building. Libby Owens Ford didn't want to buy the building, so I gave them a generous lease and an option to get out of the lease. We negotiated to sell them the machinery and the inventory.

During the negotiations, I praised Ken Kepley, our plastics manager, who had been a long time Broyhill guy. We had hired Ken for what was probably one of his first jobs and had trained him. Ken was a good man. I had put him in the company in place of some plastics people who had proved to be incompetent. After we sealed the deal with Libby Owens Ford, I assured Ken that if he went with them, he could always come back to Broyhill in as good or better a position than that which he left. He went on to make some money with them, later came back to Broyhill, and ultimately started his own retail furniture business in the Myrtle Beach area.

After some years, it turned out that the demand for the carved plastic product diminished, so Libby Owens Ford decided to combine two of their plants. Since their lease had an exit clause, they gave us notice and moved everything out of our building.

I was glad for them to vacate because I wanted to start a furniture operation in that building. They took several weeks to make the move, but they were paying rent during that period. As they moved out of an area of the building, our production people started moving in. My friend Kepley let me do that. After a few weeks we occupied half of the plant. Kepley came to me and said, "My God, Paul, you're turning that space into a furniture factory, and I'm still paying the rent."

I did turn the building into a furniture factory and was making money within a few months. We had the organization and the ability with an engineering team that when I said we were going to "do this and do that," they could get on it and get it done. That was the end of our career in the plastics business.

Prefabricated Housing

Taylor Construction, a father and sons team, had done work for us through the years. They had started a new business producing prefabricated housing components. The Taylors did the same thing to me that I had done to the people at Libby Owens Ford. They sat down with me and told me that the prefabricated parts business was a great business. In reality, they were struggling financially. They convinced me that the business would be much better under my leadership than theirs. I fell for their pitch and bought their prefabricated construction company. The technology involved lumber handling machinery, so it was a natural sideline. The building of the parts was easy for us as there was no learning curve and we had some good people we could utilize. We had a nice little plant for building the parts, which we sold to small contractors who built a few houses at a time. We did not sell to the big outfits that were building hundreds of homes.

Small builders wanted to wait to pay us until after they got paid for a house. The business worked well for a while, until a housing slump occurred as a result of the savings and loan crisis. Suddenly, all the small builders that were our customers disappeared, along with our money. At that point, what looked like a nice sideline business suddenly became a real headache. Fortunately, it was a business that we could shut down almost immediately. We could use the building and most of the machinery in our other plants. We tried to collect on the accounts as much as possible, but overall, we lost money on the prefabricated housing business.

Yet again, we turned that building into a furniture factory. In both of those instances, I turned a sow's ear into the proverbial silk purse. We had a furniture factory going there within a matter of months.

Going Southwest

Another seemingly logical diversification was to establish some production in the Southwest. At the time we were doing a lot of business there, with Houston and Dallas being the center of our activities. We bought a case goods plant in Austin, Texas, and started up an upholstery plant near Shreveport, Louisiana. Those locations made production and distribution points closer to the dealers, especially in an area that seemed to be booming.

We were able to get the factories going because, again, it was our familiar technology. However, the sales did not come as readily as we had expected. Surprisingly, our greatest competitor was Broyhill Furniture in Lenoir. We had trained the dealers so well to buy from Lenoir by combining the product line that they were not as interested in a much smaller product line in the Austin-Shreveport area. We struggled with those plants for a period of time but ultimately closed them.

Retail

One of our key accounts was Watkins Furniture in Cleveland, Ohio, run by one of my closest retail friends, Lou Rippner. The original owner of the company passed away, and the business was sold to someone who did not manage it well and who eventually wanted to sell it. I decided to buy the business at what I thought to be a good price. At that time, Watkins also had been in the furniture rental business, so using Watkins as a nucleus, we started developing furniture rental stores in the surrounding areas of Cleveland, Toledo, and Akron.

A little later, we purchased two retail furniture operations in Florida in Ft. Lauderdale and St. Petersburg. In addition to those, we developed furniture rental stores in surrounding areas including Miami, Ft. Lauderdale, West Palm Beach, Jacksonville, and on Florida's west coast in St. Petersburg, Clearwater, and Tampa. (See Appendix B, page 310.)

Lou Rippner was in charge of all those operations, and I thought with his background he would enjoy being in charge of those diverse locations. He enjoyed it for a while but eventually tired of the traveling. When he received an attractive offer in New Orleans, he decided to accept. He went on to start his own business in New Orleans and became quite successful.

Without a driving force in the retail sector, those far-flung units finally deteriorated to the point that we decided to sell the three retail operations but retained the rental component. When we eventually sold Broyhill Furniture to Interco, they were not interested in the rental business, so I kept it personally.

Most of our diversification endeavors did not turn out well. Our success had been in building business from the ground up: purchasing land, building a factory, hiring production people, developing a product line, and training sales people. In other words, our success was built the old-fashioned way, without mergers or acquisitions, just continuing to broaden and strengthen the elements that we had developed from the beginning.

15

Creative Design

Furniture

When I first started in the business, I gravitated toward design. At that time our line was small and relatively simple. In both case goods and upholstery we had European traditional and Early American styles but more than half the sales volume was from our contemporary line. Pricing for our contemporary three-piece suites started at $89.95 and went up in approximately ten-dollar increments to about $159.00. At the Harper plant, we had a small line of medium-priced, 18th century traditional case goods made of cherry and mahogany and a short line of kneehole and secretary desks. In upholstery we offered a small line of boudoir chairs and lounge chairs. During my career, we constantly added new designs to the mix with more diversity and more sophisticated styling so that eventually, we had the broadest product line in the industry that could be shipped from one shipping point.

As I turned my attention to furniture design, I also became interested in architectural design and, later, landscape design.

Chateau Broyhill

One of my first major building projects was my own home. I had been traveling to Europe every year for about 20 years and had developed an appreciation for European style. Most of the old French chateaus started with a basic H-shape and included high pointed rooflines. I drew an H-shaped floor plan and then drew the roofline and entrance.

I took the drawing to a well-known architect, Frank McCall, Jr., from Moultrie, Georgia. I saw a number of homes he had designed at Sea Island, Georgia, and liked his "design touch." I contacted him and asked if he would give me detailed drawings of the plan I had sketched. I told him that I didn't need any supervision or any onsite visits, just the plans. On that basis, he gave me a low price of $5,000, and I hired him. Then, I hired a small contractor in Hickory, Jackie Landry, a lady who was reliable and competent. I used one of my factory engineers to help supervise the construction. The home was strictly hand-built, with a crew of fewer than six people most of the time. It took about two years to complete.

Once the house started going up, I realized we still had a lot of work to do to plan the interior. I used my furniture designers to create patterns of paneling for the walls and made them in our factory. At that time, the company was purchasing carved wood parts from Spain and marble from Portugal. With those connections, I was able to buy very inexpensively the marble flooring for my entrance and a number of antique reproductions from Spain. Also, I was able to buy carpets from Spain, which I designed specifically for the rooms.

PAUL CUSTOM DESIGNED EVERY DETAIL OF CHATEAU BROYHILL.

Everything came together, and the house was completed in 1966. I have enjoyed our French chateau ever since.

Broyhill Corporate Office and Showroom

At almost the same time in my career as we worked on the house, our management team decided we needed a new corporate office building and more showroom space. I had seen pictures of the United States pavilion at the 1958 Brussels World's Fair, designed by Edward Durell Stone. When I decided on a new building, I went to New York to see if I could hire Mr. Stone to design it. I got as far as his personal assistant who was cordial, but who politely told me that Mr. Stone's fee would be several million dollars. I had planned on spending about two and a half to three million dollars total on the building and didn't think I could spend that much on the architect's fee. His assistant was kind enough to give me a small, unpublished brochure that featured a number of Mr. Stone's designs. I came back home with the brochure, sat down with my furniture designer, and based on some of Mr. Stone's ideas, drew the plans for our office building. Mr. Stone later drew plans for the Kennedy Center in Washington and also a new capitol building for the state of North Carolina. I was able to get a Stone design for the cost of a cab fare.

During the April and October markets, the dealers started in High Point. A few of the larger manufacturers had local displays, so the dealers would travel west from High Point, stopping at several factory showroom locations. We preferred to show our furniture locally rather than go to High Point. Upstairs in the new corporate

BROYHILL CORPORATE OFFICE AND SHOWROOM

office building we created a fabulous showroom and downstairs had a spacious dining room. We were able to host our dealers in Lenoir during my entire career. My final market was in October of 1985 when after 19 years, we decided to close the local showroom and move to High Point.

Broyhill Industrial Complex

By the late '60s a lot of our business efforts came to fruition; we began to make a good net profit and build our net worth. We began setting aside a war chest of cash for our largest building program, and probably the largest furniture manufacturing complex in the country. Looking down from my airplane, I was inspired by the basic design of the G.E. complex in Louisville, Kentucky. Later, I visited that G.E. plant and discovered that each building was a separate operation and that each fed into a central warehouse. We laid out a complex of buildings including a central lumberyard, particleboard plant, wall unit plant, bedroom plant, and plastics plant. All of the plants fed into a central warehouse. The overall complex was a million and a

THE BROYHILL COMPLEX, 1.5 MILLION SQUARE FEET, WAS OCCUPIED BY OVER 1,000 EMPLOYEES.

BROYHILL UPGRADES PLANTS AND EQUIPMENT

A New Predryer Building Constructed At The Complex

Americans love oak furniture. They appreciate the beauty of its grain, its strength and legendary durability. Oak is indeed a good manufacturing material, but it is a very difficult wood to dry. If allowed to air dry unattended, it may warp, split, honeycomb, and become full of a long list of other various defects.

To reduce these drying defects and increase the amount of good wood which we can cut from each board, Broyhill has recently constructed a special building called a "predryer building". By using this facility for predrying our four quarter oak lumber, we are able to greatly reduce the number of defects which occur in the wood as it dries and shrinks and at the same time, to shorten the air drying period from four months to an estimated 30 days.

The predryer building is designed to operate at approximately 80° F and use large volumes of air in drying the lumber. The predryer reduces the moisture content of the lumber from 80% to the 25% level which is required for lumber entering the dry kilns. The building can hold six kiln charges or 480,000 board feet of lumber. If placed end to end, that is enough lumber to build a walk one foot wide from Lenoir to Winston-Salem.

Designed to decrease production costs, the predryer building helps to shorten drying time, decrease inventory costs and increase lumber yield. It's one of many innovative steps which Broyhill is taking to hold down the cost of lumber, the single most expensive item which is used in the production of furniture.

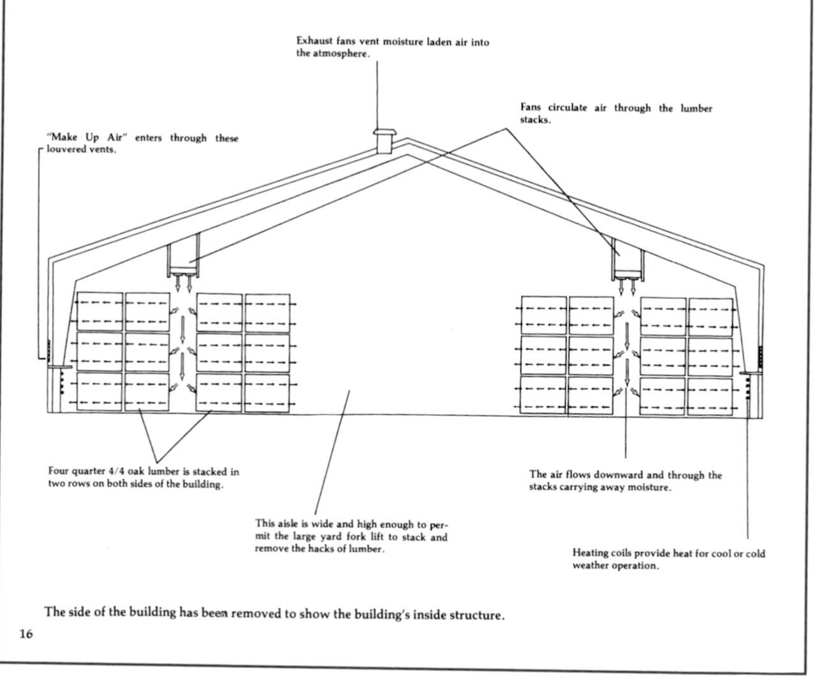
Exhaust fans vent moisture laden air into the atmosphere.
Fans circulate air through the lumber stacks.
"Make Up Air" enters through these louvered vents.
Four quarter 4/4 oak lumber is stacked in two rows on both sides of the building.
The air flows downward and through the stacks carrying away moisture.
This aisle is wide and high enough to permit the large yard fork lift to stack and remove the hacks of lumber.
Heating coils provide heat for cool or cold weather operation.

The side of the building has been removed to show the building's inside structure.

16

THE NEW PREDRYER BUILDING WAS JUST ONE PART OF THE STATE-OF-THE ART DESIGNS INCORPORATED INTO THE BROYHILL COMPLEX.

half square feet of floor space, all with brick and steel construction, filled with the latest, most up-to-date equipment. It required more than one thousand employees. The key people came from our other plants, but there were several hundred new hires.

It took us a couple of years to absorb the startup costs of the complex, but then our sales and profits started on a steady rise. With the addition of the complex, the overall company hit $100 million in volume in 1971, $200 million in 1977, and $300 million in 1981. Those numbers were all significant milestones to us, and at that time they were considered very large sales figures.

Parks and Gardens

When Faye and I were traveling, we constantly visited chateaux, palaces, and castles, most of which had beautiful gardens. We spent considerable time in the gardens, and I began to develop an interest in landscaping. My first venture was to build a private family cemetery. I purchased some land adjacent to my father's original church, Little Rock Baptist, just a few miles from his old home place

THE BROYHILL MEMORIAL PARK AND GARDENS IN BOOMER, NC

in Wilkes County, North Carolina. We landscaped the gently rolling hill that overlooks the original church with fountains, pools, and formal gardens to go along with the surrounding scenic woodlands. My father and mother lived to see the completion of the cemetery and were pleased with it. They lie there now along with my wife Faye, my sister Bettie, Bettie's husband, Will Gortner, and Allene's husband, Bill Stevens.

Sometime later, friends approached me about creating a small park in the center of Blowing Rock. The idea appealed to me, and we designed and built a lovely park around a small lake. It has become widely used and enhances the charm of downtown Blowing Rock.

We built the T. H. Broyhill Walking Park on the site of an old rock quarry in Lenoir. We cleaned out the lake, cleared out the bowl of the quarry, and created 37 acres of beautiful oriental gardens that feature unique varieties of trees, bushes, and flowering shrubs. Hundreds of people per week utilize the park for exercise and to enjoy the fresh air amid scenic beauty.

PAUL VISITS BROYHILL MEMORIAL PARK.

ENTRANCE TO THE T. H. BROYHILL WALKING PARK IN LENOIR, NC

Broyhill Family Offices

After leaving Broyhill, Hunt and I converted an abandoned country club building adjacent to the Lenoir Golf Course into our family offices. We had a lot of room, so I took two former dining areas and designed my personal office suite. For my furnishings, I used antiques and antique reproductions, most of which I purchased in Europe. Interestingly, I went back to the same carpet manufacturer

THE BROYHILL FAMILY OFFICES

in Madrid who had made the carpets for my home. He was still in business, looked up my old records, and was willing to work with me on the carpets for my new office. I incorporated large mahogany architectural elements and hired an artist to hand-paint oriental silk screening on the walls. My office is my sanctuary and I enjoy spending hours at a time there.

PAUL BROYHILL'S PRESENT DAY OFFICE

PART OF PAUL'S OFFICE SUITE WITHIN THE BROYHILL FAMILY OFFICE BUILDING

The Broyhill House

My parents built their dream home during the late 1930s. It was a stately, white brick, neoclassical home surrounded by lovely gardens. After my mother's death, we decided to donate the family home to Caldwell Community College and Technical Institute to use for

GARDENS AT THE BROYHILL HOUSE

A NEW PAVILION IN THE BACK OF BROYHILL HOUSE ACCOMMODATES OVER 100 PEOPLE AND NEW STEPS PROVIDE ACCESS TO THE FORMER POOL AREA.

meetings and to rent for parties, weddings, and other gatherings. The grounds provide a palette for their award-winning landscape department to train students. Recently, college officials wanted to be able to use the grounds outside to handle larger crowds. We designed a large pavilion that will shelter over 100 people. We added Italianate stairs descending to a pool with a cascading fountain and formal strolling gardens.

The Broyhill Logo

When we created the Premier division and started national advertising, I thought we needed a company logo. I had noticed a trend of large companies developing a unique design, and there were even companies that specialized in the development of such graphics. However, when I contacted a couple of those companies, I found that they charged tremendous fees. So, I designed the logo myself. I used an emblem that I called a centrifuge, which signified strong energy emanating from the center in a many-faceted way. However, the organization didn't pick up on the centrifuge terminology, and generally called it "Paul's pinwheel."

When I left Broyhill Furniture, I wanted a logo for our new business. The emblem of the 1940 New York World's Fair, with the sphere and pylon, influenced me with the sphere representing wholeness and the pylon representing aspirations. Our new logo combined those two images and concepts.

THE FAMOUS BROYHILL LOGO, AFFECTIONATELY KNOWN AS "PAUL'S PINWHEEL"

THE LOGO CREATED FOR
BROYHILL INVESTMENTS

Design Philosophy

I have always enjoyed projects. I like to take something old and transform it or to create something completely new, combining ideas from various sources. For years I carried a small Minox camera. The Minox camera was developed as a spy camera and used by the O.S.S. during World War II. From every trip I would come back with rolls of film to be developed. I took pictures of gardens and landscape design, of castles and mansions, and of breathtaking scenery. Most of all I used the Minox for its intended purpose: as a spy camera. I would take pictures of the competition's furniture elements and styling. I was quite adept at carrying on a conversation with a furniture proprietor while discreetly snapping pictures.

In many ways, the entire furniture operation was a design project for me. I took something that existed, used ideas that I gathered here and there, and crafted something unique. My creative formula has been "assimilate, evaluate, actuate."

16

Saying Goodbye to Broyhill

AS TIME WENT by and the company became larger and more profitable, we were approached by several large brokerage houses regarding our possible interest in selling the company. A representative from Oppenheimer came by to visit with an attractive proposal. He explained a plan whereby they could buy our business and we would pay no taxes. That sounded too good to be true, and I carefully considered the deal. Basically, their idea was to buy the assets of the company out of the corporation, paying book value, thereby not creating any corporate tax. Then the company would convert to an investment company and invest in municipal bonds, and still pay no tax. We could have a very large tax-free income. The technique was legal at the time, but later the IRS prohibited that practice. I felt the idea was too good to pass up.

We pursued the proposal with Oppenheimer until I discovered that part of their technique was to put a substantial amount of leverage on our balance sheet once the purchase was completed. I had worked hard through the years to build a strong balance sheet and was not interested in going back into heavy debt.

For the next two or three years, we were approached by several other companies. It was a time of considerable industry mergers and acquisitions. Two companies that seemed to be a logical fit for us were Warehouser and Georgia-Pacific. Actually, Georgia-Pacific held the most interest for us. I went back and forth to Seattle,

Washington, in my Learjet to meet with Robert B. Pamplin, the Georgia-Pacific chairman.

Pamplin and I negotiated and came fairly close to making a deal. He came to Lenoir and spent considerable time with me, but he kept pressing for too low of a purchase price. Due to the recession in 1975, our plants were not running well. It was not a prime time to make a sale. Finally, I turned down the offer.

A friend at Bache Brokerage Company contacted me and said that he represented a firm whose people wanted to talk with us. Located in St. Louis, Interco began in the shoe business and went on to acquire a chain of retail stores. They were looking for another leg of the stool, as they said, and were negotiating to purchase a furniture company.

We had a series of meetings with Interco. In the interim, they acquired Ethan Allen Furniture Company. Nathan Ancell, the president of Ethan Allen, was a good friend of mine, and one of the most brilliant merchandisers in the industry. I had confidence in him and in his favorable negotiations for the acquisition of Ethan Allen.

I had run Broyhill Furniture entirely without interference from my father or my family for more than 20 years. We never even had a board meeting. The family was not getting much money out of the company, as we paid small dividends. Though we had substantial personal net worth, none of us had any real money, and the family was growing larger with the addition of grandchildren and great-grandchildren. My father was 89 years old. I knew that as long as he lived I would not have any problem with the extended family. However, honestly, I didn't know what would happen after he was gone, as by that time we had more than 100 stockholders.

I learned some things from Oppenheimer and from other people, and I certainly am glad that I did not do any of the earlier deals. Oppenheimer and Georgia-Pacific each had offered a price of approximately book value. I agreed to sell to Interco for exactly the same pricing formula as Ethan Allen had sold for, and as a matter of pride, I would not take less. That amounted to a little more than book and a half. However, I had studied the Oppenheimer strategy and agreed to sell assets only. I did not sell the cash, the accounts receivable, or what my dad used to call extraneous assets, including various real estate properties that we had purchased through the years as investments.

The end result was that I retained within the corporation a net of somewhat more than double book value, or more than twice as much as the original negotiations with Oppenheimer and Georgia-Pacific. We concluded the deal with Interco in December of 1980, and I agreed to continue serving as CEO for an additional five years. Ed Beach, our Vice President of Finance, also agreed to stay on. My long-time chief lieutenants, Clarence Beach, Clarence Holden, and Bill Stevens, all decided that it was the end of an era and a good time to retire. My dad was sad, and I hated it for his sake, but I felt we had done the right thing for the family. I am sure my family would agree in retrospect that the sale gave them independence and a lifestyle that they would not otherwise have enjoyed. Our decision to sell may have been a little premature, but it turned out to be much better than selling too late, especially in light of the devastating consequences of overseas imports in subsequent years.

For the next five years, I devoted myself to business even more wholeheartedly than I had previously. I attended many of the gallery openings, flying there in my plane, having an opening, and leaving the next day. The force of my personal interest in the gallery program got it off to a terrific start.

Seemingly every year, Interco would come in with a cost savings program. Several times I told them just to take the needed cuts from my pay, even though I did not have a big salary. The most I ever made with them was about $250,000 a year. That pales in comparison to the millions of dollars that Furniture Brands, Inc., Broyhill Furniture's current owner, pays its executives, but I loved the business that much and felt the cuts would impact it negatively.

Five years passed quickly. During that time, Interco left me completely alone to run the business. I still felt as if I owned it. I loved the people. I loved the plants. I loved the products. The overall business was so much a part of my life that money made little difference.

Near the end of the five-year period, the first and only interference from Interco occurred. I was proud of our Broyhill profit-sharing program. It had not cost an unreasonable amount of money to build a retirement fund for our employees. We had a plan whereby a certain

Profit Sharing Plan Helps To Provide A Secure Future

With all the recent controversy over the soundness of our national Social Security system, it's good to know that our own Broyhill retirement plan is growing and helping to provide a more secure future for our retiring employees.

Our plan is based on the success of the company and as the company has grown, the fund has grown proportionately. It is a voluntary plan in which the company makes all the contributions.

The conversion from ESOP to Profit Sharing has resulted in very few changes. The major difference is that the fund assets are in outside investments rather than Broyhill Furniture Industries stock as in the previous plan.

The Profit Sharing Plan is designed to encourage longevity of service. Individual accounts experience a snowballing effect in later years of service. That is, the longer an individual is a participant the more it grows. Notice on the statement that the increase for the year on this actual example was $2,945.39 which is 25% of the actual salary.

An individual's participation in the Profit Sharing Plan begins when he or she meets the eligibility requirements as described on page 3 and 4 of our Summary Plan Description booklet. After becoming a participant in the plan, the account begins to grow. Each year during the month of February, plan participants receive a Profit Sharing Retirement Plan statement. Our example shown on the right is for a typical employee and it contains a sample of all the categories of information which a statement would contain.

Notice the line YR 63 100% vested. This employee became a participant in Broyhill's retirement plan in 1963 and is now 100% vested. The term "vested benefit" refers to that part of a person's retirement plan benefit which cannot be lost even if the employee leaves the company. As the vesting chart shows, the vested amount of a person's account greatly increases as years of service increase. After 15 or more years of service, an employee is 100% vested.

Under certain circumstances an employee can retire at age 55 and receive benefits from the Profit Sharing Plan, if he or she has accumulated 20 years or more of consecutive service. However, much larger benefits will be received by working longer. The longer a person works, the larger the amount of money his or her account accumulates.

When an employee continues to work, he or she is also helping to harness one of our nation's most valuable natural resources. That resource is the skill, wisdom and determination which an employee develops as he or she works on through their productive years.

Broyhill constantly encourages our older employees to continue working as long as they can. But upon retirement, the Broyhill Profit Sharing Plan, together with Government Social Security, will make up a sound retirement program.

The Profit Sharing Plan Vesting Schedule

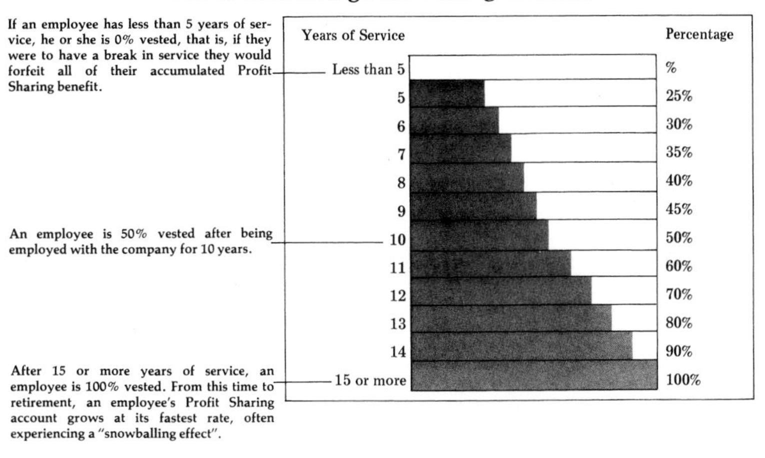
If an employee has less than 5 years of service, he or she is 0% vested, that is, if they were to have a break in service they would forfeit all of their accumulated Profit Sharing benefit.
An employee is 50% vested after being employed with the company for 10 years.
After 15 or more years of service, an employee is 100% vested. From this time to retirement, an employee's Profit Sharing account grows at its fastest rate, often experiencing a "snowballing effect".
Years of Service
Percentage
Less than 5
%
5
25%
6
30%
7
35%
8
40%
9
45%
10
50%
11
60%
12
70%
13
80%
14
90%
15 or more
100%

AN ARTICLE ABOUT EMPLOYEE PROFIT SHARING FROM *PEOPLE TODAY AT BROYHILL*

amount of money was put into a fund each year, and we tried to build it as much as we could. One of the fund's major investments was the Broyhill office building, and the fund received rent from it. Interco proposed to reduce the amount that we were putting into the profit sharing plan, and I disagreed. That was my hot button, and there was no way I was going to tell the employees that I was reducing the profit sharing. I still have old-time employees who come up to me on the street or at the grocery store and thank me for what they received out of the profit-sharing plan.

Therefore, I told Interco that I would retire at the end of the five years. I left my office December 31, 1985, and have been back in that building only three times since. I would have been glad to advise or help, but no one ever asked me until Jeff Cook, who just recently took over as CEO, declared "Paul Broyhill Day" and asked me back for a huge, welcome home event. For some reason, all the large companies that came into our industry thought they were smarter than the locals and didn't need any advice. However, none of them have been as successful as some of the original furniture families.

JEFF COOK SENT AN ENGLISH CHAUFFEUR TO DRIVE PAUL'S CAR TO THE PAUL BROYHILL DAY EVENT.

PAUL ADDRESSES THE CROWD AT THE SPECIAL EVENT ORGANIZED BY CEO JEFF COOK (STANDING BEHIND PAUL).

Over the years, the large outside companies gradually took over the furniture manufacturing industry and the original families mostly have disappeared. Mike Dugan, professor of business at Lenoir Rhyne College, wrote a book entitled *The Furniture Wars*. In it, he described the ineptitude and mistakes made by four large companies who made acquisitions in the furniture industry. Invariably, each company made exactly the same mistake of not listening to the insiders, thinking that they, the outsiders, were much smarter and had all the answers. Each tended to cut back on the organizations and to consolidate decision making into a central authority that did not know what they were doing. I was taught and always tried to push decision making down to the lowest possible level. Rather than constantly consolidating, we did just the opposite. My father used an old expression called, "Breaking down the rock." A large rock is too big to handle, but by breaking it into small pieces it becomes usable. It's unfortunate that acquiring companies failed to learn that lesson.

PAUL'S INDUCTION INTO THE AMERICAN FURNITURE HALL OF FAME. FROM LEFT: P.H., HUNT, CARON, AND PAUL BROYHILL WITH CLAIRE AND TIM GREENE.

17

Business after Broyhill Furniture

Mississippi-England

ONCE AN ENTREPRENEUR, always an entrepreneur. After selling Broyhill I just could not stand that I was not in business myself. Some people came up from Mississippi and convinced me to open a small upholstery operation there. Coincidentally, about that same time a friend from England came to see me with an idea for me to consider. I purchased a small upholstery operation in Long Eaton, England (a town adjoining Nottingham). I worked with both of those operations for two or three years but ultimately decided they were really more trouble than they were worth and sold them.

Retail Furniture

I was out of the furniture business. What now? We still owned the furniture rental business, which was making a reasonable amount of money. We had locations in Ohio and Florida.

My daughter Caron married a nice young man named John Collett, who had also grown up with ties to the furniture business. John's father headed Henredon Furniture and had developed a reputation for being a brilliant merchandiser. John had attended high school with my children in Hickory at North State Academy.

When John came to date my daughter, he wore old clog boots, a lumberjack jacket, and heavy corduroy pants. I had to clean him up and teach him some of the niceties of life. I hired him to work for me, intending that he would go into the furniture rental business. I took John with me on one of my West Coast trips and to the San Francisco market. Along the way we stopped to call on some important customers. Each time we stopped I would ask the dealer, "Where did you start your son in business?"

Invariably the answer was the same: "I always believe in starting a son in the warehouse."

After John and I made the rounds, we got back to our rental store location in Louisville, Kentucky. As I dropped him off, I said to him, "Guess where you're starting."

"Boss," he said, "I think I'm starting in the warehouse."

That is exactly where he started.

Because of John's ambition and aggression, we opened quite a few stores in the next few years. Some were successful; some were not. Unfortunately, his marriage to my daughter did not work out, and he left us to start his own real estate development business in Charlotte. John has become quite successful, and to this day I think he gives me credit for his basic business training.

After John left, my son, Hunt, finished college and came to join me in the furniture rental business. Of course, he, too, started in the warehouse, but soon he took over management. Our company continued to grow and expand its profitability. We decided to make our own upholstery and started a small upholstery plant. We bought a building, purchased equipment, and hired some of our old-time people to help get started. We had a plant, we had our own retail outlets, and we had, it seemed, a dream plan.

Manufacturing and retail marketing our upholstery seemed to be a logical progression. I thought it would be easy to do. It sounded great on paper and in theory. However, unlike the big, well-oiled machinery of the Broyhill organization that followed my lead, in that little business instead of being a general, I felt more like the Lone Ranger.

The problem with small stores is that they are entirely dependent upon the manager. If you have a good manager, the operation does well. If you have a bad manager, you lose money. We found the furniture rental business gradually changing. We set up showrooms the way we knew how to set them up, to appeal to retail customers.

However, instead of retail customers, we were dealing more and more with housing complex managers. Those managers rented furnished apartments by the week to give their customers an alternative to higher-priced hotel rooms. The complex managers started asking for rebates and under-the-table payments.

With some of the other changes in the market added to that, such as "rent to rent" and "rent to own," our business deteriorated. We decided to switch our stores entirely to retail furniture shops and to supply them exclusively from our new plant. We over-expanded locations and lost money. Needing to liquidate, we closed some of the facilities. Eventually, we liquidated the entire operation: retail, rental, and manufacturing. Though overall we made some money in those ventures, we lost a large part of it in the process of liquidation. What seemed at first to be a great business plan just did not materialize. Hunt had considered going to MBA school, but I told him that he already had an MBA education through the experience of running the rental and retail businesses and the factory.

See Appendix B on page 310 for a list of cities where we had store locations, some of which we owned; others involved lease negotiations, store up-fitting, hiring, firing, and ultimately, liquidating.

Real Estate

Through the years since my retirement from Broyhill, Hunt and I have ventured into various aspects of real estate. These include holding raw land, owning and leasing commercial properties, and developing residential lots. We generally have made some money in real estate. There is an old saying, "If you have staying power and can hang in there long enough, real estate will eventually prove to be profitable."

Trees

Hunt and I decided to put some of our raw land to work. We owned a lot of mountain property that we had purchased through the years. Our area of North Carolina is known for its Christmas tree farms; we thought we would fill some of our acreage with Fraser fir trees and sit back and watch them grow.

We planted thousands of trees and calculated our projected profits after the trees became six or seven years old. The problem that we did not foresee was that we had to cut and market a huge number of trees in a short period of time around the Christmas season. We did not do enough analysis of how we were going to sell the trees. Guys who had been in the business for years had developed their contacts. Naively, we thought people were just going to come and take the trees away from us. It was not that simple.

We decided that a much easier and more lucrative business than Christmas trees might be ornamental trees. Ornamental trees sell for higher prices. That is what we planted next. We thought that we would get rich in five or six years, but history repeated itself. Again, we could grow trees, but we had no market for them. While ornamental trees did not have to be sold all at once, if they grew too big they were too hard to handle. A large tree could bring a couple thousand dollars—that is, if we could find someone to buy it. We tried working through landscape people in different cities and also had people out selling directly, but we were not getting sales fast enough. I became disillusioned and decided to get out of the tree business completely.

My friend Bill Cooper, who managed the Dallas market complex for Trammel Crow, mentioned to me that Trammel had some agricultural sideline businesses that included soybeans and ornamental trees. Trammel's approach was to raise the trees in containers so that they could be ready for sale and transported to retail outlets like Lowe's Hardware.

I called Trammell and asked him to come and take a look at my ornamental tree farm. Trammell Crow, one of the wealthiest men in the country, actually came to North Carolina to look at my farm. The farm was beautiful. He took one look at it and said, "I'll buy it." At dinner I extolled the business, and we worked out a deal. Hunt and I never made any money in that business and, unfortunately, Trammell never made any money either. Fairly soon thereafter he, too, sold the business to some local growers who have had better success.

Broyhill Management Corporation

When we sold Broyhill Furniture, with some of the proceeds we created an investment company called Broyhill Management Corporation (BMC). We converted the shares into a mutual fund. That action required us to have more than 100 stockholders and an independent board of directors. It entailed a considerable amount of administrative paper work. That has only worsened through the years, as we have been subject not only to IRS regulations, but also to those of the Securities and Exchange Commission. We put much of the money into municipal bonds and invested the rest in the stock market and in real estate. We have held quarterly board meetings, and the fund has paid fluctuating but consistent dividends. Through BMC the family was finally able to get some personal income from the business.

Over the years we have been fortunate to have many distinguished persons on our BMC board. A list of board members, past and present, is shown in Appendix C, page 311.

Currently, BMC has an in-house administrative staff, an accounting staff, and an investment management staff. Our investment philosophy has been to be conservative and to diversify over time. We have a real estate subsidiary called P. B. Realty, LLC. Following Trammell Crow's advice, we first invested in industrial buildings.

THE GENWORTH BUILDING, THE FIRST LEED GOLD CERTIFIED PROJECT IN THE RALEIGH AREA, OPENED IN THE FALL OF 2009.

Since then we have become involved in various other types of real estate. Most recently we built a new office building in Raleigh, North Carolina. It is the first LEED Gold certified project in that area market. LEED certification recognizes and rates environmentally friendly construction from the U.S. Green Building Council. At this point only two gold designations for commercial office buildings exist in North Carolina.

Our BMC stock portfolio remains widely diversified with large cap, small cap, national, international, growth, and value. We have had municipal bonds, corporate bonds, and government bonds. That diversification has served us well and has enabled us to achieve above average results. The BMC Fund is organized and positioned in a way that it should be a long-term legacy for the family and stockholders.

HUNT, PAUL, AND TOM BROYHILL

Part 3

Building a Family

18

Flying High with My Beauty Queen

FROM 1948 THROUGH 1956, I lived at home with my parents. My brother married fairly quickly after college. My two sisters were also married, so I was the only child to live at home after the war. In my single days, I worked most nights. It didn't bother me because I did not have anything else to do. I dated a number of attractive girls and generally managed to have a date most every weekend, so I definitely had some personal life. However, I really hadn't fallen in love.

During the Chicago furniture market, I dated a couple of Miss Americas. The Lane Company used Miss America to advertise their cedar chests, and Mr. Ed Lane, a friend of my father, would let me come up and meet Miss America. I took a couple of beauty queens out to dinner and, through conversations with them, became somewhat familiar with the Miss America pageant.

In September 1955, a member of the Lenoir Junior Chamber of Commerce called to ask if I would be willing to fly to Raleigh, pick up Miss North Carolina, and bring her to Lenoir to judge a local beauty pageant, a function they sponsored.

Just a few months prior to their request, I had purchased my first airplane, a single engine Beech Bonanza. I was happy to oblige. Since I still had very little flight training, I decided to take George Reighard with me. George worked at Broyhill in sales. He was also a close friend, a member of the North Carolina Air National Guard, and current in his flying ratings.

George and I flew down to Raleigh and picked up Faye Arnold,

FAYE ARNOLD, MISS NORTH CAROLINA AND THIRD RUNNER-UP TO MISS AMERICA, 1956

the reigning Miss North Carolina. Faye told me later that she had been pleased to meet George but had not been really that impressed upon meeting me. Lucky for me, George was already married and had three small children.

The three of us flew back to Lenoir where I attempted to land at a small, dirt airstrip. I had never practiced short field landings and had never been on that particular short strip. I approached too fast, overshot the field, and had to go around. I used the excuse that

I wanted to show off the sights of Lenoir. However, I can assure you that Faye was not impressed, or pleased with the flight.

That night at the event, I suggested to Faye that I take her out afterwards. She politely declined. Undaunted, I promptly organized an affair for after the evening's event at my parents' house and invited a half dozen people to come, including her hosts for the weekend. Everyone was pleased with the invitation, so Miss North Carolina had no alternative but to join us. Later, when I took her to the home of Emory McCall, a Broyhill executive, where she stayed for the night, I walked her to the door. She had no idea that I was quite familiar with the McCall home.

"Goodnight, Mr. Broyhill. I had a good time," Faye said, dismissing me as she tried to slam the door. But I had my shoe in the doorway and eased myself in. I sat down in a chair, and I tried to pull her down on my lap and give her a hug. She indignantly brushed me off and ushered me out the door. The next day I called to see if she wanted me to fly her back to Raleigh, but she said she had made other arrangements.

At home, Faye told her mother that she never expected to see "that boy" again because I was too forward. I called her a few times, but she was quite cool to me. I obviously was not getting anywhere.

A couple months later there was an annual Thanksgiving pageant and parade to be held in Charlotte. All of the Miss North Carolina and Miss South Carolina county contestants, as well as the reigning queens of both states, were invited to participate. There were 75–100 beautiful young ladies and their escorts for the event.

The wheels of my mind began turning. I called my college friend Ike Belk of Belk Department Stores, assuming that he would be involved somehow with the arrangements. I explained to Ike that I was quite close with Miss North Carolina and planned to bring her to the parade. I asked Ike to call and confirm with Miss North Carolina that I would pick her up in my plane and take her to Charlotte. Then I called Faye and told her that the officials had asked me to bring her. I worked one against the other. I flew down to Raleigh to pick her up in the Beech Bonanza.

PAUL WITH IKE BELK AND JIM BROYHILL MANY YEARS AFTER IKE "HELPED" MAKE ARRANGEMENTS FOR FAYE TO FLY WITH PAUL TO THE PARADE IN CHARLOTTE

That time I flew alone. Unfortunately, the weather was bad, and I became concerned for her safety. I decided to make an unscheduled landing in Wadesboro, North Carolina, on a dirt airstrip near town. A man driving a pickup truck came out to meet the plane. I asked him if he would take us to where I could hire a cab. He said there would be cabs at the bus station and drove us there. Because of our unexpected detour, we arrived quite late to the hotel in Charlotte, and we made a rather ignominious arrival by taxicab. The arrangements committee was very upset with me.

Faye roomed with Miss South Carolina. In reality, I did not even have a ticket to get into the pageant, so I had to think of something. I arranged to have my dad's car and his chauffeur sent down to Charlotte. I accompanied Miss North Carolina and Miss South Carolina to the event in my dad's Cadillac. When we got out, I put my arm around both of the girls and walked in. No one asked me for a ticket.

Inside, I found out that all the young ladies were to parade through the crossed swords of cadets from a nearby military college, and that it was going to take quite a bit of time. I spoke to the lady who was in charge and told her that I would be escorting Miss North Carolina. I looked at the lady's list, marked through the escort name next to Miss North Carolina, and penciled in my name. While I waited, I went up into the seating area and sat down for a moment beside two or three gentlemen. I reached over and shook hands with them. One turned out to be the governor of North Carolina, Luther Hodges.

I watched as the line of ladies progressed. As Faye's turn came, I got up, took her on my arm, and together we went under the arch of crossed swords. After the ceremony as we danced I said to myself, "Well, I really have crashed this party!" We had a pleasant evening, although once again, the airplane flight had made another bad impression.

I continued to call Faye, but still got nowhere. She did allow me to fly her a couple of places, but that was the extent of our relationship until after Christmas.

I learned that Faye and the Maid of Cotton were to attend an event in New York City. The event happened to coincide with the New York furniture market. I did not always attend that market, but I called and told Faye that since I would be at the market anyway, I could see her in New York.

On their first day there, I escorted Pat, the Maid of Cotton (who later married the announcer Ty Boyd), and Faye around New York. That evening I took Faye to dinner in the Cotillion Room at the Pierre Hotel. When we walked in, quite a few people greeted me because they were furniture people who knew me. I think she was impressed that I seemed to be well known there. Covertly, I spoke to my service captain and told him that the young lady was going to order a non-alcoholic drink and that I wanted him to serve her champagne. Faye was so sweet and innocent. She never had drunk a single drop of an alcoholic beverage.

"We want a special non-alcoholic beverage," I said when the server came to the table. He brought Piper Heidsieck champagne.

Faye started tossing down the delicious bubbly drink quite freely saying, "Oooh, this is so good! What is it?"

"It's something special, non-alcoholic," I told her, inwardly grinning.

Faye got just a tiny bit tipsy. While we were dancing to a famous orchestra, everyone was speaking to me, which helped to impress her. When we left the hotel and got outside, I said, "Oh! We always take a ride through Central Park in the horse and buggy."

It was the middle of winter and quite cold. Since I had never taken the New York horse and buggy ride, I was unfamiliar with the procedure; however, it played right into my hands. When we got into the buggy, the driver wrapped us in a blanket and underneath the blanket set a little heater. We were snug and quite comfortable. By the time the heat got to work on that champagne, the lady got to be a little more cooperative. It was in that buggy in Central Park that I was able to get my first kiss.

After that date and our buggy ride through Central Park, getting Faye to agree to get together became a little easier. I took her several places in the plane. We began to see each other on various weekends. She had a full-time boyfriend, which of course didn't bother me one bit. I totally ignored that fact. Of course it bothered him, and I think he got mad about her beginning attachment for me. That made it easier for me, because he pulled out early in the game.

The two of us never really talked about the future very seriously. Faye had taken some courses at Meredith College but had not actually started college, although she certainly had an education from a full year traveling as Miss North Carolina. Then a phone call changed everything. I was in Chicago calling on the merchandise manager of the department store Carson Pirie Scott when the phone rang and someone said, "It's for you." I couldn't imagine who in the world had tracked me down.

My dad was on the phone. "What's this your mother heard on the radio about her son?" he asked.

I had no idea. "What did she hear?" I asked puzzled.

"She heard that her son is getting married."

I stopped to think: "My mother has two sons, Jim and me. Jim is already married..."

Taken off guard, I replied, "Who, me?"

"Yes, you!" Dad answered.

"Who to?" I asked.

My dad couldn't even remember Faye's name. He said, "Oh, you know. That Miss North Carolina down in Raleigh."

"Well, I'll call her and find out what's going on," I told Dad.

That night I called Faye and asked, "What's this my mother heard on the radio?" She burst into tears and said that she didn't know how that happened. It turned out she had been talking to somebody in one of Raleigh's clothing boutiques. Some reporter had overheard the conversation and had put it into one of the little gossip columns in *The Raleigh News and Observer,* and the radio had picked it up.

The initial report did not use my name. It read, "It is rumored that Miss North Carolina is going to marry her pilot." Of course, that pleased me very much because I'm proud of being a pilot. I said to Faye, "Maybe we'd better talk."

After our talk, Faye and I went to New York to buy a ring. My sister Allene, her husband, Bill Stevens, and her daughter, Becca, went along to chaperone. We shopped and shopped, but I could not make up my mind, so we came back without one. "Now see here," her mother said, just a little upset, "you went to New York to get a ring, but you have not yet asked her to marry you."

I finally found a ring that I liked and gave it to Faye, literally a few days before the wedding, and at the same time, I asked her to marry me. Without my having formally proposed, she had proceeded with the wedding plans. Before the wedding date, we had a pre-nuptial meeting with her minister, Dr. Douglas Aldrich. I'll never forget that meeting. Apparently, because I was an old man of 32 to Faye's young and innocent 19, Reverend Aldrich had some concerns. He forthrightly questioned Faye saying, "Are you sure you want to do this? Mr. Broyhill is quite a bit older than you and has a lot more worldly experience."

I'm not sure just what he was implying, but I kidded him about it from then on. Even at Faye's memorial service, I reminded him with a smile that we had been happily married for 46 years.

Faye and I had what we thought to be an idyllic wedding ceremony at Forest Hills Baptist Church in Raleigh, North Carolina, in August of 1956. On the arm of her daddy, she was stunning in her full, white gown. My daddy stood up with me as my best man. My sister Bettie played the organ and my other sister, Allene, sang. Only a dozen people or so were present, just our immediate families. Neither of us wanted a huge crowd. Afterwards, we had a nice family lunch at a nearby hotel, and then we flew off into the sunset aboard my plane.

FAYE AND PAUL WERE MARRIED IN AUGUST OF 1956.

We spent three days at the Greenbrier in West Virginia, and then we went to Europe. Our flight over was on a TWA Constellation plane that had a berth just like a berth in a train. That very first trip was fairly luxurious. I cannot imagine that I had not been to Europe before that, but I had been working so hard and had been so busy that I had not given Europe much thought. My bride and I spent three days in England, three days in France, three days in Switzerland, and three days in Italy. It was a whirlwind, but we had a great time. Faye joked that she saw the most beautiful ceilings in Europe! That honeymoon became the first of our annual European trips.

In September we moved into my parents' mountain house in Blowing Rock. Faye attended nearby Appalachian State University in Boone for a year. I drove down the mountain every morning to work in Lenoir. The time we spent at dad's house in Blowing Rock was like another honeymoon. Faye knew nothing about cooking, so we hired a nice mountain lady to come in and help with the cooking and cleaning. I helped Faye with her homework, and we watched TV about once or twice a week. We had a very simple but wonderful nine months.

FAYE AND PAUL ON THEIR HONEYMOON IN LONDON

THE NEW MRS. BROYHILL

AFTER THE WEDDING PAUL AND FAYE FIRST LIVED
AT J. E. AND SATIE'S HOME IN BLOWING ROCK.

One day Faye called me in tears. There had been a snowstorm and she had a little fender-bender. She had run into the median and hit a tree. According to her the tree was right in the middle of the road. I consoled her, "You know, they shouldn't be putting trees in the middle of the road like that."

Faye attended Appalachian that one year only, but later became the first female president of the university board. She also served on the Meredith College board in Raleigh where, although she had attended only briefly, she had become quite attached.

After Blowing Rock, we came back to Lenoir and bought a small house on Woodland Drive for about $25,000. We spent about $5,000 fixing it up. We lived very happily there for ten years in a quiet neighborhood. In 1966 we built the dream house I described earlier that resembled a French chateau. I have always loved that house and I still live there today.

Back in the twenties, the Broyhill family built the Lenoir municipal golf course. We all enjoyed playing there. Soon after Faye and I moved to Lenoir, some of the wives of the club members decided they would take up golf, too. They formed a ladies group and played with some regularity. However, several of us men became annoyed that the women played too slowly and were holding up progress, especially on Saturdays. The men suggested that we enact a club regulation that would forbid women from playing on Saturday mornings. We posted a notice.

Faye did not know that we owned the golf course and let's just say that when I got home on the day Faye found out about the "no ladies on Saturday" rule, I got an earful! "Do you know what *they* have done down at the golf club?" She proceeded to relate the horrible injustice and the indignation of all the women.

"You go down there and convince them to change that rule," she insisted. "You tell whoever came up with such a harebrained idea that it just won't do. The girls and I are going to get up a petition, and I want you to sign it."

"I'll do what I can," I told my wife, being wise enough not to let

FAYE AND PAUL: THE PERFECT COUPLE

on that I had a part in the plan. I went into Dad's office first thing Monday morning and said, "Dad, we've made a big mistake."

The women promptly resumed their Saturday morning play.

Faye was not only beautiful, but quick-witted too. I'll never forget the time soon after I'd received an honorary doctorate degree from Lenoir-Rhyne College that Faye asked me to take out the garbage.

"But I'm a doctor now," I replied with my nose in the air. "Give me some respect."

"Well, *Doctor* Broyhill, please take the garbage on your way out," she said without missing a beat.

I spent 46 happy years married to Faye Arnold Broyhill. She had a sweet spirit, and she used her position in life to help others. She served on numerous boards and committees, working to advance the causes of quality education, art and music opportunities, and children's well being. I enjoyed Faye's sense of humor and ease at repartee. She used to quip that she was put on the earth to keep me humble. I do not know how she handled so well all my absences and preoccupation with work, but she did. She was a fine person, a dedicated mother to our children, and a wonderful partner to me. To me, she was always the beautiful Miss North Carolina.

19

Our Children

FAYE WAS EXTREMELY supportive while I was working so hard. The business always came first, and I worked all during the week, many evenings, and most weekends. I traveled a great deal, almost every week. Having my own plane, I was able to jump in that plane and go almost anywhere on a moment's notice. I could work a day or so and then return home, but I often called at the last minute to tell her that I would not be home for supper.

When I was a kid, my dad actually met his office workforce at a downtown café in Lenoir about 6:00 in the mornings and bought them all breakfast. That's when he only had six or eight people working for him in the office. They would start to work at 7:00 a.m. and work until 5:00 p.m. Many times Dad would go back to work after dinner. With that example set for me, I followed suit, working long hours from the beginning. When I was single, I habitually worked a lot of nights.

For years, our entire office staff worked on Saturday mornings. One summer some of my executives came to me and asked that I let them off on Saturday during the summer months. I agreed. Unfortunately for me, they never wanted to go back to working on Saturdays after that. I kidded them that they really blindsided me with that suggestion that summer.

As a consequence to my being away from home, Faye practically raised our three children, Caron, Claire, and Hunt, by herself. I handled little of their discipline. At home, I wanted to enjoy my children. I wanted to play with them, and take them out and do things. If they misbehaved during the week, their mother threatened that their dad would punish them when he came home and learned about their behavior; but, I never could quite see that I was going to come home on a Saturday and start whipping up on my children. That issue was about the only one that created conflict between my wife and me. I am sure that all the advice books say that parents should approach their children from common ground. But in business, we often played the "good guy/bad guy" game. At home, I left my wife to discipline the children, and I played with them. Faye never understood why she always had to play the role of bad guy. Occasionally, she would ask me why I could not be the bad guy sometimes. She went with me occasionally to New York or Chicago or Florida, but mostly when I traveled, she stayed at home with Caron, Claire, and Hunt.

Over the years I complained that Faye was always late, especially on Sundays. I would get ready for church then sit in the car and blow the horn. One Sunday as Faye frantically herded the kids out the door, she looked at me in exasperation and said with her characteristic wit, "Next Sunday why don't I sit in the car and blow the horn and you get the kids ready?"

Because I am a bit of a Francophile, Caron's name is spelled like the French perfume, *Caron*, but pronounced with the accent on the first syllable instead of the last. Claire's name, Barbara Claire, was

PAUL AND FAYE WITH THEIR GROWING FAMILY

HUNT WITH GRANDDAD (J. E.)

a combination of her mother's name, Clara Faye, and Faye's sister, Barbara. I named our street, Claron, a blend of my daughters' names, and also called a popular suite of French-styled furniture by that name. Hunt is my mother's maiden name and my middle name. I did not want our son to be saddled with "Junior" after his name, so I did not name him after me. However, Hunt named his son Paul Hunt Broyhill, II.

My most vivid memories of my family revolve around trips. From time to time, and always at Thanksgiving and Christmas, I took my family to Sea Island, Georgia, or to somewhere in Florida. Some of our favorite places in the Sunshine State were Boca Raton, Fort Lauderdale, and Ocean Reef. In those days, we all played tennis, and the entire family would troop off to the tennis court. The children often enjoyed playing around the pool while I went to the golf course. During the years we had the big boat, we naturally went to wherever the boat was moored.

There were times that I took one of our kids on a quick business trip in my plane to such places as New York or Washington. While I was working, our pilot would do a little sightseeing with them, or they would sit around the hotel pool. It was a bit unusual to take a kid out of school, so they were always impressed when I let them skip for a couple of days to go on a quick little vacation.

FAMILY FUN ON THE TENNIS COURT

My children attended grammar school in Lenoir. Then some of us parents who thought that the public schools had begun to deteriorate founded a small prep school in Hickory called North State Academy. Children from Lenoir, Hickory, and Morganton attended the school. Our children rode a van for the 30-mile round trip to Hickory each day.

Caron went her last two years of high school to Salem Academy in Winston-Salem, but Claire finished at Hickory. Hunt spent a year at Admiral Farragut High School in Florida and three years at Episcopal High School in Alexandria, Virginia. He left Alexandria during one school year to study in France. After high school, Caron and Hunt attended Wake Forest University, and Claire went to Davidson College. They all did well in school.

CARON, CLAIRE AND HUNT

THREE GENERATIONS OF BROYHILLS

I had both of the girls wait on tables at the Green Park Hotel to give them a little work experience. Claire also waited tables when she attended Davidson. Both of the girls worked for me a bit in the business, so they each had some experience.

Hunt and I have always been pals, all the way through. As his mother did the disciplining, he was cooperative with me. I raised him with an intent to go into business, starting at a young age.

When Hunt was four or five years old, I bought him an astronaut suit, which he just loved. On one occasion I took him along with me to one of the furniture markets where we were launching a brand new, ultra-contemporary line. Hunt spent the entire market wandering around the showroom dressed in his spaceman suit. He was a spontaneous, creative advertisement and made quite a hit with the customers.

As a youngster Hunt had his own card in the time clock, and we paid him 10 cents an hour. Getting money made him want to go to the office and check in. From time to time, he hit me up for a raise.

Our three children have given us seven grandchildren. Claire has three daughters, Alaine, Satie (named after my mother), and Hunter (carrying mother's maiden name of Hunt); Caron has a daughter and a son, Caitlin and John Knox; and Hunt has a daughter and a son, Christian and Paul Hunt, whom we call P. H. So, I have two grandsons and five granddaughters! It is largely for their benefit that I am writing this personal account.

THE BROYHILL FAMILY: PAUL, CARON, FAYE, CLAIRE, AND HUNT

CARON

CARON'S DAUGHTER, CAITLIN

CARON'S SON, JOHN KNOX

CLAIRE WITH HUSBAND TIM GREENE,
DAUGHTERS SATIE, HUNTER, AND ALAINE

CLAIRE'S HUSBAND,
TIM, AND HIS
DAUGHTER, LENNIE

HUNT'S CHILDREN,
CHRISTIAN AND
PAUL HUNT
BROYHILL II

20

Chris-Crafts and Sea Rays

FAYE AND I began spending long weekends at Florida's Ocean Reef Club just north of Key Largo when Ocean Reef was just a small fishing village. We enjoyed watching the club expand through the years. The original club included a small lodge where we stayed and an airport, which made travel convenient for us. Eventually, we bought a home there. Though hurricanes hit Ocean Reef from time to time, it was spared any substantial damage until 1992 when it took the brunt of Hurricane Andrew. After that, because of the threat of severe hurricanes, we moved across the peninsula to Naples, Florida.

When I was single, I owned a 24-foot cabin cruiser on Lake James near Marion, North Carolina. I loaned the cruiser to some of the boys from the plants from time to time. One time, Beef Johnson was pouring gas into the tank when the boat blew up and sank. Fortunately, no one was hurt. When my dad read about the incident in the paper, the reporter had mistaken my name for Bernhardt. "See," said my dad, "I told you those things were dangerous." He didn't realize it was actually my boat.

When I began dating Faye, I told her I had a boat at Lake James. I didn't tell her that it was actually *in* Lake James. When she said she wanted me to take her boating, I quickly shopped and bought an 18-foot Chris-Craft Runabout. It was a classic with mahogany trim.

After our marriage, we did not go to the lake often, and I eventually sold the Runabout. While the children were small, I did not own

THE DIXIE RUNABOUT

a boat. I talked about buying another one, and from the time I first began going to Florida, I walked up and down the docks and admired them. They looked as pretty to me as pretty girls. Somehow I never dreamed that I would really own a large one, but I still bought boating magazines and looked at the sale advertisements like a wish book.

One time when we were at Ocean Reef, I asked Hunt, who was about 12 years old, if he would like to go into Lauderdale and look at the big boats. Hunt said, "Dad, you're never going to buy a boat. I think you are just fooling me."

For some reason his comment challenged me, and that day I saw a boat that I wanted at a price that I could afford, and I bought it on the spot. It was a 70-foot Chris-Craft Roamer. Chris-Craft, of course, is a well-known name. Chris-Craft bought out a company called Roamer, which at the time was making boats larger than typical Chris-Crafts. Roamer also was utilizing aluminum in their construction. Aluminum was considered to be advanced technology for the time. Fiberglass, so far, was used mostly on smaller-sized boats. Larger ones were made primarily of wood or steel.

THE 70-FOOT CHRIS-CRAFT ROAMER PURCHASED ON THE SPOT AFTER A DISCUSSION WITH HUNT

THE ROAMER AT SEA

A FAMILY OUTING ON THE BOAT

We hired a captain and took the boat to Ocean Reef. We alternated mooring it there and at Lauderdale, where we sometimes stayed at Marina Bay, a considerable distance up the New River. In the summer, we occasionally stayed at Hilton Head and moored the boat there. We took it as far north as the Chesapeake Bay. From time to time, we entertained customers on the boat, and I also let some of my executives use it for entertaining.

Not long after I bought the boat, Trammell Crow flew in his plane to visit me in Hilton Head. He brought his wife and Bill and Sue Cooper. Bill and I had become very close over the years. He was a pilot, and even though Trammell employed a pilot, he allowed Cooper to help fly the plane, which he really enjoyed. I invited all of them to come out on the new boat. We sailed from Hilton Head to Savannah.

Savannah was built on a river that has an outlet to the sea, so it is a port city. There is an inside route and an outside route between Hilton Head and Savannah. The inside way goes through some winding canals, and it is an interesting trip that takes two or three hours. We took the inside route and spent a pleasant afternoon sitting on the back of the boat and enjoying the scenery. We arrived in Savannah in late afternoon. Much of the area around the docks has been restored historically and has beautiful squares for strolling. After dinner on the docks, we returned to the boat for the trip back to Hilton Head.

My captain called me aside and said, "We can't go, Mr. Broyhill. A fog has rolled in." I told the captain that Mr. Crow needed to leave Hilton Head early in the morning, so we really needed to get back.

"There's no way that we can go," replied the captain. "The fog is too dense."

"I'll show you how to take this boat home," I told him confidently.

I had brought my plane pilot along with me on the boat trip, and I asked him to help me navigate. It was just like flying blind in an airplane, which I had done many times. I had radar on the boat and it indicated the buoys, so I steered by the compass heading, just as I would have done in a plane. I sent my pilot to the front of the boat to help spot the buoys and call out their locations. Between his calls and the radar screen I steered from buoy to buoy. I did not look outside at all; I could not see through the dense fog. Eventually, we emerged into the Atlantic and turned north towards Hilton Head. We made it back by hitting the buoys, never being able to see outside the boat. When I brought that boat back into Harbor Town that night and docked it, the captain just shook his head. He could hardly believe that we made such a treacherous trip without incident.

The punch line to that story happened a few weeks later. Again, I started back from Savannah on the same route that I had taken that night, but it was broad daylight and I wasn't being as careful as I had been the night of the fog. I ran aground. The situation was not too serious, and probably if I had run aground that foggy night, I could have backed off. When you run aground in boats, depending upon what you hit, very often you can back off and move on. Sometimes you cannot, of course. I used to run aground a lot, because in those days I was not as careful in the boat or as watchful of the charts as I was when I flew an airplane.

The night of the fog the Crows, the Coopers, and my wife were down below in the back of the boat having a good time. None of them realized the conditions I had faced. If you were to ask me if I would do that again, I would say *definitely not*! I have taken lots of chances in my life that in retrospect I wouldn't do again. That certainly was one of them.

When Hunt was at Admiral Farragut Academy in Tampa, Florida, he felt quite alone. As a doting father, I bought a 24-foot sailboat and joined a small yacht club close to his school so that he had a sailboat to play with on weekends. That summer we took the sailboat up to Hilton Head, and in addition to it and the Chris-Craft Roamer we also had an 18-foot Dixie Runabout. We had quite a flotilla that year!

Having a boat was a lot of fun, but at the same time, a lot of aggravation. There were always maintenance problems and always personnel problems. We had our Chris-Craft Roamer about five years and hired four captains during that time. It didn't take me long to lose interest in having a large boat. We felt more or less obligated to use the boat on our free weekends. Eventually, we decided to sell the boats and to buy our Ocean Reef vacation home. We found that having the vacation home was more comfortable and more fun for us than being tied to the boats and worrying about their maintenance and crew.

HUNT AND HIS 24-FOOT SAILBOAT

When we were at Ocean Reef, we needed a small boat to get around the reef, so I purchased a 24-foot Formula Cruiser that could be berthed in a boat barn. That boat was so much easier to enjoy than the bigger boat. If we wanted to ride on the boat, a lift pulled it down from the barn, and away we would go.

My sister Bettie and her husband, Will Gortner, had been in Clearwater for a long time but had moved to Naples and had become involved in the social life there. When we decided to leave Ocean Reef in 1992, they were already well established in Naples, so that influenced our own relocation direction. They were in the process of building an apartment in a new condo building. Because they had a lot of friends and were members of the clubs, we felt that we could fit into Naples life very easily.

When we moved to Naples our condominium had a dock and a boat slip right at our door. It was just too big a temptation not to have a boat there. We traded the 24-foot Formula for a 33-foot Sea Ray that was still small enough to handle without a crew. I have kept that boat through the years. However, whenever we go up and down those docks at the yacht club, I'm still looking.

21

Rolls-Royce and Learjet

LIKE MANY MEN, I have been fascinated with cars and have taken pride in owning prestigious models.

When I was in the military I had that sporty, maroon 1938 four-door Packard touring sedan with the spare wheel up on the side. At

PAUL IN HIS VERY FIRST CAR

school I had the two-door Plymouth known as "Red Ted." After I got out of school, I decided a two-door vehicle was sportier than a four-door, so I bought two-door Buicks or Oldsmobiles, always maroon.

My dad drove Cadillacs. I still have the last two Cadillacs my dad owned: a 1974 Brougham and a 1976 Limousine. When Lincoln brought out some of their outstanding models, I bought them, as I wanted to be different from my father. After Lincoln, I changed to Mercedes and have owned most of their large models.

Faye's first car was a 1956 yellow T-bird convertible. That was a classy car and she loved it. When Caron and Claire graduated from high school and went to college, I bought each of them a classic two-door Mercedes coupe.

In 1978 I bought my first Rolls-Royce, the two-door Camargue. Somehow the two-door Rolls didn't seem to be quite as classy as the four-door, and it was not long until I sold it and bought a 1980 Silver Spur. It was the last year of that body style. A few years later, I sent that car to our Florida home, where it stayed for many years. Of course, I needed another Rolls for North Carolina. I bought a 1984 four-door Silver Spur that I later traded for a 1989 Silver Wraith. In

DESIRING A FOUR-DOOR, PAUL UPGRADED FROM HIS FIRST ROLLS-ROYCE TO A 1980 SILVER SPUR.

PAUL WITH HIS 1989 ROLLS-ROYCE SILVER WRAITH

early 2010 I sold the 1980, with only 30,000 original miles. As of this writing, I still own the '89 Rolls and leave it in Florida.

Currently, my wife drives a Mercedes 500 and I have a Bentley Arnage. I have enjoyed driving the Bentley, but it has an entirely different feel than a Rolls and handles more like a sports car than a limousine.

For the first few years I was in business, I rode a train whenever I traveled because I easily became motion sick in cars, planes, trains, and especially boats. That was the era when the airlines were using the DC-3, an un-pressurized tail wheel airplane that was not really very comfortable. Even before we left the ground, I would begin to feel motion sickness in the DC-3. After about five years of commercial train travel, I started renting small aircraft with a pilot for short, quick trips. I quickly developed the urge to learn to fly.

While cars fascinated me, planes were my passion. I started flying in July 1953, and for two years I rented Cessnas at Hickory Flying Service, owned by John Terrell. My instructor was Max Freeman. Max later joined Lowe's Food Stores and became their chief pilot. Early on, he received some Lowe's stock and retired with a very nice income from their profit-sharing plan.

PAUL'S FLYING INSTRUCTOR,
MAX FREEMAN

In those early days I flew Cessna models 140, 150, 170, 180, 172, and 182. The first four were tail-wheel airplanes. The last two were nose-wheel airplanes. I got my initial training in tail-wheels, a distinction that makes us old-time pilots feel somewhat superior to the younger crowd.

I bought my first airplane in August of 1955 from Greensboro Flight Service. It was a 1952 Beechcraft Bonanza, which was a single-engine, high-performance aircraft for that time and is still being made with modifications today. Hughes Tool Company (Howard Hughes) originally owned that plane. At the time I purchased it, I had flown approximately two hundred hours, most of which were cross-country, and I had had very little intensive training. That was the plane I was flying when I picked up Faye the first time after having owned it only about a month. A lot of businessmen, young lawyers and doctors have killed themselves in that kind of plane because they were just like me. They would jump in and learn how to take off and land, but they did not have much intensive training.

High performance airplanes fly high and fast and are capable of long trips; consequently, the flights are more vulnerable to weather variations, especially if trips extend over several days. When the weather is bad for the return flight, pilots can be tempted to skim the treetops. That is where trouble begins. I did my share of that, and I was fortunate that I did not kill myself. Because of my inexperience, there were many times when I should not have been flying due to bad weather. Somehow, I got by with it. Thank goodness I never had an accident. I think about John Kennedy, Jr., and just how quickly an inexperienced pilot can get into trouble.

The most feared weather phenomena for most pilots are thunderstorms and icy conditions. All of my twin-engine planes had radar and de-icing boots. Radar looks ahead and detects thunderstorm activity. Wing-mounted, rubberized boots pulsate, breaking up any ice that may form.

Initially, my dad opposed my owning an aircraft. To get around his disapproval, I bought the Bonanza personally and did not put it in the company name. My father was a great one to tell me not to do something and then do it himself. After I bought the plane, he began to take it on trips, all the while telling me that I should not be flying. His justification was that he was taking a good pilot with him.

A year or so after buying my first plane, I talked Dad into buying a company plane. It was a Twin Beech E-18S. That type of plane had been used during the war, mostly for personnel and supplies transport. That particular one was built after the war, and they had made some modifications. Arthur Vining Davis of Arvida Company owned the plane before me. Davis was a major real estate developer in postwar Florida.

The plane was big and heavy with large radial engines. It was a tail-wheel airplane, but it was comfortable. It was fairly slow, attaining about 180 mph. I used that plane quite a bit. When I was in it, I was the pilot and our professional pilot acted as the co-pilot. I actually earned my twin engine rating in that plane, which is sort of crazy.

As part of the training requirement for the rating, I had to chop an engine and fly with a single one. That big, old plane had a tremendous amount of torque and required pilot skill to generate a positive climb rate on only one engine. It was supposed to climb 200 to 250 feet a minute on one engine, which is not much performance.

We hired an old-time pilot, Hamilton "Ham" Holder. Ham had flown before the war and was part of a civilian instructor group used by the Air Corps to help train its initial wave of pilots. He flew for us for more than 20 years and was very close to my family and me. On most business trips I used the Twin Beech, but I continued to use the Bonanza for my personal trips.

Once my dad started using the plane, he grabbed his golf clubs and went hither and yon, all across the country playing golf with key account customers. Dad usually called on the larger dealers who played golf, and they just loved to see him. He was a great ambassador for the company.

I continued flying my single engine Bonanza for fun. After working all day, I would jump in the plane and fly to nearby destinations

OFF TO A FAMILY VACATION

such as Raleigh, Greensboro, Charlotte, or Asheville. I would have dinner at those various airports then fly home at night. On a lot of those night flights, George Reighard accompanied me. On Saturdays I would fly to the Atlanta airport, have lunch, get a haircut, and then fly home. It was not long, however, before I was taking more extensive trips. I enjoyed taking my family to Florida on most of our breaks.

For several years I flew without an instrument rating because I had been just too busy to make time for the training. However, I logged a lot of actual instrument time while I flew with the co-pilot. When I finally obtained the instrument rating, my ability and safety greatly improved. I began training two or three times a year at FlightSafety International, and I earned the following ratings: single engine land and sea, glider, twin-engine land, instrument, commercial, and Learjet.

I considered myself to be well trained, competent, proficient, and safe. To actually qualify as "safe," a pilot has to be able to fly solely with instruments and land in bad weather. I insisted that Hunt start with FlightSafety right from the beginning of his flying career so that he could avoid some of the misadventures I experienced in my early flying days.

I have owned 15 different aircraft (see Appendix D, page 313), the most sophisticated of which was the Learjet. We traded the Twin Beech for a DC-3, which was a large airliner-type aircraft. It was comfortable but slow.

We traded the DC-3 for the Learjet, which is small, but fast. Built in 1966 the Learjet would climb to 41,000 feet in about 15 minutes and would cruise at 475 miles per hour. Instead of de-icing boots, it had heated wings. Because it only had about 3 hours and 15 minutes of fuel range, we had to stop every two and a half hours in order to keep the required fuel reserve. However, we could easily travel 1000 to 1200 miles between stops. That would get us to California with two fuel stops. For the return trip, oftentimes we would come back with only one stop, as the prevailing wind is west to east. I flew back and forth across the country many times in the Learjet. I sold it when we sold the company.

THE LEARJET AND THE SILVER SPUR

PAUL AND THE LEARJET, COMPLETE WITH BROYHILL LOGOS

I traded the Bonanza for a twin engine Cessna 310. I traded it for a Cessna 320. Over the years I owned a Cessna 411, a Beech Duke, three Cessna 340s, a Cheyenne II, and finally a Cheyenne II XL, which I own as of this writing.

The Cheyenne is a fast, high performance, turbo prop plane that carries a lot of weight. It travels about 285 miles per hour and has a range of 1000 to 1200 miles. I have owned that plane for more than twenty years, so I have had a lot of experience in it. Hunt started out flying the Cessna 340, but he graduated to the Cheyenne II XL. He and I have been to FlightSafety many times together for intensive recurrent training and we consider ourselves to be proficient.

Fairly early in my flying career, I bought a World War II trainer plane called an SNJ. It was the Navy version of the famous Army Trainer AT-6. Ham, my old-time pilot, had instructed in that kind of plane and he thought I should have some training in it. It had a large radial 650HP engine and was hard to handle on the ground. It certainly contributed to my being able to fly the E-18 Twin Beech and the DC-3. On Sunday afternoons, I would fly the SNJ Trainer from Hickory to Lenoir and buzz my house. My little children would come running out, wave at me, and yell, "That's my daddy!"

On one occasion, I made a 70-mile flight to Charlotte in a Cessna 340 to pick up two of my buddies, Larry Crockett and Bill Cooper. They were coming to Lenoir for a meeting of my mutual fund board. Both Larry and Bill had been pilots during the war. After departing the Charlotte airport we heard a loud clunk. My right engine had just

PAUL IN THE COCKPIT OF THE CHEYENNE II XL

"Like flying airplanes, FlightSafety training runs in the family."

PAUL AND HUNT BROYHILL of Lenoir, North Carolina

Flying has been a large part of Paul Broyhill's life for almost 50 years. In fact, he met his future wife in 1955 while flying her to an event during her reign as Miss North Carolina. He continued to fly while running his family's business, Broyhill Furniture Industries, which was sold in 1980. Today, he is Chairman of the BMC Fund, Broyhill Investments, Broyhill Realty, and the Broyhill Family Foundation. As a seasoned pilot with 11,000 hours – including 2,000 hours of jet time – he trains with FlightSafety, often with his son Hunt, who followed his father's footsteps in both business and aviation. Hunt is now CEO of Broyhill Asset Management, LLC, and President of Broyhill Investments and the Broyhill Family Foundation. In 1987, he received his pilot's license and has since logged more than 3,000 hours.

AFTER NEARLY 50 YEARS OF FLYING AND MORE than 11,000 hours in the left seat, Paul Broyhill has had plenty of in-flight experience. Since 1953 – the year he bought his first Beech Bonanza for $12,000 – he's also received lots of instruction. But to stay proficient, he still feels the need for frequent, high quality training – and for that he turns to FlightSafety.

"I first came to FlightSafety in 1984, when I started flying my Piper Cheyenne," he recalls. "I saw immediately how their training could make me a better pilot, and I've been their biggest fan ever since. So when my son, Hunt, started flying, I insisted he learn from FlightSafety."

Thanks in part to Paul's insistence, FlightSafety training has become a family tradition – and also an important component of the Broyhill family business. As father and son fly their Cessna 340 and Piper Cheyenne 2XL to meetings along the East Coast, they rely on the confidence and the proficiency they gain from the leader in aviation training. So despite their demanding schedules, Paul and Hunt train together at FlightSafety four times a year.

"One of our companies manages venture capital investments and financial risk management, which means we prefer as little risk as possible," Hunt explains. "We like to think of FlightSafety as risk managers for aviators." In fact, the younger Broyhill credits his training with helping him act correctly during an in-flight emergency a few years ago. "I'm living proof of the value of training from FlightSafety."

"Actually, at 76, I'm the *real* proof," says his father. "There's a saying that you can be either an old pilot or a bold pilot, but you can't be both. For me, that means putting safety first, and that's why I keep coming back to train with FlightSafety. In fact, I want to be their oldest client."

Highest Quality Training for Owners of Light Aircraft.

Please call (800) 227-5656 or (316) 220-3200. Fax (316) 220-3239.
Or write us at P.O. Box 12304, 1951 Airport Road, Wichita, Kansas 67277.

PAUL AND HUNT IN A FLIGHTSAFETY PROMOTIONAL

stopped. I was near the Charlotte airport, but rather than declaring an emergency and going back like I should have done, I said to Larry and Bill, "The hell with it; this plane will fly just fine on one engine; let's go on home."

We were reasonably light. There were just the three of us and we did not have a lot of luggage on board. I made the 30-minute flight on only one engine. We landed just fine in Hickory and I had my plane at home instead of in Charlotte. The two guys were impressed that I was so cool and calm about it all. On three separate occasions I lost an engine. Each of those instances was uneventful due to my being trained for such emergencies.

When I first started flying, the chief navigation aid was a low frequency radio beam, the same frequency as on a home AM radio. On one side of the beam you would get a dot-dash. On the other side you would get a dash-dot. When you got a steady signal it meant you were "on the beam."

During my career, I saw the introduction of the VHF (Very High Frequency) communication system and the VOR (Variable Omni Range) navigating system. That navigation system is still in use today, but gradually newer ones are outmoding it. I saw the advent of the DME (Distance Measuring Equipment), the mass usage of Airborne Weather Detection Radar, later the Collision Avoidance Radar, then the LORAN (Long Range Navigation), which was a predecessor to today's GPS (Global Positioning System).

I had a brief attempt at learning to fly a helicopter. I thought it would be useful to be able to fly around to our various plants, so I bought a Brantley 305 helicopter. It was almost brand new when I bought it and was a really good-looking machine.

Ham Holder had a few hours of helicopter training, so he adapted to it very quickly. To this day, I probably have only fifteen or so hours of helicopter time. Fairly soon after we bought the Brantley, a bank in Atlanta lost one of their helicopters in a crash. It happened to be the same model as ours. As a result, the entire fleet of Brantley 305 was grounded until the manufacturer could determine the problem. When I bought the aircraft, I had been told that helicopters never crashed. I thought that if the motor stalled, you would simply windmill down and easily land. Of course, I was disillusioned when I heard about the crash. I was further disillusioned when I tried to sell the Brantley and found that the market value for that model had plummeted. The helicopter sat idly in the hangar. However, from time to time, I took my five-year-old son and we would sit in the helicopter, shake the stick, kick the rudders, say, "Woo-woo-woo," and pretend we were flying it.

I often joke that some fathers buy their kids a toy helicopter to play with but that I bought my son a real one. Hunt continues to fly our plane and commutes in the winter to Ocean Reef, Florida, dropping off Karen and me at Naples. He is as dedicated a pilot as I was.

Flying was a way of life for me. I was generally in the plane once or twice a week. Whether going somewhere on business or going somewhere on the weekends for pleasure, flying enabled me to do

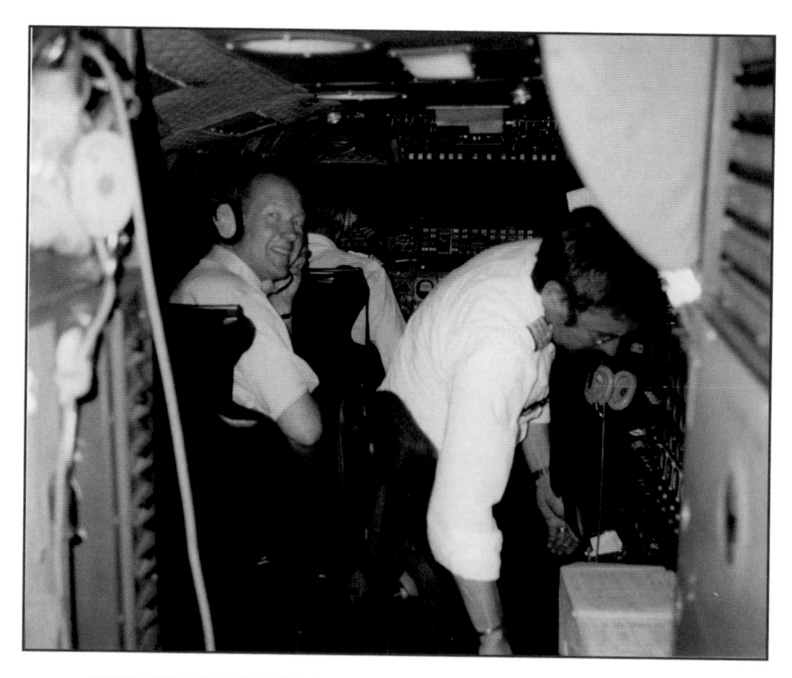

PAUL IN THE COCKPIT OF THE SUPERSONIC CONCORDE

so much more with my time than I possibly could have done without that capability; both professionally and personally. Overall, I flew 200 or 300 hours a year.

I have actually flown more than 13,000 total hours. I calculated that with an average work year being 2,000 hours, I flew 6 ½ work years. That means about 10% of my work life was spent in the air, but I do think that was productive time. Faye said that I spent more time with my pilot than I did with her.

THE CONCORDE

22

Second Time Around

FAYE AND I lived happily for 46 years, raising three children and enjoying seven grandchildren together. We had known each other for a year before marriage, so that comes to 47 years being together.

Suddenly in 2002 Faye became very ill. It was such a shock because everything happened so fast. She got sick in late August and passed away in early October. After she was gone, I was completely devastated and thought that my life was over as well. Her death was so unexpected and so quick. In retrospect, the short time frame may have been a blessing in disguise. We all tend to say that we would like to go quickly, and I am glad that she did not suffer very long. However, I was absolutely distraught. I could hardly continue a normal routine.

I was so lonely that I started dating again soon after I lost Faye. The wives of some of my close friends disapproved of my going out so soon, but that is something everyone has to decide for himself. It was not an indication that I did not love my wife; it meant that I loved her so much that I could not stand to be alone on weekends. I have never been a particularly emotional person, but sadness consumed me for at least a year. I cried every time that I thought about Faye. I tear up thinking about her even now.

I never thought I would be seriously interested in another woman. However, after staying home for a few weeks, crying and feeling sorry for myself, I was making myself sick. I decided I needed some company. I called a lady whom Faye and I had known previously at Linville Ridge Club. Over the following year, I went out with her as well as

KAREN RABON BROYHILL

with several other women. I told all of them that I was 59. At 78 years old, trying to be 59 can be pretty hard work, but I gave it all I had.

My daughter Caron and her friend Jenny Hall decided to assume the role of matchmakers. For some time they talked to me about meeting Jenny's mother, Karen. Truthfully, I had some reservations. I did not want anything I might do to affect Caron and Jenny's friendship. I had to promise my daughter that I would be a perfect gentleman.

On the first date arranged by the girls, I found Karen to be very attractive. She had been a high school beauty queen. We attended a pre-wedding cocktail party in honor of one of Karen's friends. After the party, we went to an antique show fundraiser at the Mint Museum in Charlotte. It was the type show where small vendors set up in individual spaces to display their goods. Faye and I liked that sort of thing, so I felt comfortable. As it turned out, some of the vendors recognized me. I enjoyed showing Karen around.

We found that we had a lot in common. We were both raised in the small town environments of Lenoir and nearby Salisbury. Both of us attended a Baptist church and we held many of the same beliefs. We had attended public schools. Karen was easy to be with and from that first date, we have been together almost every weekend.

Karen had been an avid cross-country runner and had run in several marathons. She loved to play tennis, and though she had always wanted to play golf, she had little experience. She had taken half a dozen lessons and had recently purchased a set of clubs, so we started golfing together. I had played tennis when I was young, so I took it up again. We were playing tennis in the morning, golfing in the afternoon, and dancing at night. I was reliving my youth.

We established a routine of being together that worked well for us. She lived in Charlotte and I lived in Lenoir, about an hour and a half apart. During the week she pursued her real estate career, played tennis with her friends, and enjoyed the company of her two adult children, Chris and Jenny.

I worked at my office every day during the week. On weekends in the winter, she would meet me at the Hickory airport and we'd fly to my home in Naples; in the summer, she came by my house in Lenoir and we drove together to my home at Linville Ridge in the mountains of North Carolina. We were comfortable in the relationship, and I felt my old confidence return.

JENNY AND CHRIS WITH THEIR MOTHER, KAREN

During my early dating years I had managed to avoid marriage until I was 32 years old. I dodged that bullet with a number of girls because I was practiced in not getting seriously involved. When I met Karen, I was at a different stage in my life. I was no longer 30 years old, but in my late 70s. After Karen and I had dated for about a year, I decided that I should do her a big favor and ask her to marry me. I arranged a fancy dinner. I did not actually have a ring, but I bought a beautiful necklace. After dinner I announced that we had been together happily for a year and that it was about time to talk about marriage.

Karen put me off. She said she was honored but that we ought to think about it a little longer. Frankly, I was in a state of shock. I could not imagine anyone turning me down. Both personally and professionally, I was used to being in control and getting my way. For the first and last time in our relationship, I was upset—and she knew it.

Undaunted, I went ahead and bought a ring. On the night I presented it to her, Karen put it on and wore it during the evening, but then she gave it back to me. She said that we still needed more time to think.

At Thanksgiving, Karen began her usual preparations to entertain her entire family: her two children, her three sisters, her brother, their families, and her mother. They traditionally stayed for three or four days. I did not want to get involved in all that family stuff, so I said that I was going out to Santa Fe, New Mexico, to visit with a lady friend. When I told Karen my plans, she bristled.

"Well, we're not engaged," I said coolly. "I don't see why I can't continue to play around a little bit."

She turned around, narrowed her eyes, glared at me for a moment and said, "Give me the darn ring!"

She took the ring, jammed it onto her finger and said, "Now are you satisfied?"

"Yes, I'm satisfied," I answered.

"So, are you going to Santa Fe?" she questioned.

"I guess I'll just spend Thanksgiving with my family," I said, stifling a victorious grin. That was not a very romantic proposal, but it worked.

Karen enjoyed showing off the custom-made ring to her friends.

It was quite an attention-getting canary diamond. After she grew accustomed to the idea of being engaged, I again brought up the subject of marriage. Her answer: "Let's think about it a little longer."

I took matters in hand and called Dr. David Smith, my minister in Lenoir, and asked him if he would marry us. I knew that I wanted to get married in the mountains, so I called Blowing Rock Baptist Church, where my father and mother had gone in the summers. The church had an organist and a vocalist. I knew a florist in the mountains, ordered flowers, and hired a photographer. In just a short time I planned the entire wedding and only lacked one small detail: a bride.

I called Karen and asked her for a date on November 10th of 2007 and told her that I wanted her to wear her best dress. Suspiciously, she asked me, "What's the occasion?"

"We're going to get married," I stated.

"I haven't talked about it with my mother or my children," Karen protested.

"Well, you better start talking," I said.

THE HAPPY COUPLE

THE WEDDING PARTY FROM TOP LEFT: HUNT (PAUL'S SON), CHRIS HALL (KAREN'S SON), STEDMAN STEVENS, AND TIM GREENE (CLAIRE'S HUSBAND). FRONT: LEANNE (HUNT'S WIFE), JENNY HALL (KAREN'S DAUGHTER), KAREN AND PAUL, CARON AND CLAIRE (PAUL'S DAUGHTERS).

Our wedding turned out beautifully. It was sweet and intimate. It was just us, with our children and their spouses as attendants. Although it was small, we had all the elements of a big wedding. The men wore tuxedos and the women wore black dresses. By contrast, Karen and I wore off-white, she in a lovely suit and I in a dinner jacket. Hunt, who stood with me as my best man, and the other groomsmen waited at the altar while the four bridesmaids walked down the aisle carrying their flowers. Chris, Karen's son, escorted her down the aisle and gave her to me. Everything came together. The music, the flowers, the homily—it all turned out perfectly.

After the ceremony, we all gathered at our Linville home, ate a nice dinner, and enjoyed a lovely wedding cake. Karen and I danced to our favorite song, *The Second Time Around.* The evening was a prelude to the fairy tale life we share together. We are now living happily ever after.

THE LINVILLE RIDGE HOME

INSIDE THE LINVILLE RIDGE HOME

THE BROYHILL HOME IN NAPLES, FLORIDA

While we brag to our friends that we never have had a fuss, that is not entirely true. From time to time, we have had little tiffs over my trying to give her golf lessons, or getting us lost in Europe. Once when she was trying to hit out of a sand trap and was banging away as if she were trying to kill a snake, I tried to tell her how to get out, but she would not listen. After the game, I insisted that we go to the practice sand trap.

She answered in an unfamiliar, firm, tone of voice, "I am not getting back in any sand trap today! I'm out of here; I'm going home and get a glass of wine!"

I couldn't help but laugh.

European trips have been a once or twice yearly ritual for me since my honeymoon with Faye in 1956. Karen has accompanied me now for six years. On those trips, Karen drives and I navigate. I think I have a pretty good sense of direction, but I have quite a history of getting lost. On our first trip to Europe, we were in England going around one of the circles that they call "rond-a-boot" (roundabout). Those circles have six or eight outlets. I was not sure of the direction, so I kept saying, "Let's go around one more time."

After I had said that three times, Karen said in that same firm tone I had heard on the golf course, "I am not going around this circle another time. Figure out where we're going."

When we are in Europe, we get lost at least once a day. Of course, I never admit that I am lost. I just say, "We're taking the scenic route." When we get lost, I can blame it on our companion, Tom. Our Tom-Tom GPS system has been a big help, but his verbal instructions sometimes can be a little confusing, causing us to make a wrong turn. If you go off one of those big autobahns at the wrong exit, sometimes it takes you a while to get back on. In my opinion those "side trips" just add to our fun.

So far, Karen and I have traveled throughout Western Europe. We have been to England, Belgium, Germany, Austria, Switzerland, Italy, France, Spain, Greece, and Croatia. We never have gone with a tour group because I cannot stand someone herding me around. I have a lot of books on Europe, and part of the fun is reading ahead of time where I want to go. I try to plan a daily itinerary, first booking the hotels. I love the country hotels and the countryside more than the cities. After I plan the lodging, I try to find something to do or see closeby. Most of the country hotels have beautiful grounds as well as pools and spas. Those beautiful landscapes have inspired me to recreate them closer to home.

Karen and I are compatible golfers. We play by the Broyhill rules. We take mulligans if we want them, and I keep the score. I do not write down anything more than a double bogey. We say that we play *honest golf.* We will say, "That's a five, but it wasn't very honest," or "That's a fairly honest five," or "That's a really honest four." I always know about what she is going to make, and I pretty well know what I am going to make.

A part of what has made our marriage successful is that Karen and I continue the routine we established while dating. She maintains her life in Charlotte during the week while I am working in Lenoir. She still works in real estate sales, has her tennis friends, and has time for her family. Both Karen's children, Chris and Jenny, have successful careers, but neither is married. Her father recently passed away, so Karen regularly visits her mother in Salisbury and helps her

PAUL AND KAREN AT THE GREENBRIAR

with whatever she may need. I joke with her that I'm not married Monday through Thursday. She just grins and rolls her eyes.

Since the beginning, I have had a pleasant relationship with Karen's family. I did have one adjustment though with the most pampered member of the family. I lovingly refer to her as the "D. D." Mollie, Jenny's three-pound miniature Chihuahua, does not know she is a dog. I learned fast that it was a package deal: Love me; love my dog. When Jenny travels in her work, Karen keeps the dog. They dress Mollie, bathe her, perfume her, and hug and kiss her. The dog has never slept alone. When I want to sleep with my wife, there is that Damn Dog in the bed.

My acceptance of the D. D. is ironic. When I was married to Faye, a friend of ours left a lovely wife and married one of those "sweet young things." The new, younger wife had a little dog. At dinner one night the guy was making quite a fool of himself over the dog. I just could not stand watching that man fawn over the dog in order to please his wife. Disgusted, I turned to Faye and said, "See what a fool he's making of himself? One thing's for sure; I will never do that for a woman!" Now what is worrying me is that Faye may be looking down on me from heaven, laughing at me over the Damn Dog.

Karen has chosen to live with an older man. Though our marriage is a bit unusual, it is not one-sided as we both enjoy the relationship. She enhances my life. I try to enhance hers by offering her unique experiences as well as compatibility. It works both ways.

At this stage in my life, time is precious and I am wise enough to know how blessed I am to have a companion to share it with, especially one who is attractive, interesting, agreeable, and fun. I always enjoy being with Karen and each day I try to let her know just how much she means to me. I used to joke with Faye, "I love you so much; it's all I can do to keep from telling you." I have improved a little now and constantly tell Karen how much I love her.

MOLLIE (D. D.)

Part 4

Life Goes On

23

Dad's Spirit of Generosity Passed Down

MY DAD WAS generous and believed in sharing what he had. Soon after the war, he decided to start a charitable foundation. His original idea was to set up a fund to make loans for young people to go to college. He never had a lot of schooling and felt strongly that everyone should have the opportunity for a good education. Dad established the Broyhill Education Fund with a little personal money, and then we annually donated a small percentage of our corporate profits into it.

Dad established a board of directors, developed by-laws, and obtained non-profit status from the state of North Carolina so that the corpus of the fund could be invested and the proceeds could be used to make loans and charitable donations. Through those loans, we helped several hundred students continue their schooling. Very honestly, we had such poor repayment history on the loans that, in reality, they turned out to be scholarships rather than loans.

As the fund grew larger, I succeeded Dad as chairman of the board. Because of administrative hassles, we got out of the loan business and gave our existing loan balances to the North Carolina College Fund, a state-administered organization that was in business to loan money to deserving students. We began sending contributions directly to small church-related colleges in Western North Carolina.

Later we broadened our scope of giving and established categories of interest including the arts, local charities, health and hospitals, schools and colleges, parks and recreation, and youth development. Because of the wider range of interests, we changed the name to the Broyhill Family Foundation.

In the early days, we only donated to colleges in Western North Carolina that had religious affiliations because state schools were strictly government funded. Through time they, too, have established departments of institutional advancement to fund some of the research and special programs that they offer. We have endowments at a number of colleges and universities in Western North Carolina, and we underwrite some of their special programs, especially in business, business ethics, and leadership.

My father and mother met at Appalachian College when it was small and privately owned, so we always have had an affinity for it. When the state of North Carolina took it over, the school focused on training teachers. With state and private support, the college expanded to include a business school and other departments. Today it is a full-fledged, well-respected university where we continue to have particular interest. My wife Faye had the distinction of being the first female president of the Appalachian board of trustees.

Some years ago, I became quite interested in the concept of the community college as a way to make education more accessible and affordable. We were active in establishing our local community college, and we urged officials to include a technical component to train students for work in various trades. In 1966, Caldwell Community College and Technical Institute was founded. In recent years, we helped to create a career center at the college, which is a combined effort between the college and the public schools. One day as my brother and I were lunching with Appalachian State University leaders, they were lamenting that they had no room to expand. At that lunch, we came up with the idea of ASU partnering with CCC&TI to have a presence on their campus. The idea came to fruition with our donating money to help with construction of the Faye A. Broyhill building to house an ASU teaching center at CCC&TI. Under the program, a student could go for two years to the community college, transfer to Appalachian, and literally walk across campus to earn a four-year teaching degree. With our county commissioners on board with the idea, that became the first partnership of its kind to involve

Broyhill ASU Center donation

The Broyhill Family Foundation recently presented Caldwell Community College and Technical Institute with $200,000 toward the Appalachian State University Center project. Pictured left to right are Paul Broyhill, James Broyhill and CCC&TI President, Dr.

PAUL AND JIM PRESENT AN INSTALLMENT FOR THE ASU TEACHING CENTER TO DR. KEN BOHAM, PRESIDENT OF CALDWELL COMMUNITY COLLEGE AND TECHNICAL INSTITUTE.

the community college system, the university system, the public sector, and the private sector. Since then, Appalachian has partnered with other area community colleges to offer degrees in other fields. That concept was, and still is, an innovative one. It saves a tremendous amount of money and truly makes education more available.

By far the two largest giving categories for Broyhill Family Foundation are colleges and hospitals. Besides our endowments at schools such as Wake Forest, Converse, Lenoir-Rhyne, Gardner-Webb, Lees-McRae, Meredith, and Mars Hill, we have a giving history at a number of medical centers. Those include Caldwell Memorial Hospital, Watauga Medical Center, Wake Forest Medical Center, Duke University Medical Center, and the University of North Carolina Medical Center. We support both the Mayo and Cleveland Clinics. Because one of my granddaughters has a condition called myasthenia

THIS PORTRAIT OF FAYE GRACES THE LOBBY OF THE FAYE A. BROYHILL BUILDING AT CALDWELL COMMUNITY COLLEGE AND TECHNICAL INSTITUTE.

gravis, we have donated to neuromuscular research. Since Faye's death, we are interested in cancer research, especially brain cancer.

One of the most significant areas of our foundation's interest is youth development. During the late 1980s Michael Broome, a young man from Appalachian, approached us with an idea to develop summer camps for young people. He desired to have a hard-hitting program that would orient youth towards leadership, individualism, conservative morals, and just plain "business sense." Almost 1,000 people a year have attended the Tomorrow's America *Broyhill Leadership Conferences*. From its inception, Michael and his wife, Karen, have done the work, and the Broyhill Family Foundation has

1998 Broyhill Leadership Conferences

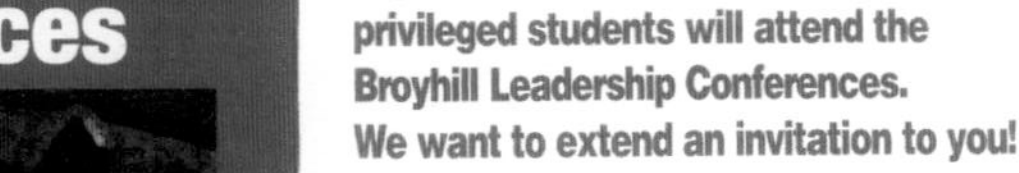

Charting a Course for Youth

Since 1982

This summer, over two thousand students across America will be chosen to participate in one of the most unique experiences of their lives. These privileged students will attend the Broyhill Leadership Conferences. We want to extend an invitation to you!

Michael Broome

From the moment you arrive, you'll be taking part in an adventure that will help strengthen your leadership and communication skills, and develop goal setting and positive thinking abilities. Your self confidence will grow and you'll begin to view your problems as challenges. You will become keenly aware of our priceless freedoms and the blessings of our free enterprise system.

The opportunities you'll encounter at the **Broyhill Leadership Conferences** will include hearing humorous and motivational speakers, seeing inspirational and entertaining films, and participating in energetic group activities and discussions. You will also enjoy a dance, talent show, Olympic-style athletic events, and have the pleasure of making a multitude of new friends!

The 200-page **BLC** Handbook and six-tape cassette series are great tools and resources that you will be able to use in your school, organization, and personal life. "Textbook" does not describe the Handbook - it is written specifically for young people.

It is considered an honor to attend the **Broyhill Leadership Conferences**. I hope that you will be able to join us!

The Broyhill philosophy is one that encompasses a belief in perseverance, self-reliance, and service to others. These are not mere words, but a way of life for Paul Broyhill and his family. They have always had a special interest in the development of youth as evidenced by their commitment toward the **Broyhill Leadership Conferences**.

At **BLC**, young leaders are taught to apply the same principles that have enabled the Broyhills to make many lasting contributions to their community, state, and nation.

The founder of Broyhill Industries, James Edgar Broyhill, said, "God forges us on an anvil of adversity for a purpose known only to Him. That is the way He prepares us for life."

Surely the Broyhills are fulfilling their purpose by helping so many youths to accomplish their dreams.

In an age when heroes are hard to find, we are grateful to be associated with a family that exemplifies heartfelt generosity and that dares to be great.

Our nation needs more leaders of this caliber and the **Broyhill Leadership Conferences** are developing them. We look forward to seeing you there!

Paul Broyhill

TOMORROW'S AMERICA BROYHILL LEADERSHIP CONFERENCES FOCUS ON YOUTH DEVELOPMENT.

furnished the finances. That program is more on a personal level than just donating to an institution. The enthusiasm of the young people impresses me. My advice to young people today on how to be successful is simply to combine that enthusiasm with hard work and dedication, and apply it to a career they enjoy. My dad said, "If you enjoy what you do, you will never have to work again, because your work becomes fun."

Another organization where we have significant interest is Baptist Children's Homes. My dad and mother were instrumental in the establishment of the western campus of Baptist Children's Homes, called the Broyhill Home, in Clyde, North Carolina. Linda Morgan has been the director there for three decades, and she recalls visits from

THE PLANNING STAGES OF BROYHILL HOME

JIM, J.E., SATIE, BETTIE AND PAUL ON THE BROYHILL CAMPUS OF BAPTIST CHILDREN'S HOMES IN THE WESTERN NORTH CAROLINA MOUNTAINS

my parents well up into their later years. They loved to see the children provided with a safe, secure, and loving environment. Though it is sad to hear of their former despicable circumstances, it is touching to hear stories of children overcoming their backgrounds to live productive lives.

From the time of our honeymoon in Europe, Faye and I enjoyed our annual overseas visits to parks and gardens. We were drawn to beautiful homes and landscaping, especially in France and England. Everywhere we went, we took a lot of pictures. Those visits inspired us to help develop a small park in Blowing Rock. After that, we decided to do something similar in Lenoir, only on a much larger scale. My Uncle Tom had owned some land, a portion of which was used by the Civilian Conservation Corps as a rock quarry. He donated the land to the city of Lenoir to build a municipal swimming pool. Some years later, the city constructed a sophisticated fitness center and pool on another site, and the old pool fell into disrepair. When Faye and I visited Bouchart Gardens in Vancouver and saw the lush gardens built on the site of a former rock quarry, I conceived the idea of turning the neglected Lenoir site into something similar. The idea grew when we visited Clivedon, the Astor estate on the outskirts of London. There we saw the Japanese pagoda that was built for the 1889 World's Fair in Paris and that was later purchased by Lord Astor for his wife, Nancy.

With the help of furniture designer Bill Early and landscape architect Harry Yates, I fashioned an oriental-themed walking park that covers 37 acres. An oriental pergola stands at the head of the large lake as a focal point. A replica of Lady Astor's Japanese pagoda stands near a small upper pond that is flanked by up-lighted rock cliffs. When we finished the park, we donated it to the city of Lenoir. It is heavily used by citizens from all "walks" of life. Not only for exercise and play, it has become quite a popular place to provide scenic backgrounds for wedding and prom photography.

THE T. H. BROYHILL WALKING PARK WAS DESIGNED ON THE SITE OF A FORMER ROCK QUARRY.

THE FAYE ARNOLD BROYHILL BRIDGE AT THE WALKING PARK

DRAMATIC WATERFALL AT THE FAYE ARNOLD BROYHILL BRIDGE WITH PAGODA AND ROCK FACE IN THE BACKGROUND

THIS PAGODA AT BROYHILL WALKING PARK WAS MODELED AFTER LADY ASTOR'S JAPANESE PAGODA.

LADY ASTOR'S PAGODA AT CLIVEDON, ENGLAND

HISTORIC MARKER HONORING THOSE WHO HELPED MAKE THE T. H. BROYHILL WALKING PARK POSSIBLE

We have made two other donations that I would like to mention. The house where Jim, Allene, Bettie, and I grew up still stands on the corner of College Avenue and Norwood Street in Lenoir. For a number of years we leased it to the Caldwell County Arts Council, but recently we donated it to them as a permanent location.

The home my parents built later, the place they lived until their deaths, is a stately, white, neoclassical home surrounded by lovely gardens. We donated that home to Caldwell Community College and Technical Institute. They use it for meetings and rent it out for special events. We continue to help maintain the home and to add landscaping details. It is one of the area's most popular sites for weddings and receptions.

Through the years, the corpus of the foundation has grown until today it is one of the largest foundations in Western North Carolina. It certainly does not compare to Reynolds or Duke foundations; nevertheless, it is large enough to make a significant impact in our area. We run it with minimum administrative costs, but have a

THE FORMER COLLEGE STREET BROYHILL HOME NOW HOUSES THE CALDWELL ARTS COUNCIL.

THE FAMILY DONATED THE ESTATE TO CALDWELL COMMUNITY COLLEGE.

strong executive director, Sheila Triplett-Brady, who evaluates all our requests. We joke with her that we lured her with an easy job of giving money away. However, I think she has found that every day we have to deny requests for many good causes and worthwhile projects, and it is not much fun turning down such requests.

I know my dad would be pleased with the size and scope of the Broyhill Family Foundation because he loved helping people. He taught us well. While many buildings, programs, and initiatives bear the Broyhill name, we actually try to keep a fairly low profile. By Dad's example, we do not seek recognition; rather, we seek to give back to the community a portion of what we have received.

Reception July 14th Officially Designates Hospital's New Outpatient Rehab Center In Honor Of Satie Hunt Broyhill

Staff, friends and supporters of Blowing Rock Hospital's new Outpatient Rehab Facility were on hand on Tuesday, July 14 to honor the lifetime devotion and contributions of the late Satie Hunt Broyhill and that of the Broyhill family. Because of the interest and generosity of the Broyhill family the new facility opened recently will bear the name of The Satie Hunt Broyhill Outpatient Facility, a tribute to Mrs. Broyhill and her family for years of service, not only to the hospital, but to the community of Blowing Rock. With the naming of the Outpatient Facility in her honor, the Broyhill influence in Blowing Rock is now even more evident. Broyhill Chapel at First Baptist Church and Broyhill Park are both named in honor of Mrs Broyhill's late husband, J.E. Broyhill. Pictured above during the reception this past Tuesday are (from left to right), Senator James T. Broyhill and his wife Louise, Faye and Paul Broyhill, Allene Broyhill Heilman and her husband Robert E, and Willard A. Gortner and his wife, Betti Broyhill Gortner. Behind them is the new portrait of Mrs. Broyhill painted for the lobby of the new facility named in her honor. At the lower left is Diane Davant, who was the interior decorator for the new facility, pictured with Cheryl Kilby and Marguerite Taylor Moore who painted the strikingly beautiful new wall mural of Grandfather Mountain at the new west entrance to the Outpatient complex.

THE FAMILY HONOR THEIR MOTHER WITH A GIFT FOR AN OUTPATIENT FACILITY AT BLOWING ROCK HOSPITAL.

FAYE AND PAUL WITH MARS HILL COLLEGE PRESIDENT FRED BENTLEY

PAUL PRESENTS A CHECK TO NORTH CAROLINA GOVERNOR JIM HUNT FOR THE SMART START PROGRAM.

2A—Watauga Democrat, Boone, N.C., Feb. 21, 1990

JAMEY FLETCHER/Democrat staff

Broyhills honored

Paul Broyhill, chairman of the Broyhill Family Foundation, accepts an award from Jerry Burns, chairman of the Centennial '89 Committee for Blowing Rock, during the Blowing Rock Chamber of Commerce's third annual awards banquet Tuesday night at the Meadowbrook Inn. Mr. Broyhill and the Foundation were honored as 1989 winners of the chamber's civic beautification category which recognizes improvements to the environment in the town of Blowing Rock. The Broyhills were major contributors to the restoration of the old Mayview Lake and the construction of the new Broyhill Park. Eight other awards to individuals and businesses were presented by the chamber.

PAUL RECOGNIZED FOR BLOWING ROCK PARK

Historic Lea Lab Recently Restored And Dedicated As Broyhill Hall

Wake Forest, NC - Lea Laboratory, built in 1888 and now the oldest building on the Southeastern Baptist Theological Seminary campus, has been restored and dedicated as Broyhill Hall in honor of industrialists J. E. Broyhill, his son Paul, and their families.

The beautiful Colonial Revival style structure has been unused for several years, awaiting the day when the Southern Baptist Convention seminary could secure funds for its restoration. Originally built in 1888 as one of the first chemical laboratories on a southern college campus, the structure was named for Sidney Slade Lea, a wealthy Caswell County, N.C. farmer and his wife Fannie E. Lea. The original cost of the central portion of the building was $13,000, paid for by a gift from the Leas. Later, two wings were added, making the building an intriguing blend of Colonial and Victorian elements.

Lea Lab was one of the buildings inherited by Southeastern Seminary when the Southern Baptist Convention purchased the campus of Wake Forest College in 1950. The 146-year-old campus was used jointly by the College and the Seminary until 1956 when the College moved to its new campus in Winston-Salem. Following the College's move, the building was used as a book store and campus soda shop. With the completion in 1968 of Mackie Hall student center, Lea Lab was no longer utilized. Because such extensive renovation was needed, the building was almost demolished. Fortunately, it was saved, and a drive was begun to secure funds for its restoration.

Seminary President Lolley (right) presented a framed sketch of Broyhill Hall to Mr. J. E. Broyhill, and his sons Paul, left, and James.

Extensive rennovations were required to bring Lea Laboratory back to good health. Because of the gifts of many generous benefactors, the new christened Broyhill Hall will soon begin a second century of service.

The drive for restoration gained additional momentum in 1975 when Lea Lab was entered in the National Register of Historic Places. Its unique purpose as a pioneer classroom building for the study of science qualified it for that recognition.

The dedication has signaled the completion of a determined effort by the Seminary to preserve a historic and valuable building. The effort was begun by former Seminary President Olin T. Brinkley and continued by his successor, W. Randall Lolley. Leaders in the fund drive were former trustees of the seminary, James E. Broyhill and his son, Paul, furniture manufacturers of Lenoir, N.C. Because of their generous gifts, the Seminary's Board of Trustees have re-named the building in their honor.

An additional gift of $100,000 was received from the Kresge Foundation of Troy, Michigan, a foundation well-known for its generous support of projects to reclaim historic buildings. Also, the Southern Baptist Convention made a significant contribution to the cost of its restoration.

With its nine chimneys, walls of Flemish bond, and delicate detail, the newly refurbished Broyhill Hall is providing a pleasing view for the Seminary, community and visitors. The interior refurbishing has created new meeting rooms for the Board of Trustees and Faculty, the Formation in Ministry program, and the Student Placement program. In addition, the Seminary's communication offices, offices for faculty members and a conference room will also occupy space in the building.

Through the long labors of concerned individuals Lea Laboratories has been resurrected, refurbished and rechristened as Broyhill Hall. As it enters its 94th year, this historic building houses new tenants and fulfills new goals. It should serve the Seminary well for many years to come.

EXCERPT FROM *PEOPLE TODAY AT BROYHILL* RECOGNIZING BROYHILL HALL AT SOUTHEASTERN BAPTIST THEOLOGICAL SEMINARY

24

Broyhill Politics

THE BROYHILL FAMILY holds an established tradition of conservative Republican politics. In 1948 my father became a Republican National Committeeman and held that position for 20 years. He was involved in recruiting candidates for various public offices and was very much involved in fundraising, both locally and nationally. In those days most of the wealthy businessmen were Democrats, and Dad had the tough job of breaking the ice and getting them to devote some of their resources to the Republican Party.

My brother-in-law Bill Stevens made an unsuccessful run for Congress in 1954. Several years later the Republicans recruited my brother, Jim, to run against an entrenched Democrat congressman. No one thought Jim Broyhill actually had a chance to win, but he surprised everyone and became a United States Republican Congressman, an office he held from 1963 to 1986.

RE-ELECT
JAMES T. BROYHILL
YOUR CONGRESSMAN
FOR LEADERSHIP, DEDICATION, AND SERVICE TO THE 10TH DISTRICT
ALEXANDER - AVERY - BURKE - CATAWBA
CLEVELAND - GASTON - CALDWELL - WATAUGA

"JIM BROYHILL FOR CONGRESS" CAMPAIGN BROCHURE

BEHIND THE POLITICAL SCENES

In 1986 Governor Jim Martin appointed Jim Broyhill to fill an unexpired United States senate term left vacant by John East. He served the balance of the term but was defeated in the next election. After that, Governor Martin recruited Jim to be North Carolina Secretary of Commerce. Jim was well suited for politics. He had patience, he was likeable, and he had good judgment. Those qualities have served him well all his life. As a conservative, business-oriented congressman, he was able to get along well with both sides of the aisle.

Emory McCall, a longtime, early Broyhill employee, ran for Congress, was defeated, and then ran locally three times. He was finally elected as the first Republican county commissioner in Caldwell County. That was a coup for local Republicans.

In 1971 Bill Stevens was elected to the North Carolina House. He served ably, not only as a member of the state General Assembly, but also on a seven-person committee that made decisions regarding where roads were going to be built in the state. Bill Stevens was responsible for the first four-lane leg of Highway 321 North that bisects Caldwell County and is now its major corridor. He accomplished that before he left his post in the House of Representatives to run in 1974 for the United States Senate at the encouragement of then-governor Jim Holshouser. Unfortunately, Bill was unsuccessful in his bid for senator.

With my father, my brother, and my brother-in-law being so involved in politics, I worked behind the scenes helping to organize and to raise campaign funds. I had the opportunity to meet a lot of congressmen and senators as well as the Republican presidents.

Today, I keep some of the pictures of those personages on my wall at the office. People who visit my office enjoy seeing the scores of pictures of our posing with Presidents Hoover, Eisenhower, Nixon, Reagan, George H. W. Bush, and George W. Bush, as well as with other government leaders.

J.E. WITH TOM DEWEY (LEFT) WHO RAN FOR U.S. PRESIDENT IN 1948 AGAINST HARRY TRUMAN

J. E. MEETS WITH HERBERT HOOVER.
SEATED L–R: HERBERT HOOVER AND GENERAL WOOD,
THE HEAD OF SEARS, ROEBUCK AND COMPANY.
STANDING: JOE KENNEDY, BERNARD GIMBEL, J.E. BROYHILL.

J. E. (FAR LEFT) IN THE OVAL OFFICE WITH
PRESIDENT EISENHOWER

ROBERT TAFT (PRESIDENTIAL CANDIDATE IN 1952 AGAINST EISENHOWER), SATIE, MRS. TAFT, AND J. E.

PAUL, HUNT, AND J. E. WITH PRESIDENT GERALD FORD

PRESIDENT RONALD REAGAN AND PAUL

To Paul and Hunt Broyhill
With best wishes,

HUNT AND PAUL WITH PRESIDENT GEORGE H. W. BUSH

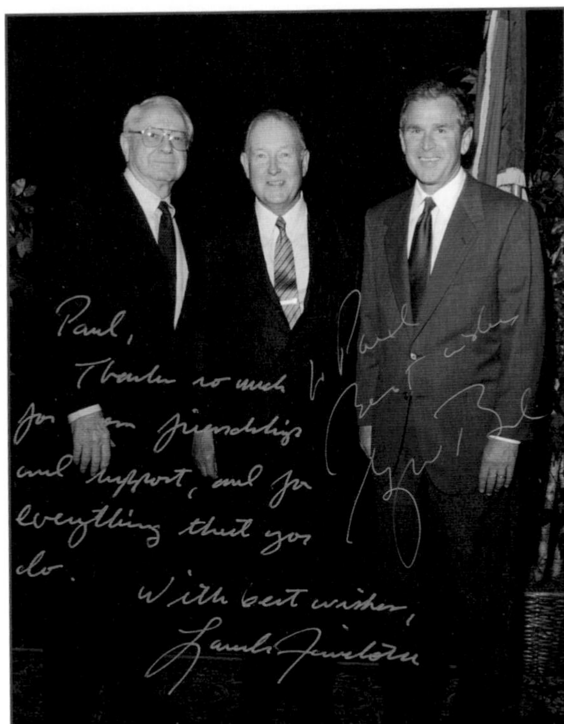

SENATOR LAUCH FAIRCLOTH (R-NC), PAUL, AND PRESIDENT GEORGE W. BUSH

FAYE WITH SENATOR AND MRS. RUSSELL LONG AT OCEAN REEF. SENATOR LONG'S MEMORABLE SAYING WAS "DON'T TAX THEE AND DON'T TAX ME; TAX THAT FELLOW BEHIND THE TREE."

PAUL WITH SENATOR BOB DOLE (R-KANSAS)

Paul—I love your shirt and tie! With heartfelt thanks to a
great friend and my very best wishes,
Elizabeth Dole

LOUISE AND JIM BROYHILL, SENATOR
ELIZABETH DOLE (R-NC) AND PAUL

SENATE MAJORITY LEADER TRENT LOTT,
PAUL, HUNT, AND SENATOR BOB DOLE

PAUL, NORTH CAROLINA GOVERNOR JIM HUNT, AND HUNT

I think the older a person gets, the more skeptical he becomes about the future and where our government leaders may be taking the country. My personal philosophy, and that of my family, has always been that government has to be kept in check so as not to erode individual freedom. Our forefathers came here to escape the overpowering governments of England and Europe. Governments have been oppressive all through the ages as they have sought to finance their activities through enlarging the tax base and tax rate. We built this country to be a republic, not a democracy, so that there would be a minimum of government. In a democracy the majority has unlimited power. You get to a situation where two foxes and a lamb are voting on what to have for dinner. Only in a republic, with government limited by the constitution to certain enumerated powers, are you sure of individual freedom. Our country has evolved away from a republic to a democracy and I find that more and more disturbing.

As a republic, the United States was supposed to be controlled more by the states than by the central government. Switzerland's government also was founded to be a republic. I find it interesting that Switzerland has maintained the republic model whereas we have not. As a result, Switzerland is still one of the freest countries in the world. Here, our central government has grown in control and continues to grow. The situation reminds me of Europe after World War II. People won their freedom, and immediately the government tendency was like it had been in Greece in 250 BC. They wanted to tax the wealthy minority and give everything to the majority. Our Constitution was written to protect the minority, but gradually Supreme Court decisions have given more and more power to the government. It is my fervent hope that the rights of the individual and the free enterprise system will survive and will flourish in the years to come.

25

"Have I Told You That Story?"

Paul Broyhill loves to laugh. He has a mischievous streak in him and a gleam in his eye. When I see that gleam I know he is going to come out with his characteristic line, "Have I told you that story?" For effect, he punctuates these tales with a grin and elicits sporadic exclamations of "Oh, my gosh!"

Sheila Triplett-Brady

DAD AND I were to play golf with a New York banker at Blowing Rock Club. Back in those days a banker was very important to us. The banker called me ahead of time to say that he was bringing his girlfriend with him and that she could round out the foursome. I did not tell Dad that. Back then it was a man's world, especially on the golf course.

When we gathered at the clubhouse, I said, "Dad, you take the young lady as your partner." I could see his expression cloud because he wanted to team up with the banker. With a troubled expression, he went ahead and teed off. The banker and I followed.

The banker's lady approached the ladies tee with confidence. With a strong swing, she far outdistanced all three of us men. Dad's expression and demeanor promptly changed. With a smile, he said what came to be a cliché in our family, "That was pretty good—for a girl."

She and Dad had no difficulty in beating us that day. Afterward Dad was jovial and charming, acting as though their teaming up had been his idea.

A COUPLE OF GOLFING BUDDIES POSE WITH ARNOLD PALMER AND PAUL, WHO WAS ALWAYS UP FOR A ROUND OF GOLF.

On one occasion, Ed Beach, Allene, Allene's husband Bill, and I were on an outside elevator with some other people in a Marriott Hotel in New York City. We were on our way down after having eaten at a rooftop restaurant. To go all the way to street level, we had to get off at the lobby and change elevators.

Thinking I could avoid having to get off and change elevators, I started pushing random buttons, one after another. All of a sudden, the elevator stopped; then, it started jumping, something started popping, and the lights went out. Suddenly, the door opened. Unfortunately, we were between floors. An angry woman who had been loudly berating me instinctively jumped out of the elevator into a dark hole. The door closed, the elevator immediately started down, and it went all the way to the street level without stopping—just as I had intended. The last we heard from that woman, she was yelling, "Help! I have tickets to *Phantom of the Opera!*" I wonder if she ever got out of that black hole.

Faye really was a good sport. When Faye was only around 20 or 21 years old, I took her to the Bahamas in my plane. We stayed in a nice place on Eleuthera and used the plane to fly around sightseeing during the day. We flew around the Out Islands, looking at the beautiful sights and the clear, blue water. We had to land in Nassau to refuel.

When we were ready to take off again, the controller told us that it was "officially" dark, so we could not leave. Of course, as was my custom, I tried to reason with him, saying that it was a good while before dark, and that it was only a thirty-minute flight back to where we were staying.

No matter what I tried, the comptroller would not allow us to leave. Faye and I were forced to go into town and find lodging, but everything was full. We finally found a place that was dingy and dirty. We went out for dinner and to a drugstore to buy toilet articles. In the store she and I were briefly separated. "I felt very conspicuous while you were gone, like people were staring at me," she said.

"I don't know why," I said. "I just bought a toothbrush, toothpaste, and a pack of rubbers."

She was mortified.

Over the years we had numerous instances of men flirting with my wife. She was beautiful, innocent, and personable, the very qualities that attracted me to her. I loved to tease her about them just to get a rise out of her.

Faye and I visited Spain several times. I admire the Spanish guys. We American guys, particularly when we are young, are not necessarily good lovers. We don't know how to talk nice to a woman. We sit around tongue-tied. I've always said that I was trained by John Wayne rather than one of the smooth Latin lovers. I can talk much better today, and I talk beautifully to Karen, but I didn't do it nearly as well with Faye. I was sweet to her, but perhaps not as verbal. Those Spanish guys would come out and start telling Faye how beautiful she was. They would dance with her, and then they would start hugging her. She'd come back from dancing all aflutter. She'd say, "That guy out there was trying to kiss me on the dance floor."

We had such an experience in Peru in the early '60s. We were flying over the Andes Mountains on our way to Cusco. We met a gentleman who was attracted to Faye, and he invited us to have dinner at his home in Cusco. Not having any other plans, we accepted the invitation and were his guests for the evening. We were served a sumptuous meal. When I excused myself for a few minutes, our host took Faye down the hall, showing her various pictures on his wall and telling her stories about some of them.

On the way home Faye was upset. She said that while I was gone, the man was hugging her, trying to kiss her, and was nibbling on her ear. I replied that I thought it was such a good dinner that it was worth a little ear nibbling. She was not amused.

I apparently made an impression on David Rockefeller. At the time we were accumulating cash to build the Pacemaker facility, called the Broyhill Complex. I got the idea for its design from flying over a General Electric plant in Louisville, Kentucky, where there were four different product lines feeding into one warehouse. We embarked on our single largest building project of one million square feet, and later expanded into a million and a half square feet. That project was going to require more expenditure than we anticipated, so Ed Beach and I went to New York to establish a credit line with a New York bank. An old friend arranged introductions for us at Chase Bank. The executives looked over our financial figures, but they took so much time doing so that I thought turn about was fair play. When they finished and said they wanted to do business with us, I replied, "Before we make any final decisions, I would like to see *your* financial statement."

The bank officials were shocked and thought I was joking, but I made them produce a statement, which I perused carefully. Then we arranged a credit line and continued to do business with them for several years.

One day when I was introduced to David Rockefeller, he said, "You're the fellow who asked to see my statement." Somehow the word had gotten all the way up to him that I asked to see his financials before doing business.

I saw him several times after that, and he never forgot me because of that incident.

Gerald Ford was a friend of ours back when he was a U.S. congressman. He was spending a long weekend at the Green Park Hotel in Blowing Rock and I was having dinner there with him one night.

During dinner we heard that Vice President Spiro Agnew had resigned. I asked Gerry whom he thought would be selected to take Agnew's place. He answered vaguely. I told him that I thought he was the man for the job.

Shortly after dinner, I went to Jim Broyhill's home. He and I discussed the news and decided to call President Nixon. We called Mr. Nixon and told him that we heartily endorsed Gerald Ford to fill the vacancy.

Gerry had told me that he would be very surprised if the job were to be offered to him. But, the next day, he was called back to Washington and the rest, as they say, is history. Gerald Ford became our vice president and later, of course, President of the United States.

During a Chicago furniture market, when I was still a bachelor, I happened onto Ike Belk with an attractive girl on his arm. They were holding hands in front of the impressive Art Institute of Chicago on Michigan Avenue. I walked up to them and said with concern, "Young lady, do you know who you are out with? This guy is a friend of mine and I have heard his line many times. A nice girl like you should be very careful of him."

Ike introduced Carol Grotnes as his fiancée and said they were planning to be married soon.

"Oh, he tells that to all the girls," I teased.

Sure enough, not long after that chance meeting in Chicago, Ike married Carol. That was in 1948 and they have been together ever since.

During my career I constantly traveled and often spent at least a couple of nights a week away from home. Having the Learjet enabled me to jump around quickly, and sometimes it was hard for my staff to keep up with me. One night a telephone operator called my home to ask my wife where I could be located. Faye had a hard time convincing the operator that she had no idea where her husband could be found. The operator finally felt sorry for Faye and told her, "Mrs. Broyhill, if we find him, we'll call you back and let you know where he is."

Whenever I'm asked to give advice to newlyweds, I always tell this story: my friends, a happy marriage is similar to an oyster. When sand irritates an oyster, it forms a soothing substance over the irritation. Each time the oyster becomes irritated, it layers on more of the soothing substance. Ultimately, layer upon layer becomes a beautiful pearl. The same thing happens in marriage. If we smooth over all the little irritations, the marriage ends up like a lovely pearl.

I love quotes, especially those by historic personalities. At this stage in my life, two of my favorites are from the great American humorist, author, and lecturer of the 19th century Oliver Wendell Holmes, Sr. Holmes said, "Men do not quit playing because they grow old; they grow old because they quit playing." He qualified that statement with, "Old is fifteen years older than I am." I wholeheartedly agree. That's my story and I'm sticking to it.

Part 5

Perspectives from Family Members

26

Perspective on the Early Days from Allene Broyhill Stevens

Allene Broyhill is the eldest of J.E. Broyhill's children, two years older than Paul.

MY SIX CHILDREN have often said that growing up in Lenoir in the 1950s and '60s was like growing up in Mayberry. Likewise, for my three siblings, Paul, Jim and Bettie, and me, growing up in Lenoir in the '20s and '30s was like stepping out of a Norman Rockwell painting.

We lived close to the center of town in a white frame house with a wide porch on three sides that saw a lot of children's play and a bit of courting later on. A big, fenced-in back yard served many purposes at different times: a play yard with swings and sand box, a ball field, a rabbit hutch and billy goat habitat, always a vegetable garden and the indispensable clothes line that often served as a chinning bar.

ALLENE AND PAUL WITH THEIR MOTHER, SATIE

The basement of that house was a dark and scary place for a small child. On one side there was a monster furnace that had to be fed shovelfuls of coal several times a day. On the other side there was a single light bulb dangling above a behemoth washing machine. The washer was quite modern for its time because it had two rollers on top that would wring the rinse water out of the wet clothes before their trip to the clothesline outside. That was, of course, before the days of electric dryers.

I describe this basement in such detail because it is the first memory I have of our father's business. He started the Lenoir Chair Company when I was about four years old, and our basement was used to store samples of new chairs. I can remember the chair frames stacked up between the washing machine and the furnace, and that men in trucks came to take them away.

Our neighborhood was full of children; I guess we were the baby boomers of World War I, although that term was reserved for another generation. On summer evenings after supper we would gather in someone's yard to play games: red rover, kick the can, sling the statue, or tug of war. When it got dark we would catch fireflies and put them in Mason jars with holes punched in the lids for ventilation. In spite of our loving care, not a one of those lightnin' bugs ever survived overnight.

ALLENE AND PAUL TAKE A RIDE.

BIG SISTER, ALLENE, TAKES CARE OF LITTLE BROTHER PAUL.

We played hopscotch and we jumped rope, but those were mostly girl games. The boys chose sides and played football and baseball. We all climbed trees; we put on theatrical performances on one end of our large Victorian porch; we made swings using boards attached to a rope slung over a tree limb; and we played hockey using tin cans and our mothers' worn out brooms. In winter, there was lots of snow and lots of sledding on empty city streets. If there weren't enough sleds to go around, we borrowed the garbage can lids.

We built tree houses every summer. Paul tells the story of my pushing him out of our tree house resulting in his broken arm. I can't understand why he remembers that so vividly. All I remember is his interrupting our tea party by proclaiming, "No girls allowed in this tree house!"

When he was about thirteen Paul fell in love with horses. After much cajoling he was allowed to keep a horse across the street in "Grandpa" Shearer's barn. The deal was that he had to feed and groom the horse, exercise him, and take care of his stall. For several years Paul spent most of his free time with his horse, Chief.

Our family honored the fourth commandment. On Sunday all of us, parents and children alike, put on our best bib and tucker, and went to the First Baptist Church for Sunday school and the 11:00 a.m. service. During the week we were back again, almost as often as the doors were open, for youth groups, choir practice, midweek prayer meetings, women's missionary society, and deacons' meetings.

Sunday afternoon was our special family time. Both Mother and Dad came from rural communities, so it was "over the river and through the woods to grandfather's house" that we looked forward to every Sunday.

There were eight children in our father's family and nineteen of my generation who were first cousins. It was not unusual for half of us to show up at Grandma Broyhill's house in Boomer on Sunday afternoon. While the adults sat on the front porch in rocking chairs, drinking iced tea, we kids had the run of the farm. Well—almost. The place that held the most fascination for us was the well house, but it was strictly off limits unless there was an adult to help lower that old oaken bucket into the water many feet below and to help crank it back to the surface. Water is heavy stuff for kids.

We explored the corncrib and considered it our lucky day if we found a red or purple ear. We watched Grandpa Broyhill "rob" his precious beehives and then present us with a jar of delicious sourwood honey to take home.

We helped Grandma Broyhill feed her chickens. She would allow us to get handfuls of corn from the pouch she made of her apron. Then she showed us how to scatter the kernels of corn to the chickens, surrounding our feet with a little flick of the wrist—and how to communicate correctly by cluck-clucking at them. We played hide and seek in the barn stalls and hayloft until it was time for the cows to come home to be milked. A few times I tried to milk a cow, but I never seemed to get the hang of it.

A trip to Grandpa Hunt's, Mother's home in Grandin, held other fascinations for the four of us. Grandin was a ghost town, the remnant of what was originally a railroad terminus and shipping point for Grandin Lumber Company. After two devastating floods washed out the railroad, Mr. Grandin retained my grandfather to stay on and dispose of his huge tracts of timber in several mountain counties.

What remained of the little town of Grandin was a delightful playground for children. There was the old planing mill containing pieces of rusty stuff small enough to go home with a child explorer, stuff that Mother would eventually discard. There were old railroad tracks that led to nowhere. There were the office and warehouse where there were all sorts of goodies: old bills of lading, check stubs, and memo pads that found a home in our pockets. Just poking around in those dusty, abandoned buildings was like a Tom Swift adventure.

In the early days there was no electricity at either grandparent's home. At dusk the oil lamps were lit so that when you needed to go from room to room you carried a lamp (or a candle) with you. If you wanted to go to the bathroom, it was a dark and scary trip outside and down a well-worn path to a little structure somewhat removed from the house. The outhouse had one door with a half moon aperture at eye level. Inside was a long bench with two holes cut into it. You can imagine the scene: the Sears Roebuck catalogue in lieu of Charmin, the cold air emanating from those holes on wintry nights, the ever-present danger of splinters in delicate places.

One thing I never understood—why two holes?

If you were to ask anyone of my generation what were the most defining events of his life, I'll bet the answer would be, "World War II and the Great Depression."

I was seven and Paul was five when the booming stock market came crashing down on October 24, 1929. Black Thursday was the beginning of a worldwide depression that lasted until World War II.

Rich people became poor people overnight. We saw pictures in the newspapers of men dressed in expensive clothes standing in long lines to get a handful of bread or a bowl of soup. There were stories of men in the big cities who jumped to their deaths from skyscrapers rather than face being penniless. In our small town, we didn't have any skyscrapers to jump out of, but there were plenty of desperate people out of work and out of money.

Often we would answer the door to find an embarrassed, shabbily dressed man asking if we could spare some food for his hungry family. Mother never turned anyone away empty-handed. We were lucky that we had farm connections and never left Grandma's house without a chicken or ham or freshly ground flour from Grandpa's little mill.

Almost one-fourth of the total labor force was unemployed at the depth of the depression; thirteen million people were out of work and out of money. One of the first things President Franklin Roosevelt did after his inauguration in 1933 was to declare a four-day "bank holiday" until Congress could pass a bank reform law. During those days while the banks were closed there was practically no currency available. I remember our father paying his employees with "scrip," a piece of paper promising to reimburse the holder in real money at a later date. It makes me proud to remember that Dad was so respected that his scrip was used all over town just as if it were the real thing.

Even as young children, we were very much aware of our father's business. There were no restaurants in town other than a couple of simple cafés, so Dad brought all his out-of-town customers or salesmen home for dinner. We came to know some of those business associates as friends whom we cherished for their entire lives.

Sometimes Dad would be missing at the breakfast table, but we never had to ask where he was. Frequently he took his entire office staff, about six people, to one of those cafés for a 6:00 a.m. breakfast and pep meeting. His oft-repeated motto was: "If you get up early enough, and work hard enough, you will succeed."

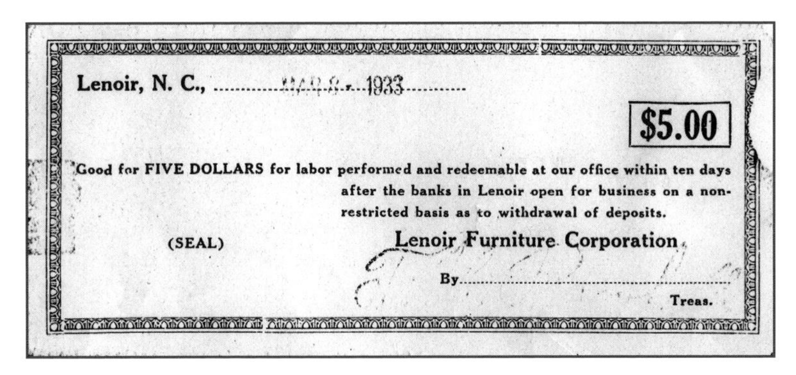

Lenoir, N. C., ... [illegible] 1933 ....

$5.00

Good for FIVE DOLLARS for labor performed and redeemable at our office within ten days after the banks in Lenoir open for business on a non-restricted basis as to withdrawal of deposits.

(SEAL)

Lenoir Furniture Corporation

By..

Treas.

DEPRESSION SCRIP THAT J. E. ISSUED TO EMPLOYEES FOR CURRENCY WHEN THE BANKS WERE CLOSED. THIS "BROYHILL MONEY" WAS USED ALL OVER TOWN.

As we got older, we all were expected to work at the company during school vacations. Paul did backbreaking work on the lumberyard for a couple of summers. Both he and Jim eventually advanced to the sales force after they were out of college. I got the cushiest job of all as switchboard operator.

During our high school days there was a lot of competition amongst our friends and amongst each other for good grades and music proficiency. The Lenoir High School Band was known as one of the finest high school bands in the nation. Although Lenoir High School no longer exists (all the county schools were consolidated in 1977), its band still holds the record in North Carolina for the most "superior" awards in state and district contests.

Both Paul and Jim played flute in the band, achieving "first chair" status. Bettie played bass fiddle. Since she couldn't carry that big thing in the marching band, for football games she substituted a glockenspiel. When Jim was a senior and Bettie was a junior, they had their first 15 minutes of fame as the only brother-sister drum major duo in the state. My interests turned elsewhere, and I became active in glee club and drama.

Having majored in music in college, our mother certainly fostered our love of music. She insisted that we all learn to read music as soon as we could read print. Many years later, Mother's efforts were publicly fulfilled when all four of her children were among the founders of *An Appalachian Summer*, the summer arts festival of Appalachian State University.

27

Perspective from James Thomas Broyhill

Retired Senator Jim and Mrs. Broyhill. Jim is the third of four children of J.E. Broyhill. He served in the United States Congress and Senate for 24 years.

IT WAS NOONTIME, January 3, 1963. I was in the big city of Washington, D.C., and this was a day my life was going to change forever. I was in the United States capitol building, in the House of Representatives, and about to be sworn in as a United States Congressman.

Just that past November, I had been elected to Congress from North Carolina's 9th congressional district after a long, hard-fought campaign, winning out over a ten-year veteran congressman, Hugh Alexander of Kannapolis. At that moment, I had no idea that the United States capitol was to be my address for the next 24 years.

Born in 1927, I grew up in the small town of Lenoir, N.C., during the 1930s and early 1940s. I always will have fond and nostalgic memories of those years. I was the third child of James Edgar and Satie Hunt Broyhill. My sister Allene and brother, Paul, were older than I. Bettie, my younger sister, was 18 months younger. The fact that I had

JIM BROYHILL BEING SWORN INTO OFFICE, JANUARY 1963

to repeat the 4th grade because of an illness meant that Bettie and I were only one class apart all through school, and thus we were much closer to each other than to the other siblings. In fact, we often double dated during our high school years. My older sister, Allene, finished high school six years before I did. She had finished Converse College and was married well before I graduated from high school. My school years with Paul overlapped only one year, 1940–41.

After finishing the six grades at East Harper Elementary School, I went to the 7th grade, located at that time in the same building as Lenoir High School. Thus, we junior high kids had daily contact with the older kids. I began playing the flute and piccolo and was in training to become a member of the famous Lenoir High School Band. I chose the flute because that was the instrument Paul played.

At the end of the seventh grade, the students who qualified were admitted to the senior band. To qualify, a student had to be able to play his instrument competently and to march expertly, because the LHS band was also a superior marching band. In the early spring of 1941, I was admitted to the senior band and was a proud member of the flute section. Paul was first chair; I was sitting last chair!

Let me digress here to explain a little more about the famous Lenoir High School Band. The band was started in the mid 1920s. After WWI, the local American Legion, an organization formed after WWI to represent veterans, had sponsored a community band. When interest in the effort waned, the Legion donated the instruments to the high school for the purpose of organizing a school band. Captain James C. Harper, a local businessman and a veteran of World War I, had been active in the American Legion band. He volunteered his time to conduct the high school band. It was not long before Captain Harper became the permanent director. He spent the rest of his life dedicated to teaching young people to play instruments and to teaching us some of life's lessons. He drew the analogy between the personal discipline we needed to master our instruments and the necessity to play in tandem with other instruments, to the skills we needed to be successful in life.

Paul decided to forgo his senior year at LHS and to attend Culver Military Academy. He was probably one of the few senior plebes in the history of Culver. However, I am sure that the experience was greatly responsible for Paul's achieving membership in Phi Beta Kappa when he went to Carolina a few years later. He told me that the only way he could avoid the hazing and harassment of a plebe was to stay in his room and study. I believe those study habits stayed with him throughout his college career and beyond.

During high school, I took my first job at the old Collins-Pridmore department store on West Avenue in uptown Lenoir, the Christmas season of 1942. In the spring of 1943, I took a weekend job at Smithey's department store. Founded in the late 1800s by E.J. Smithey of Wilkesboro, Smithey's was a small chain with locations in Wilkesboro, Lenoir, Taylorsville, Sparta, and West Jefferson. Smithey catered to the country trade. Those were the folks who came into town on weekends from the country to conduct their business. The store was adjacent to "Hog Waller," which was an area where the country people parked their vehicles and sold or traded wares, animals, or garden produce.

Smithey's sold merchandise at discounted prices. The idea of self-help or self-serve shopping was a new concept found at larger grocery chains such as Winn-Dixie and Piggly Wiggly. On the contrary, Smithey's still used the old system: customers came in the door, gave you a list of what they wanted, and you got up the order, added up the cost, collected for the order, and put the cash in the cash register. When I worked there, it was the era of rationing, so we had the added responsibility of collecting ration stamps for certain items such as sugar.

Not long after I began working at Smithey's, Jim Odell, manager of Winn-Dixie, offered me a job with a substantial raise in pay. He offered to pay me 25 cents an hour, so I jumped at it. There, the shopper used a grocery cart and gathered his own items from the shelves, then took them to a checkout counter to make payment.

I did some bagging of groceries, but soon Jim had me stocking the shelves and operating a section of the store where customers could check their purchases, go on about town to do other shopping, and come back later to pick them up. I was in charge of keeping track of the checked bags.

In early 1944, my father asked me to come to his office to help out with a chore or two. Before long, I resigned my job at Winn-Dixie and went to Dad's office just about every day after school and on Saturdays. Back in those days, the office was open and fully staffed every Saturday from 8 a.m. until noon.

Like keeping up with the checked bags at Winn-Dixie, the first job I had at Broyhill was to keep track of the sales quota system. At the outset of World War II, Dad found that due to shortages and increased demand, he could sell anything he made. He easily could have sold his entire output to just a few retailers in the larger markets. However, Dad decided early on that his output was going to be divided among all his customers who had bought from him and who had been loyal to him in the past. So, he developed an intricate system to keep track of the sales to each customer. That was long before the days of computers. We established a dollar quota for everyone, and I manually entered the dollar amount of every order for every customer onto a card system.

Not long thereafter I was given a far more responsible job in the purchasing office. I prepared every invoice for payment. I verified the purchase, checked it for accuracy, obtained receiving reports from the factory to assure it had arrived, and attached the report to any freight bills. Then, I entered the information by hand in a ledger with the vendor's name, product, amount, and accounting for the purchase: cost of goods or capital goods. Before I got the hang of it, I charged off some sewing machines as cost of goods rather than putting them in the capital column.

In early 1944 Dad had the idea that I should get some actual experience selling furniture on the road. Like my brother, Paul, I had attended most summer markets at Chicago and at High Point with Dad since 1938, so I was familiar with the line and, of course, knew every Broyhill salesman and many of the major customers.

Dad gave me two territories to cover: eastern North Carolina and eastern Virginia. Talmadge Biddix, Dad's former driver, had been promoted into sales and had become a seasoned salesman in Lenoir. He and I scrounged some rationed gasoline stamps and started out. In Virginia, we covered Richmond, Norfolk, Newport News, Charlottesville, Lynchburg, and the towns in the Shenandoah Valley. From there we moved down into North Carolina, covering Raleigh and everything east. What a great experience, and we didn't have to work to sell a thing! Everyone welcomed us with open arms and took any product we gave them, even if it were only two or three suites of furniture and a half dozen chairs. However, we made a lot of friends for the company. We were just about the only sales people they had seen in months.

I must hasten to add that this was all before the days of Broyhill Furniture Industries. We had more than one order blank. Every company was a separate corporation, except for the two Lenoir Chair companies, one bedroom plant, and one upholstering plant. So, each company's order had to go on a separate order blank: Harper Furniture on Harper, Otis Broyhill Furniture of Marion on another, and so on.

After that first trip with Talmadge Biddix, I started taking trips through the two territories on my own. I worked the summer markets and waited on customers who attended from those two territories. In those days we didn't show many goods. We didn't have to. We could sell everything we made by telephone. However, Dad encouraged the salesmen to make goodwill contact with the customers, saying, "Boys, the war will be over soon, and I want them to remember who you are and who took care of them when things were in short supply."

In 1946 we started showing the line again at the High Point market (not Chicago), although we did not have much trouble selling the output from the factories. Since the war was over, demand for furniture increased as veterans were back starting families and setting up housekeeping in their new homes. That was when I was saddled with the responsibility of getting the samples ready for the shows and making sure the showrooms were set up for market.

About that time Paul was discharged from the Army. He immediately re-enrolled at Chapel Hill where he had already finished one year of college. Paul and I were at Carolina together for two years. Although we did not take classes together, we saw each other every day at the Phi Delta Theta house where we were members. We both took our meals there. As I recall, Paul and I took two big trips together while we were at Chapel Hill. One trip was to New York on the train, and another was by car to the Republican National Convention that was held in Philadelphia. While in Philadelphia, we met many Republican Party leaders of the time including Senator Bob Taft, Governor Thomas Dewey, Congressman Carroll Reese of Tennessee, the chairman of the Republican National Committee, and many others.

I remember an incident that occurred on the way to Philadelphia. Even to this day, Paul enjoys telling stories about how tight I was with money. On that occasion we were passing through Colonial Heights, just north of Petersburg, Virginia, on U.S. Highway 1. I was driving when a siren sounded behind us, and I was stopped for speeding. Paul was asleep in the passenger seat. I remember waking him up and saying, "Wake up and pay the man!" I didn't have a cent on me.

Receipt from Town of Colonial Heights

P. O. Petersburg, Virginia

No 1090

$ 16 25/ June 25 1948

Received of James T. Broyhill

Address Box 775 Lenoir NC

Sixteen & 25/100 Dollars

Account of Bur Police Court June 28/48

Excessive Speed Charge

Town of Colonial Heights

Balance $ — By D. W. Hawkins JP

JIM WOKE PAUL TO PAY FOR A SPEEDING TICKET.

All through college, on weekends and during the summer months, I continued to serve territory sixteen: eastern North Carolina. We employed a young man, Kemp Honeycutt from Hickory, North Carolina, to take over the eastern Virginia territory, and he did a fine job. However, in the late '40s we decided that the territory needed a permanent man, and we hired Tommy Culbreath, a young man Paul and I had gotten to know at Carolina. Tommy had worked his way through school doing various jobs. He had a personality that fit in well with the customers in the eastern part of the state. I was still helping out, making sure the market samples were prepared and the market showrooms set up. Paul also did some traveling in those territories. Both of us called on dealers all across the country.

As the tastes of the average furniture consumer changed, we had to work harder to make a sale. The company had to pay more attention to styling and design. Paul had a flair for that part of the business and early on began spending more and more time working with the design team to streamline the line and to merchandise it. Our line was neither the lowest priced line in the business nor the highest priced line. We had a nice niche in the middle and that is where we stayed through the years, offering a line of well-styled furniture that fit the taste and the budget of middle-income Americans.

In 1951 I asked my best girl, Louise Robbins from Durham, to marry me. We married on June 2, the same weekend she graduated from Chapel Hill. Because Tommy Culbreath had been drafted into the Korean War and I temporarily had taken over his territory, Louise and I had to work our wedding and honeymoon plans around the dates of the Chicago and High Point summer furniture markets. After she and I were married, the company hired our friend Bruce Chester of Lenoir to take over the eastern North Carolina territory. He represented the company for many years thereafter. When Tommy returned from the war, he took over South Carolina, and he, too, remained for many years with the company.

I saw the need for a member of the family to be involved with our plants, and I became interested in the fledgling personnel program we had at the time. We were expanding fast and needed trained supervisors. Quite honestly, we were also concerned about administrative efficiency, particularly regarding order flow and inventory control.

We installed an IBM punch card system. It never worked well because of the volume of punch cards needed to account for every item we produced. We purchased another IBM system, the IBM 1401, which was the first computer on the market and probably the first to be used in the furniture business. It was an outstanding success. Through the years Broyhill continued to update and upgrade the system as new technology became available.

As I stated, Paul had a talent for the merchandising side of the business and for styling the line. He had a knack for knowing what would sell. He also developed a successful management style. Every quarter the top managers were required to come before their peers, other top management, and the family to report on their performance and to present their goals. In other words, every segment of the business had a business plan, and each manager of that segment was accountable. Paul would give ample attention to each segment of the business in order to determine how they were doing in achieving their goals. He made personal visits to keep abreast of progress.

In early 1962, I was persuaded to become a candidate for the United States ninth congressional district. The ninth consisted of Caldwell, Watauga, Allegheny, Ashe, Alexander, Iredell, Rowan, Cabarrus, and Stanley, North Carolina counties. I was successful in 1962, but in the election of 1966, redistricting removed Iredell and Alexander counties and added Avery, Wilkes, and Surry counties. In spite of the redistricting, I was reelected. Again, in 1968, the state General Assembly redistricted and placed my home county of Caldwell along with neighboring Watauga County in the 10th district, which at that time was represented by Congressman Basil Whitener, a Democrat from Gastonia. The counties in the 10th district were Gaston, Cleveland, Burke, Catawba, Caldwell, Watauga, Avery, and Alexander.

Notwithstanding the attempts to defeat me by redistricting, I was successful in ousting Whitener, and I beat him again in a rerun in 1970. After that, the reelection campaigns were not nearly as difficult or as expensive. All through the era of my bids for office, my brother, Paul, and my late brother-in-law Bill Stevens were most supportive and acted as my campaign fund-raisers. Because of them, I never had to worry about that important part of a political campaign.

I served in the Congress from 1963 until 1986 when North Carolina Governor Jim Martin appointed me to the seat left vacant by the death of Senator John East. I was unsuccessful in my bid for reelection and retired from Congress in 1986. Soon after, Governor Martin asked me to come to Raleigh and take the position of state Secretary of Commerce and Chairman of the North Carolina Economic Development Commission.

From that day in 1963 when I left Broyhill to pursue a different direction from my brother, Paul, I knew I made the right decision. We were brothers and from the same background, but we each had different talents and interests. Though our career paths diverged, we both followed in our father's footsteps. My dad had been passionate about Republican politics and was active on local, state, and national fronts. He was proud of my work in the House and later in the Senate. Paul carried on Dad's business and took it to a level of incredible success. Because our parents placed within us a sense of commitment, we both intensely approached our different fields with a feeling of obligation to our constituents: my voters, his employees. As brothers, we have supported each other and have always had a good relationship. Paul helped me realize my dream by working on my campaigns, and I helped him by serving as a board member at Broyhill. We continue to have mutual respect and admiration for each other's accomplishments.

YOUNG CONGRESSMAN AND MRS. BROYHILL

Working For You — And Our Nation

— Congressman James T. Broyhill —

Washington is an exciting place these days, according to Tenth District Congressman James T. Broyhill, who is serving his 10th term as a member of the United States House of Representatives. He has served with six Presidents—three Republicans and three Democrats.

"It is especially interesting at this time because of the tremendous leadership and support which President Reagan is receiving from the Congress and the American people," Broyhill said.

Commenting on the two big victories for the President's Economic Recovery Program, Broyhill said, "I sincerely believe we are now on the right economic course. High inflation and high interest rates are unacceptable. We have experienced poor economic conditions for the past four years and recovery will not come overnight. I hope we will have the patience to deal with those who are already criticizing our recovery rate. The President's Program only took effect on October 1 and it will take time for the changes to begin working."

While Congressman Broyhill does not try to take credit for passage of the President's budget cuts and tax reduction package, experienced Washington observers say he has considerable influence, "Jim Broyhill is one of the most respected members of the Congress" one Washington insider recently said. "His leadership in the business community helped secure passage of the President's program."

Broyhill was especially active in the budget cut fight, which is continuing through the regular appropriations process at the present time. "Many more cuts, across-the-board, need to be made if we are going to balance the budget by 1984," he said. "Frankly, I wish we could do it before then. Many of my people back home say we are not cutting enough out of the $700 billion budget. I agree."

Broyhill, who is well known in Washington and in North Carolina for the high quality of service to his constituents, has seen many of his legislative ideas enacted into law. He has seen growing support for his economic and regulatory ideas. "It is now popular to be on the side of balancing the budget, cutting federal spending, and reducing taxes," Broyhill said in a recent interview.

The Big Prize

However the big prize has thus far eluded the popular Lenoir native . . . a committee chairmanship. All House committees are chaired by Democrats and that's the way it has been since the Congressman left Broyhill Furniture Industries in 1962 to seek the congressional seat. In fact, the Republican Party has not controlled the House in 26 years and that means no member of the GOP has held a chairmanship because the party in the majority controls all committees.

TAXPAYERS BEST FRIEND—Congressman James T. Broyhill receives an award for his work to reduce taxes and federal spending by Len Rippa of the National Taxpayers Union. Fewer than 10 percent of the members of the Congress received this award.

Gaining Influence & Seniority

However, Broyhill has steadily gained in seniority and influence. He now sits next to the Chairman of the powerful Energy and Commerce Committee as the top-ranking Republican. Broyhill now ranks ninth in seniority among the Republicans and 35th among the entire membership.

"Our committee ranks in the top three in legislative activity," Broyhill said. "We consider nearly all the legislation in the fields of energy, health, transportation, consumer protection, environment, communications, and highway safety."

With a Republican President and Republican Senate, Broyhill's activity and influence have increased greatly. As the top Republican on the Energy and Commerce Committee, he sits on the six subcommittees and directs a staff of 26 professionals.

The Reagan administration is doing an "outstanding job" of consulting with the Congress on appointments and legislation, according to Broyhill. "Nearly every day various persons being considered for top jobs in the administration come to talk with me," Broyhill said. "While the Congress can and should change many of the regulations, one of the most effective ways to bring about positive change is to place people with common sense and ability into the regulatory agencies."

BROTHERS ON DIFFERENT PATHS BUT STILL WORKING AS A TEAM
AS SEEN IN THIS EXCERPT FROM *PEOPLE TODAY AT BROYHILL*

28

Perspective from Claire Broyhill Greene

Barbara Claire Broyhill Greene is the middle of Paul Broyhill's children. She is married to Tim Greene and has three children.

STORIES RECOUNTING THE deafening roar of cannons or the clashing of swords on a battlefield may not be at the top of a pediatrician's list of soothing nightly rituals for children. Most parents read sweet books about moons and talking animals and living happily ever after, but my dad is not like most parents. My bedtime stories were about Ulysses' travels, Hannibal's crossing the Alps, Roman battles, and French emperors. My father has a very intense aspect to his personality.

With the same effortful way he held my jaw and scrubbed clean my teeth, Dad would relate detailed accounts of fierce battles and of kings cutting off the heads of wives of whom they no longer approved.

I think he told that story so my siblings and I would share it with Mom the next day.

Dad approaches everything in life with the same intensity and commitment as he did his storytelling. Once he makes up his mind, it is hard to convince him otherwise. I remember Dad's mother telling me a story about how he had a tricycle that he would ride into their house and park under her piano. Nana was a pianist and also very particular about her house. She said that she admonished Dad and punished him repeatedly, but that he still rode his tricycle into the house and parked it under the baby grand. Dad told Nana that his tricycle had to have a garage and that under the piano was the best one he had found. Nothing was going to change his mind (although I'm sure Nana eventually won that battle). Obviously, Dad's determination and commitment were present even at an early age.

Drive and determination were always evident in every aspect of Dad's life. He is an avid reader, particularly of history. He and Mother traveled to Europe for the first time on their honeymoon, and he has returned every year since. He loves to visit battlefields and castles, and to spend hours and hours and hours driving along tiny roads in the English, French, or Italian countryside. One aspect of Dad's fierce determination involves only looking at a map once, never turning around, and never admitting defeat. Whenever we heard our mother say, "Paul, you just missed the turn; Paul, did you hear me? We need to turn around, Paul," we knew that was our cue to lean back and take a nap.

Dad had a firmness of purpose and commitment in the way he approached work or hobbies. He was devoted to Broyhill Furniture and was always the first one at the office in the mornings and the last one to leave at night. He would drag us to hit balls at the driving range on Sunday afternoons or to spend hours flying with him in his plane.

Dad played the flute in his high school band and was actually one of the best high school flutists in North Carolina at that time. I remember he would say that "you have to practice, practice, practice," or "you have to prepare" to be good at something.

Dad taught Sunday school and spent time every Saturday preparing his lesson. He was very disciplined. When I was young, children had to go into the sanctuary and sit with their parents during the church service once they were of school age. We were not coddled like children are today who go to a fun, after-Sunday-school hangout room. One of my earliest memories is sitting on the hard benches at First Baptist Church of Lenoir, going a little crazy having to sit still and be quiet, and then looking over at my father who was writing on his church bulletin. I didn't understand why he could write in church when my siblings and I got into trouble if we did that. Mom always gazed pleasantly toward the minister, and Dad scribbled on his bulletin. With age, I began to realize he was taking copious notes on the sermon. I remember his doing that every Sunday, at least until I graduated from high school. After the service, we would always leave through the front doors of the church and stop to say hello to the minister. Dad would tell him how much he liked the sermon—and how he could maybe improve upon it the next time. One of Dad's favorite things to do was—and is—to give advice!

29

Perspective from M. Hunt Broyhill

Hunt is the son and business partner of Paul Broyhill.

I'VE HEARD IT said that bringing work home isn't healthy. I can't help but chuckle at that as I think of growing up in the shadow of our family business, Broyhill Furniture. The business was an extension of the family; or we were an extension of it. It was as if the business were a fourth sibling, one that suffered first child syndrome and demanded a significant share of my father's attention.

My contention is that counting back nine months from twice-a-year national furniture markets, each of us children was conceived. Pre-market and market times Dad was totally focused on product introductions, showroom details, merchandising, and sales. Only between markets could he even somewhat be diverted.

My earliest memories relate to the business. When I was just four years old, Dad gave me my own office. Admittedly, it was a switching closet for the phone wiring, but I had my own desk, my own key, and my name on the door. I even had an adding machine. In fact, it was the first adding machine at Broyhill and I still have it. I was important enough to have my own time card, and I loved to punch the time clock. I made 75 cents an hour!

Later, at the end of the elementary school day, someone would drop me by the corporate office where I ran up and down the vast halls and harassed employees. One or another of them would befriend the boss's kid. In some cases I learned more from them than I did at school. For example, if I have any artistic talent today it is because Dad's furniture designers took me under their wings and taught me to draw.

When I was in first grade, the Apollo space program was at its height. For Christmas, Dad bought me an authentic-looking astronaut costume from FAO Schwartz. The following April at the Lenoir furniture market, Broyhill featured an ultra-contemporary collection called Chapter One. Certainly such an introduction needed a real, live astronaut. Dad took me out of school for the entire week so I could meet and greet customers in my costume.

BOY SCOUT HUNT BROYHILL HANDS THE U.S. FLAG TO HIS DAD AT THE DEDICATION OF THE NEW FLAGPOLE IN FRONT OF BROYHILL'S MAIN OFFICES AS HIS TROOP LOOKS ON.

I vividly remember that the 1970s brought a strong surge of organized labor efforts to infiltrate southern factories. They used two strategies to try to take over a company's labor force. One was to push for a vote across the entire organization, an all-or-none tactic that was quite risky for them as well as for the company. More often, like letting the proverbial camel's nose into the tent, unions would target individual factories and build success one by one. After one victory they projected that others would follow, creating a domino effect. However, the unions underestimated the family-like attitude of Broyhill employees.

Dad's tactic was a personal "focus on the family" approach to stay in touch with his workers, to build morale, and to assure them of their value to the organization. He knew he could hold the fort one factory at a time but that he might be vulnerable to a cross-company vote. He used reverse psychology on the unions by requesting an overall vote. They insisted on a vote per factory, which played right into Dad's hands. The few times the unions challenged us, Dad "licked 'em good" and sent them packing back up north.

Dad had worked particularly hard to encourage a non-union vote at our upholstery parts plant in Summerville, South Carolina. When we were successful in rebuffing the union, I went with him to the plant to celebrate the victory. I had been with him a number of other times to Summerville and I enjoyed those trips because I had made friends with a Black man named Eddie who operated an outdoor lumber forklift. Those outdoor lifts were much larger than the inside ones, and I was impressed. On our visits Eddie would let me ride around with him to pick up pallets of lumber scheduled for production and stack them high.

Before the luncheon, Dad had looked for me; when he couldn't find me, he went ahead with his speech. He praised everyone, encouraged the group, and ended by saying rhetorically, "If anyone needs anything, just let us know." Since he wasn't looking for an immediate response, Dad was surprised when a small hand rose in the back of the crowded room and I said loudly, "Eddie needs a new forklift!" Dad promised Eddie his new machine, even though it cost in excess of $50,000.

Another time, at one of the Lenoir plants Dad had been holding small group meetings. He had discovered a management training program from the American Management Association that was designed to teach managers how to motivate workers and how to keep control in potentially volatile situations. In one of those group meetings a mouthy guy who had the reputation of being an instigator challenged everything Dad said. Dad stayed calm. After the meeting Dad pulled the man aside. He held out a one hundred dollar bill. He always carried, and still does, an "emergency" hundred dollars. Nonchalantly, he ripped the bill in half, handed half to the man, looked him in the eye, and said, "You're bright and you have potential. If you finish high school, you can advance in the company. When you finish school or obtain your GED, come and pick up the other half." It took a while, but eventually the man collected. That incident demonstrated Dad's ability to turn a potential negative interaction into a positive motivation.

Even our family vacations were business connected. We took trips with families that were Broyhill customers. My parents had a particularly close relationship with Lou and Carol Rippner from Ohio. Like us, the Rippners had two daughters and a son who were close in age to my sisters and me. Several of our early Christmas and Easter vacations were to the Sea View Hotel in Miami with the Rippner family. Other outings included a Bahamas fishing trip with Rawson Haverty and trips to the Florida Keys with Mike Baker and his family.

Dad had a love of history. When I was little, at bedtime he told stories of Xerxes, Alexander the Great, Napoleon, and other great figures. I guess that fueled my own love of history. To this day I have to "know my stuff." If I try to challenge him about an obscure historical piece of trivia, he can likely recite the people, places, and events from memory even though he is 86!

Dad's fascination with history influenced his and Mother's foreign travel. While most trips were to Europe, Mother and Dad traveled to almost every continent. Dad visited the castles of his "old friends" from the history books. Of course, he used the trips to research international manufacturing technology, to study European design, and to visit with international dealers, but those trips were as close to a real vacation as he ever took.

After hearing our parents' stories and seeing pictures of

magnificent faraway places, it was a thrill when we traveled with them. Each of us children had a one-on-one trip with Mom and Dad following our graduation from eighth grade and prior to entering high school. We took other family trips later, but we each cherished that special trip.

We never went anywhere that we didn't visit furniture stores so that Dad could take pictures with his Minox camera of an arm or a leg element or the curve of a sofa. Because Dad would become absorbed with furniture or architecture and Mom with shopping, our trips weren't complete without one of us kids being lost or left behind. Early on, we learned to designate an emergency meeting spot. It was not "if," but "when" one of us kids would become separated from our parents, or more commonly, Dad from us. We learned not to panic, that Mom or Dad would realize we were missing and eventually come back to retrieve us.

Twice a year, in January and July, Broyhill showed their product line at regional furniture market exhibitions in New York, Chicago, San Francisco, Dallas, and Atlanta. In May and October they showed at the national market in North Carolina. While we children had little one-on-one time with Dad, he often treated us with trips to one of the regional markets. Those excursions exposed us to interesting people and to magnificent cities that little Lenoir, North Carolina, just couldn't match in excitement.

One of those trips occurred when I was 12 or 13. I accompanied Dad on a cross-country trip in the Learjet to the San Francisco market. On our way west we visited Horton's Furniture in Wichita, Kansas, and the Nebraska Furniture Mart in Omaha owned by the Blumkin family. On the return trip we visited the Lake Tahoe home of loyal Broyhill dealer Bill Bruener. We even worked in a side trip in the Learjet with the Brueners to Vancouver, Canada. That experience opened my eyes to the vastness of the country and introduced me to many iconic people connected to the furniture business.

The April and October markets impacted our home life. For 10 days every six months, we opened our home to Broyhill furniture dealers and sales representatives for nightly entertainment. We hosted them at our hotel, the Green Park, in the nearby mountain resort town of Blowing Rock. Because many of Broyhill's customers

THE BROYHILLS USED ARTHUR WURTZ'S BOAT TO ENTERTAIN THE HAVERTYS. WURTZ OWNED THE AMERICAN FURNITURE MART IN CHICAGO.

were family-owned businesses, this family-to-family type of entertaining not only gave the dealers a respite from the frantic pace of the market, but also it gave them a kind of six-month reunion of genuine old friends who also happened to be business associates.

At the end of every market, on two consecutive Sunday afternoons, we held an open house in the showroom for all employees. Dad would stand and shake hands for more than two or three hours while several thousand people came through the line.

The business encompassed even our church life. Some people referred to the First Baptist Church of Lenoir as "Broyhill Baptist." In reality, that wasn't far from the truth. Not only was the Broyhill family the church's largest financial contributor, but also the executives of Broyhill Furniture held most of the lay leadership roles in the church. Because of those two factors, Dad wielded significant influence over the major decisions of the church and its direction.

Our factories closed for a week for the Fourth of July and a week at Christmas. The employees eagerly anticipated those breaks. Dad had a custom of providing in-house barbecue lunch parties for them in July, dinners at Thanksgiving, and covered dish lunches at Christmas.

He held more elaborate annual dinners for factory department supervisors and managers at places such as Cedar Rock Country Club. We kids were not required to attend all the parties because many of them occurred during school hours. However, I fondly remember standing in greeting lines with Dad and Granddad, shaking hands with the employees. Today, almost thirty years later, folks approach me and remind me of those times. Obviously, Broyhill employees felt as if they were treated like family.

Dad had a passion for aviation. I am convinced that since he used airplanes to leverage his business time, he earned the equivalent of at least an extra day a week over his competitors who did not use private aviation. Naturally, he used his plane to fly the family, and as a result, I wanted to be a pilot like my dad. For many years, Dad and I attended required biannual FlightSafety training together. During the three days of training, he and I explored a common passion that was generally unrelated to business. We pushed each other to master and hone the requisite skill sets essential for safe and professional aviation.

Because Dad and I flew as single pilots except during FlightSafety, we tended to have different approaches to handling an aircraft. Yet, our evaluators often marveled at the synergy we had in the team exercises. With one of us as pilot and the other as copilot, we anticipated each other's actions and often communicated without words. Perhaps that was because we were father and son; perhaps it was because we were so close. For whatever reason, I knew what Dad was going to do before he did it. Ultimately, Dad gave up single pilot aviation, and today is content riding in a rear passenger seat. However, I do recall that he flew his Piper Cheyenne, N500PB, on a trip on his eighty-first birthday. There are few folks who can make that claim!

As I grew up, I worked with Dad more and more. Markets continued to be the time marker on our calendar. When I was in high school, I remember working at the Dallas market to set up the showroom. Showroom prepping was physically taxing and emotionally stressful. Our work would shape the customers' first impressions of the Broyhill offerings. We had only a few days to unload ten to twelve semi-trailers of furniture, move it to the showroom, and then prep and accessorize the showroom space for market. The unloading was hot, heavy work. Also it was tightly scheduled because other manufacturers had to unload at the same limited truck dock facilities. I recall one of our factory guys asking me one day why I worked so hard since I was the boss's kid. I told him, "Look at that name on the side of the box. It says, *Broyhill*. Dad always raised us to be a Broyhill first."

Be My Guest
I'm Hunt Broyhill
and I'd like to invite you to
use our Custom Sofa Gallery
showroom as your personal
design studio. You and your
clients can work comfortably
in a beautiful setting, with
an array of fabrics and
accessories close at hand.
Take a look inside for a
better idea of just how much
we'd like to work with you.
And please be my guest,
Hunt Broyhill

HUNT ON THE COVER OF CUSTOM SOFA GALLERY BROCHURE

For my entire life Dad has been my mentor and my colleague. By example and by direction, he taught us pride in being a Broyhill. The company loomed large and was an ever-present entity that demanded my father's attention. Now, as an adult and a parent, I am grateful for my dad's dedication. I admire him for his loyalty to his extended family—the 7,500 employees that kept the plants going. As a manager of our investment fund and its real estate arm, I feel the same responsibility to the stockholders. I also know the pressures of providing a good life for my children. While I want them to pursue their dreams, I also want to instill in them the values that began with my grandfather, were passed to my father, then taught to me, and are their legacy.

Part 6

Perspectives from Business Associates

30

William Stevens

Senior Vice President

The following excerpt is taken from the book *Anvil of Adversity: Biography of a Furniture Pioneer* by William Stevens, copyright 1968. Stevens married Allene Broyhill, Paul Broyhill's older sister.

HAVING FREQUENTLY HEARD his father's maxim that "water seeks its own level," Paul determined early to establish his level in the business at a high-water mark. Just as Ed Broyhill had been happy that Tom let him seek his own level, Paul was happy that his father permitted him to be the master of his own destiny. He did not want to be placed in command. He wanted to assume command.

In his rise to prominence at Broyhill, Paul has emulated the best of his father, and has added virtues of his own. "He is a perfectionist," says Allene, "right down to the last detail." A perfectionist he is, it is true. But also dynamic and determined, he aspires to head the most nearly perfect furniture company in the industry and has put forth a prodigious personal effort to make his dream come true.

Paul is not exactly a chip off the old block, despite his physical likeness to his father and his unconscious effort to capture some of his father's personality traits. He is, rather, an innovation all his own. Unlike his father, Paul is not the least shy—or, if he is, no one knows it. He is more like Ed Broyhill's idol, Ken Wherry, in that he can wade into any roomful of people and make his presence known. He is absolutely unabashed at social encounters. More highly polished by education than his father, he is understandably more smoothly articulate, appearing perfectly at ease on any rostrum or in any business group. Cool, assured, in perfect control, he leads a business conference with force and clearly thought-out direction. Despite the differences between father and son, they are yet enough alike that Ed Broyhill will live on at Broyhill as long as Paul is around.

Paul has worked furiously to match his father's accomplishments, as though in his father's shadow a little success would be unnoticed; only a big accomplishment would do. He felt he could do it, and he has. From the time of his first plunge into designing and merchandising in 1948, his influence spread over the company in ever-widening ripples. In addition to designing and merchandising, he asserted himself in sales, manufacturing, purchasing, personnel and plant expansion, veritably covering the waterfront, until by 1955, he was signing his name over the title of general manager, and by 1963, over the title of president.

PAUL AND HIS BROTHER-IN-LAW, NORTH CAROLINA STATE CONGRESSMAN AND BROYHILL VICE PRESIDENT, BILL STEVENS

Brent Kincaid

Customer Service, Sales Manager, Purchasing, President, Chief Executive Officer

MY EMPLOYMENT WITH Broyhill lasted 41½ years. Prior to that, I had been teaching school and was not in the market for another job. However, through a school event, I met some people from Kent-Coffey, a Lenoir furniture company. They asked if I would interview for a sales opportunity. I informed them of my current contract with the school and explained I could call them at the end of the school year.

The day after school was out the Kent-Coffey people called me requesting an interview. I went, and they offered me a sales position. That night Jim Broyhill called me. "I heard you went down to Kent-Coffey today for an interview. I didn't know you were leaving school," he said.

"Well, I just went down to follow up on a commitment I had made," I answered.

"Before you make a decision, how about coming down and talking to us," Jim said.

Between Jim, Paul, Bill Stevens, and Mr. J.E., I spent one full day interviewing at Broyhill, and *they* offered me a sales position. The rest is history.

Before I started my sales work, Paul suggested that if I really wanted to make progress in the company I should be in administration. He had an opportunity for me in the credit department. I took the job.

We did something new and combined credit with customer service. That meant that if a customer had a problem with any of our products, they could call and not only get that situation resolved, but also determine if their open line of credit with us would earn an opportunity for greater business. It had not been uncommon for customers to claim that they were not paying their invoices because they had problems with Broyhill furniture. Paul eliminated that issue by combining the two departments.

After Paul and his dad built a new corporate office building, Paul made a major decision in regard to administration, one that I think propelled Broyhill far ahead in the industry. He laid out the office to create departments serving specific needs of customers: data processing, customer service, traffic, and purchasing and accounting. I was given the opportunity to manage the customer service department.

The beauty of the arrangement was that the customer could call one person assigned to his account and obtain full information regarding the status of their order, the status of their account, inventory availability, and shipment information. That strategy put Broyhill's customer service far ahead of any other company in the industry. When you provide personal service, you build relationships with the customers, and thus have an opportunity to expand your business.

In our experience, the customers felt comfortable calling specific people, and friendships developed over the phone. When the customers came to market—at that time we had many of the furniture shows at the corporate office in Lenoir—oftentimes one of the first things they wanted to do was to talk with those people with whom they'd had telephone contact.

Paul developed a personal relationship with our customers, and he treated them all the same, regardless of the account size. They were special and important regardless of the amount of business they did. I honestly can't remember a customer that, regardless of volume, did not believe that Paul Broyhill was his personal friend, and that Paul's golden arm could reach out and placate any of their concerns.

Paul supported the decisions made by his employees. As an example, a customer might come in for a credit line increase. Even if my decision to limit their credit might not have been a good one, Paul would say something like, "Well, you know, we want to do as much business with you as we can, but you understand that I've got to support my employees."

Paul had a way of providing extra opportunities for persons at Broyhill if he believed that person might make a contribution in a certain area. I specifically remember that I became interested in politics at a very early age, serving in a statewide office in the Young Republican organization. My interest led Mr. J. E. Broyhill, who was a national committeeman at that time, to invite me to accompany him on a number of trips. Mr. J. E. was kind enough to take me to Washington and to other places for major political gatherings, always purchasing my tickets because I couldn't afford them. Those visits, of course, increased my interest in politics.

I was sitting in my office one day when I got a telephone call from upstairs. Bill Stevens said, "Brent, I want you to come up to my office. Paul, Jim, and I want to talk to you."

"What have I gotten myself into now?" I wondered. I hadn't been with the company very long at that time and was a little unsure.

There, in Bill Stevens' office, they asked me to become Jim Broyhill's campaign manager. I knew Jim had been exploring the possibility of becoming a candidate for Congress. When I pointed out that I had no experience as a campaign manager, they said, "Well, we want you to do it." And Paul used that golden arm of his. He put it around my shoulders and said, "Don't you worry. We're going to see to it that you get the proper training."

The amazing thing about that decision was that it was a bold step to take against an entrenched conservative Democrat congressman. I attended campaign school in Washington, and Jim went up at the same time for candidates' school. The thing that I may have brought to the campaign was that I had some organizational skills. More than anything, I thought selling the candidate would be just like selling the product. I decided that if we could sell the Broyhill name as a candidate for office, Jim would be elected.

The Election Day margin of victory was about 1,200 votes. A lot of people take credit for Jim Broyhill's winning that election, but his brother Paul supported him in every way he possibility could, within the legal limits of financial contributions, and Paul opened the door for many others to support the campaign.

Jim served 22 years in Congress and today is primarily responsible for the growth of the Republican Party in Western North Carolina. His dad was the forerunner. His dad gave him the interest in politics, his brother Paul has always had an interest in politics, and I think any businessman today who doesn't develop an interest in politics is making a mistake. We must strive for good government that promotes a healthy business climate.

I was in my office one morning and Paul Broyhill called. "Brent, there's a sales management position open in Bedroom in our company, and I want you to take that position. You need to get some sales experience, and now is the time. You need to make that decision today, because the Dallas market starts in two weeks, and you need to get prepared to go to it."

When a man tells you what to do in order to make progress in the company, you take the challenge. I became Sales Manager for Bedroom and during my sales management experience had practically every state in the nation at one time to manage.

Next, they wanted me to manage the purchasing department. I made the transition, which gave me tremendous opportunity to learn more about the manufacturing side of our business. In that position I became involved in the procurement of everything that Broyhill used. I communicated with our suppliers and communicated with the plant management. A person in that capacity couldn't help but absorb something about every facet of our company.

Sometime later I was summoned again. That time they wanted me to become Chief Operating Officer of the company. I accepted that responsibility and subsequently moved up with Broyhill Furniture as Chief Executive Officer, and finally as President and CEO, a position I held for six years.

It was my good fortune to have been associated with Paul Broyhill and the Broyhill family. Through the years I absorbed things that he taught me about running and managing a business profitably. My tenure as President and CEO was during a period that was fantastic for business across America, a golden age of furniture manufacturing.

T.V. Promotions Bring Broyhill Into America's Homes

What happens to a TV game show winner after the announcer offers congratulations, the studio lights go down, and the cameras are switched off? For a growing list of persons, the original excitement of winning prizes on a TV game show is being followed by the delivery to their home of a room full of Broyhill furniture. The chain of events which brings about that happy ending begins in a New York consulting agency and at Broyhill's main office in Lenoir.

Broyhill's involvement in TV began in 1957, as the first furniture manufacturer to participate on network game shows, and has been producing publicity, exposure, and excitement in ever increasing quantities. In 1981, more than 240 persons won Broyhill furniture on 11 different game shows and the number of winners continues to grow. Even though we have been on game show programs for almost a quarter of a century, we did not have a North Carolina winner until July 1980. Since then we have had three North Carolina winners.

The promotional process which brings Broyhill furniture to the TV programs, and subsequently to many homes, begins when the Edward E. Finch and Company, our merchandising consultants, contacts Broyhill's Advertising Department and announces the availability of air time on an upcoming show. After considering the opportunity and making the initial commitment to contribute merchandise, the furniture is carefully selected. When selecting the furniture, many factors must be considered including popularity and future availability of each fabric, frame, or case goods piece. It is important to present the best possible image when we appear on national TV. Careful selection of merchandise will insure that the viewing public sees the best that we have to offer.

After selecting the merchandise and receiving directions from Edward E. Finch and Company, the furniture is sent to the TV studio. At the present time, most of the TV game shows which feature our furniture are filmed in Los Angeles, California. As a result, merchandise which is to be advertised on a show is sent to a Broyhill warehouse in Los Angeles where it is uncrated and deluxed before being delivered to the TV studios for taping.

After a TV contestant wins a prize of Broyhill furniture a chain of events occur. First, Edward E. Finch and Company is notified by the show's producer of the winner's name and address and first date to be aired. Edward E. Finch and Company in turn sends this information to Broyhill's Lynda Melton, in the Advertising Department. She receives the notification and proceeds to write up the order which is acknowledged and then Ann Hatton in Traffic coordinates the shipment. Generally a loyal Broyhill dealer is selected nearest to the winner's home for shipping destination. The dealer uncartons, inspects, and makes any and all adjustments and repairs. Following this step, the furniture is delivered to the winner's home.

Our first North Carolina winner was Cindy Hicks of Roxboro, N.C., who won merchandise on the daytime Price Is Right show. With her is Norman Chambers, our Bedroom Division salesman for eastern North Carolina.

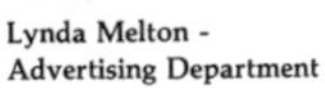

Lynda Melton - Advertising Department

Ann Hatton - Traffic Department

Ms. Hicks won this Chatsworth II bedroom group. A Broyhill dealer in her area delivered the merchandise to her home.

Winning Broyhill furniture brings enjoyment to the individual and nationwide recognition of the Broyhill name and the company's products. Of all the shows involved, the Price Is Right daytime, Hollywood Squares nightime and Gambit are currently the most fruitful, providing the largest number of winners and most exposure for Broyhill's products. Game show promotions are an integral part of the Broyhill promotional plan—a concentrated effort to make Broyhill a household word for quality, reliability and value.

AN EXCERPT FROM *PEOPLE TODAY AT BROYHILL* DESCRIBING BROYHILL'S TELEVISION PROMOTIONS

We achieved record sales in excess of $700 million, the greatest percentage of profits in the history of the company. I attribute a great amount of my success to the training and mentoring that I received from Paul Broyhill.

Before I retired, Broyhill was the largest manufacturer in terms of dollars-shipped of any single furniture brand *in the world*. Broyhill had grown from practically nothing in the early days to become the largest producer of furniture under one brand.

Some of the things Paul pioneered were four-color advertising, shelter magazine ads, TV spots, newspaper ads, and radio spots. Broyhill partnered with customers so that as the customer advertised his store, he also advertised the Broyhill brand. That's what grew our company. It *is* the best-known brand in the world. I've tested it many times by asking people at random what brand of furniture came immediately to mind.

Paul didn't just grow a company, he grew people. I'm proof that his methods worked. They worked for me, and for many others like me.

PAUL, KATHRYN KINCAID, LAUCH FAIRCLOTH AND BRENT KINCAID

32

Harold Lawing

Information Technology, Sales Manager, Division Manager

MY EMPLOYMENT WITH Broyhill began in April of 1961. Upon arrival for my first interview I introduced myself to Myrtle Miller, the receptionist, and told her of my appointment with Mr. Broyhill. She replied, "Which one?" The only name I knew was Ed Broyhill.

After a nice conversation with Mr. J. E., he turned me over to his son-in-law Bill Stevens. Paul also interviewed me on that visit. During my interview with Jim Broyhill, he brought in Clive Laney, Brent Kincaid, and Al Wilson to talk. I later received a phone call from Jim Broyhill asking me to meet with Beef Johnson at a Duke University motel for Beef to administer some tests to me. One was an aptitude test for programming computers.

I vividly remember my first golf game with Mr. J. E. Before the game, some of the guys instructed me to give Mr. J. E. the short putts. On the first hole I picked up his ball, giving him his putt, and tossed it to him. He dropped the ball and very quickly said to me, "Harold, I like to play golf, but I do not play catch ball." From then on, I handed him the ball instead of tossing it.

When I was employed, Mr. J. E. was still active in a limited way. Paul, Jim, and Bill Stevens were transitioning into the leadership of the company at that time. That was a period of time when Paul showed his leadership by expanding the company, which became a giant in the furniture industry. He built a large dining room plant in

Rutherfordton and then developed the huge Broyhill Complex that consisted of a large bedroom plant, a plastics plant, the central warehouse, a particleboard plant, central lumberyard, and dry kilns.

Broyhill was always on the cutting edge of computerization. We started with a computer from the Punch Card Company, which later became known as IBM. We bought one of the first IBM computers for our size business. From that beginning and as new technologies developed, we made countless updates to the system so that production would be as efficient as possible. The Anthon Company in Germany created a computer specifically for Broyhill's particleboard plant. The purpose of that computer was to operate the saw, successfully gaining a higher yield in the cutting operation.

As Paul moved me up the corporate ladder, the company offered numerous training opportunities and new challenges. When Paul made me a sales manager in the dining room division alongside John Kastan and Worth Osleger in 1974, my first project in the new position was to design a computer program for scheduling production of dining room furniture. In 1977 he promoted me to vice president of the Occasional division, which was the smallest of the four divisions, but was becoming the fastest growing division in the company. He didn't just turn me loose, though. Rather, Paul simply told me that I was to discuss with him any major decisions that needed to be made, and we then made them together. He accepted responsibility for the outcome. He urged me to search out the knowledge of others, which was in abundance within our company.

In 1980 Paul again promoted me to vice president of the dining room division. That year Broyhill was the largest producer of dining room furniture in the world, in the range of $80 million a year.

Also in 1980 Interco bought Broyhill. Interco realized just how important Paul was in the successful operation of the company, so they made an agreement for him to stay on for five years.

Paul started turning over the leadership role of the company to Gene Gunter in 1984. Gene started making changes in management right away, including demotions of several key people. That really was the beginning of many other changes that occurred during the next several years. Interestingly, when I began my career at Broyhill, Paul

BROYHILL UPGRADES PLANTS AND EQUIPMENT

The New 4341 Computer System

— It's Creating a Revolution in the Way We Handle Information at Broyhill. —

She arrived in March and is already taking on jobs that her predecessor could not even touch. She's Data Processing's new I.B.M. 4341 computer system and she promises to revolutionize the method in which we handle information at Broyhill.

Our old system, the I.B.M. model 360, was acquired in 1969 and has served us well operating 24 hours a day, five days a week, for 12 consecutive years. As the company grew, however, the total amount of information which we handled on a day to day basis also grew. We finally reached the point that the 360 and its system were too small to readily handle the amount of data which we processed on each day. The need for a system with a larger memory and a capacity for improved data handling prompted the acquisition of this new, vastly improved system.

The new system with its four meg storage capacity (10 times larger than the old system's), faster operating times, and remote terminal capability, is already affecting our daily operations. For the first time, designated operators within each plant are able to "punch in" or "talk to" the computer through their plant's CRTs or "remote terminal and printer" and receive information from the central memory. Remote terminals can now provide information to each plant on such matters as inventory, production tags and shipping labels. The categories and amount of information which are available to each plant terminal will certainly increase in the months and years to come as the need for that data increases.

Data processing and information handling are becoming an ever more important part of our daily operations at Broyhill. This new 4341 system should make that task easier for the Data Processing Department and for each plant which works on a day to day basis to produce Broyhill furniture.

The Heart Of The New System

This is a view of the main components of our new 4341 system. Missing from the photograph are the 3273 CRT controller and the 3705 CRT controller.

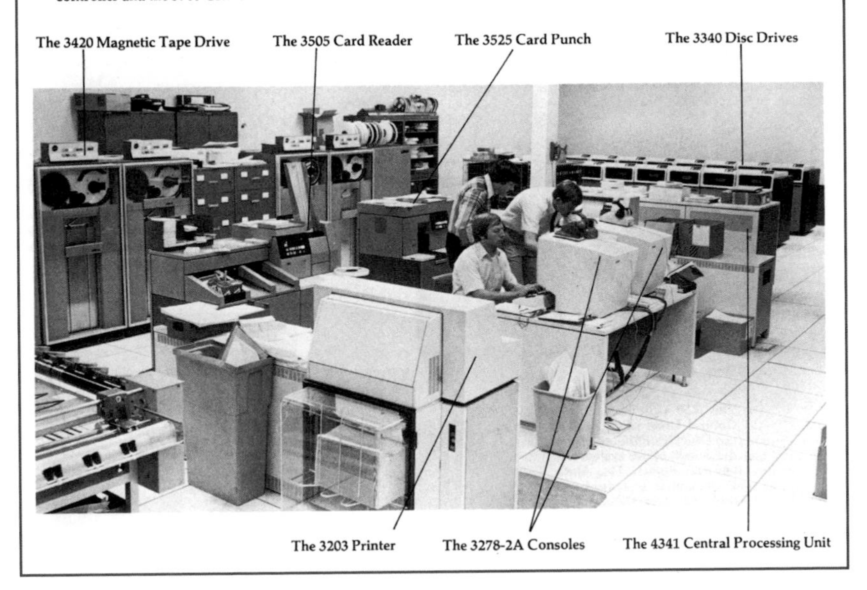

THE NEW COMPUTER SYSTEM, AN EXCERPT FROM *PEOPLE TODAY AT BROYHILL*

was just beginning to take over the reins, and we ended our careers on the same day in 1985.

Paul possessed many wonderful skills in his leadership role. He was a great listener. He would talk to several people about a given subject matter, and then he would take that input with his own knowledge and make decisions. He recognized just how important training was. The emphasis on training his employees enabled him to promote from within the ranks. By that type of management he was able to surround himself with qualified, dedicated, and loyal employees.

My employment at Broyhill for 25 years was exciting and challenging. I appreciated all the opportunities that Paul gave me during my career.

HAROLD AND JOYCE LAWING

Larry Freiman

National Sales Manager and Key Account Manager

MY BACKGROUND IS in furniture: my father was a furniture retail salesperson at one of New York's largest furniture stores, Ludwig Bauman. I attended NYU and graduated in Business and Finance. After graduation, I found a Broyhill Furniture ad in *New York Times* that read: "IF you are ambitious and you want to get ahead in the furniture business . . ."

Broyhill was the only company in the furniture business, and maybe one of the few companies around, that would hire a salesman who had no experience selling the product. You didn't need to know a dresser from a chest. Broyhill had a training program that was the envy of the furniture industry. Paul Broyhill knew that other companies were always waiting to pick up salesmen that Broyhill had trained, but it didn't make any difference to Paul; he felt that it was for the good of the company and the whole industry for Broyhill to train people the way they should be trained. They started us out going to the factory, watching the furniture being made, going into the finishing room and the other departments, and learning all about production. At that time, it was an eight-week program.

At the Chicago market, I walked into the sales meeting on New Year's Day and when the sales meeting was done, they handed me the price book and they said, "You go around and study everything, and when too many customers come in for one salesmen to handle, you take them around while he finishes up." That was a great learning experience. I would explain to the customer, "Look, I'm just starting and I need some forbearance."

At my first High Point market when I went down to breakfast, Paul Broyhill was there and invited me to join him. That was really the first time that I had spent any amount of time with Paul. I think that morning established the relationship that lasted my entire career. At that breakfast, a lot of the things about Paul's character came out, quite a few wonderful characteristics that I later saw play out during my career at Broyhill. With Paul, his word was his bond. If he said something, he followed through.

Paul Broyhill had vision. There was a time when fabric prints were out. Prints were either in or out. For years they were terrific, big sellers, and then they would die, and they'd be out until the trend turned again. During one of the "out" periods, Paul and I were in a famous high-end furniture store in the city. I can picture us standing on the showroom floor and Paul looking at new prints on the furniture. Paul took out his Minox spy camera and took pictures of anything that caught his eye.

"We have to get back into prints," he said.

We went back to the factory and got hold of Jim McCall, the vice president of Upholstery. Paul showed him the pictures and said, "I want to put prints back in the fabric swatches" (we were not showing any prints). Of course Paul was right; prints came back strong and we were right in there.

Another episode was when Montezuma, the Spanish look, was the big thing in furniture. Most of the carvings then were made of plastic. We were making money hand over fist with plastic; we just couldn't make it fast enough.

Paul realized that plastic was beginning to die, that it was going out, that all that plastic stuff was over. The vice president of Dining Room, Bill Zoller, said, "But we are making money on it!" Of course we were, because plastic didn't cost that much. Bill didn't want to stop making it, but Paul made the decision to move out of it. That decision gave us a jump on our competitors.

Product Innovation —

A Key To Successful Marketing

Broyhill products are shown at major markets four times per year — twice per year in Lenoir and twice per year in regional markets located in Atlanta, Dallas, and San Francisco. At the last market, our products were shown to a large number of customers, producing excitement and dealer orders. A few of the newest introductions are shown on the following pages.

Bedroom Division

This 4205 "Criterion" suite is one of our successful Bedroom introductions. Its face is actually a basket pattern, woven with genuine sliced rattan made in the Far East. The look is casual and natural, easy to live with, easy to decorate with and light hearted — clearly class!

Dining Room Division

Broyhill's 7100 "Brittany Province" collection captures the warmth, charm and robust nature of the old Brittany Provinces of northwestern France. Featuring pine solids and veneers with a weathered aged look and compatable hardware, "Brittany Province" captures the hand painted look — a truly authentic adaptation of the painting on an old French blanket chest.

PRODUCT INNOVATION, AN EXCERPT FROM *PEOPLE TODAY AT BROYHILL*

The company built an enormous furniture factory in Taylorsville to make occasional chairs. It was a tough business to be in, and Paul realized that it was not going to work out. So, he said, "I know what I'm going to do; I'll make Early American sofas and matching chairs there," and that is just what he did. We made lots and lots of money at Taylorsville. In later years they shipped about a million dollars of product a week from that plant. That started out as a chair plant, and just like that, he changed it.

Paul had the vision to build the Broyhill complex. Talk about betting the farm on that deal! It was a real gamble. Nobody at that time would have thought of doing that, but it worked out great.

Though Paul had vision, he also realized when he had made a mistake. In fact, he once told me, "Some of the mistakes I've made, if I had not owned the company, I would have been fired."

When Paul and J. E. ran the company and things got tough, the salesmen received letters reminding them that they were responsible for the employees, their families, and everyone—the responsibility to keep people working. There were contests that salesmen could win, and during tough times we were given incentives for meeting our quotas. I remember we had a special promotion on a particular French suite. We salesmen got quadruple points toward our quotas for selling it.

If we made our quotas, we could go on trips. Mr. J. E. had the best times on those trips. He enjoyed the beach in Acapulco, socializing with the wives. I remember going to Mexico City and not being able to get back to the Chicago market because of a snowstorm. I had to lay over in Mexico. There were trips to Florida, and even one to Havana.

At Broyhill we all had a working family relationship. At the year-end meetings, basically the State of the Company address, when Mr. J. E. would come in, Paul would direct everyone to stand to his or her feet. I was always impressed by how Paul treated his father. I was invited to small dinner parties for Mr. J. E.'s birthday. For his birthday, he gave presents—Cross pens. I still have mine. There were no presents for Mr. J. E., but there were gifts for the attendees.

Along with a working family attitude, the Broyhills provided opportunity. You could work your way up from the mailroom or anywhere. Because of such an attitude company loyalty was so built into me that even when the Broyhill family no longer owned the business, I still felt I belonged to Broyhill.

LARRY FREIMAN WITH M. SHAIVITZ BUYERS

Keith Suddreth

Engineering, Plant Manager, Production Manager

AS A COMPANY Broyhill Industries welcomed innovation. They were not afraid to take calculated risks. That trait combined with a respect and appreciation for their employees was their secret to success.

I started working at Lenoir Furniture Corporation in the summer of 1956, right after high school. Not only did my dad, Atwell Suddreth, work there in maintenance and engineering, but I had uncles working there too. Dad came right off a submarine and hooked up with the company when he got out of the military. Because of his training, he was the best boiler man in the area. He could fix anything.

Since I didn't have a car, I got a job over at Corporation where I could ride with my dad. I went to work for $1.00 an hour, the starting rate. After I had worked at Broyhill for a year or so doing different jobs in different plants, I was working at the veneer plant when I talked to Henry Medlock, a young division superintendent, about ideas for automation. As a result of our conversations, I made some crude drawings to illustrate my suggestions. At that time we relied entirely on manual labor: we rolled logs with a can hook and peeled logs with a spud.

One morning I was working on the yard, cutting and sawing logs. It was hot, and I had my shirt off. I was just a kid, about 20 years old with no credentials other than enthusiasm. Henry came out and said, "Get your damn shirt on, boy. We're going to the main office. Bring your drawings."

In Mr. J.E.'s office Henry said, "He's Atwell's boy." He turned to me, "Show Mr. Broyhill what we're thinking about." We laid the drawings of a log conveyor on the desk. Mr. Broyhill looked them over and gave us the approval to proceed. That first project cost about $41,000.

Encouraged by Mr. Broyhill's interest, we decided that we might even be able to get a debarker. There were some new styles of debarkers called Rosserhead; the design came from Sweden. Oh, it was state-of-the-art. I never will forget it. By using a machine like that, productivity increased. That was the start of my interest in production engineering.

Mr. Broyhill and Paul hired a consultant, Curt Joa, to kindle ideas to increase factory output. He suggested that we start a research department. My dad and Ray Walker, the first engineer the Broyhills had hired, created Research to start building specialized machinery. After Ray Walker, Jack Buss headed the Research team and asked me to join. When Jack left to start his own engineering business, Bill Sale took his place. Bill ran a successful engineering department and charged me with automating the veneer mill. I put state-of-the-art equipment in United Veneer, National Veneer, and Lenoir Veneer.

I remember talking to Green Suddreth who was a superintendent at the veneer plant. He said one day, "Keith, why do you continue to spend so much money?"

"Look how much we're saving you, Green," I quickly answered as I started to rattle off what we were saving.

He looked at me seriously and replied, "Well, we can't afford for you to save us any more money!"

Many of my extended family members already working in the Broyhill plants became managers: plant managers, department managers, and assistant department managers. I became a plant manager.

Most everybody remembers Paul Broyhill as quite a pleasant guy. As a plant manager, I learned one time, however, that if you get a little product quality problem, all hell would break loose. When I was the plant manager at the Marion plant, Z. O. Riggs was the chief finishing coordinator for our lacquer. Because of a customer complaint, we realized that the packaging tissue was sticking to the tops of the bedposts. We had shipped the product everywhere very quickly, appar-

Lumber Savings Continue To Increase

A tree must undergo a great many changes as it leaves the forest and becomes part of a piece of furniture. The lumber that is sawn from that tree must pass through many manufacturing steps before it can become a drawer front, table top, or other furniture part. Since each machining step results in a loss of wood, and lumber continues to increase in price, we are becoming increasingly careful throughout our plants to save every amount possible . . . Considering the huge amount of lumber which we use at Broyhill, even a small increase in lumber yield can mean a large savings in production costs over a year's time.

One of the newest innovations in lumber savings is brought about by the use of abrasive planners. They plane the lumber as it enters the rough mill enabling the cut-off saw operators to increase their operating efficiencies.

Our rip saw operators, who also cut out wood defects, are accomplishing their tasks with a minimum of waste. That requires skill and good judgement.

As they saw lumber into shorter pieces, our cut-off saw operators are being extra careful to cut out wood defects while saving the most wood possible from each piece of lumber.

After the lumber has been planed, it is sent through the edging saws. These saws smooth the edges of each piece of stock while removing the least possible amount of wood. The careful use of edging saws can save up to 5% of an average board.

LUMBER HANDLING, AN EXCERPT FROM *PEOPLE TODAY AT BROYHILL*

20-30 YEARS—Left to right are Paul Broyhill, who made the award presentations; Betty Carter, 30-year award winner; Keith Sherrill, George Boutwell, Virginia Craig and Iris Laney, 25-year award winners; and Atwell Suddreth and Warren Ford, 20-year award winners. Carl Clarke and Malta Hamby, 30-year award winners, are not shown.

CENTURIES OF SERVICE

Over five centuries!

That's what you get when you total up the years of service of those who were honored at the office Christmas party.

Thirty-nine employees, whose combined length of service is 510 years, received the awards from Paul Broyhill.

Watches and pins were presented to Warren Ford and Atwell Suddreth, both of whom have reached the 20-year milestone. All other award winners received pins.

J. E. Broyhill greeted the guests upon their arrival and Bill Stevens served as master of ceremonies.

Held at Lenoir Country Club, the annual event was attended by over 400 persons.

15 YEARS—Shown with Paul Broyhill are, left to right, Joe Pritchard, Tommie Keyes and Louis Land. The other 15-year award winners were Marie Hartley, Ann McMillan and Bill Zoller.

10 YEARS—Left to right are Keith Suddreth, Lee Pritchard, Nancy Penley, Susie Grist, Betty Jenkins, Barbara Love, Mary Norris, Jackie Norris, Leona Bryant and Paul Broyhill. The other 10-year award winners were Charles Bush, Worth Hamilton, Venoy Pearson, Dick Stewart and Pat Taylor.

5 YEARS—Left to right are George Reese, Ralph Laney, Diane Holman, Jean Summerlin, Paul Broyhill, Pat Goforth, Marie Crotts and Harold Lawing. Other recipients were Phyllis Andrews, Ray Bubien and Barbara Cline.

KEITH SUDDRETH AFTER 10 YEARS OF SERVICE WITH OTHER HONOREES

ently before the lacquer was dry, so we had a week or two of product that had to be reworked.

Paul came up to the factory. Before then he had always been so cordial. He would put his arm around me and push and shove me in fun. Boy, I tell you, on that occasion he was so stern, it was like he was at a funeral. I told my wife, "I saw a side of Paul Broyhill that I don't ever want to see again." I never forgot that Paul had a lot of responsibility.

On one of Paul's rounds through the Pacemaker factory, which was new and struggling, Raymond Saunders, a division manager, spoke to him about the need to return to a conventional finishing room. We had installed a new, innovative flat finishing system that was not working well. The new project would cost around $500,000. Within a week, Paul called a meeting. He got everyone on board and put in a conventional finishing room where we could glaze and we could spray lacquer. That prepared the plant for anything that came its way.

After I left Marion and moved to Pacemaker, a major challenge came during the winter of 1976. There was an unbelievable fire at the Marion plant where they made New Bedford, our hottest selling product. New Bedford represented Broyhill. It was an industry leader.

We didn't know what we were going to do because the product line was 20 weeks or more oversold. The fire destroyed the factory; $6 million worth of inventory lost in a day. That was on Thursday. Friday, what little was left was still burning. Saturday morning Paul called the division corporate guys, the plant manager, and the engineers to the Holiday Inn. He told us that we would move the product line to Pacemaker, and that not a single Marion employee would be laid off. They would be absorbed into the other plants until Marion could be rebuilt.

Moving the product from Marion to Pacemaker was a challenge. We already had a full staff at Pacemaker, so we started a second shift. Six days after the fire I remember going down to Pacemaker and seeing a banner that read "Welcome Marion to Pacemaker." We had about 300 employees at Marion. About 150 of those came to the second shift at Pacemaker and started the first cutting just one week after the fire.

They ran New Bedford at Pacemaker for years and then created a similar second-generation product called Fontana. Between those

Broyhill Upgrades Plants And Equipment

"One of our greatest strengths at Broyhill is our constant modernization of plants and equipment. This enables us to attain greater efficiencies and lower costs. This creates more security for all of our employees."

New Wall Systems Plant Located At The Complex

Located deep inside the complex, Broyhill's new Wall Systems Plant is in full operation, manufacturing a wide range of wall system components. Most of the new plant is separated from the surrounding Pacemaker Plant by walls, doors and aisles. A few Wall Systems operations, however, such as panel sizing, edge banding and printing, are carried out in the surrounding Pacemaker Plant.

The new plant's manager is Raymond Saunders, the former production manager at Pacemaker. His Wall Systems Plant offices are located to the left of the Pacemaker offices, at the location of the former Panel Plant offices.

The new Wall Systems Plant has several innovations, most noticeably, a special finish line floor conveyor. This conveyor is designed to carry each piece of furniture through each spray booth two times. On one pass, the spray operator applies one finishing material. On the second pass a second finish material is applied. The cases come through the spray booths in a staggered order so that the first case is sprayed with one material and the second case is sprayed with a second type of material.

With many dedicated employees, modern equipment, and a highly efficient plant design, the new Wall Systems Plant is Broyhill's answer to the growing demand for our wall system merchandise.

Let's look at some of the people and processes which are making this new plant so successful.

As the stock enters the Wall Systems Plant, it undergoes numerous machining operations such as sizing, dadoing, shaping and grooving. This ultra-modern Torwegge tenoner is able to perform a multitude of these operations at a dizzying pace. Many panels are also grain engraved through a multi-step process that involves sanding, filling, base coating, grain engraving, and a top lacquer coating.

After the major machining and grain engraving steps have been completed the stock (above) is ready for assembly. First the ends, shelves and tops, the basic components, are put together, clamped and tightly fastened. After being turned upside down the cases are then "based out" (right). In this step, brace blocks, leveling blocks and skids are applied.

THE FLEXIBILITY OF PACEMAKER AND THE COMPLEX AS HIGHLIGHTED IN AN EXCERPT FROM *PEOPLE TODAY AT BROYHILL*

two suites—like a Ford and a Chevrolet—those were the best two products ever made. Paul Broyhill took a risk to invest in that finishing room at Pacemaker, a decision made less than a year before the Marion fire. Because of it, we were prepared from a manufacturing standpoint for that emergency.

Paul rewarded employees who displayed discipline, hard work, and loyalty. He was all about employee morale, all about the team. I once was the recipient of a special check after a particularly hard personal time, not a little check, either. I said to my direct boss, "I can't believe this has happened." And he said, "Well, there may have been fifteen or twenty of those across the company today."

If you're in the Lenoir area, you can go to Wal-Mart or some other public place and you will probably see someone wearing a Broyhill jacket. If an employee worked every single day for a year, despite the hardships, he would receive a jacket. We gave away thousands of those jackets.

For sales force awards Paul gave blue blazers with the pinwheel lapel logo, which the salesmen wore with pride to the market. Those people who earned that distinction became part of a sales council for that year.

Employee length-of-service awards were given in five year increments. At the twentieth year it was a watch. Boy! When somebody got the watch, they had "arrived." Award ceremonies were given much attention and lots of pictures of recipients were taken with Paul and other executives.

Paul introduced the Broyhill corporate flag. If you were leading the division in a factory, you would get to fly the flag. I remember how zealous we were to get to fly the Broyhill flag. We got so competitive that we would actually go to another factory and steal it. The Broyhill flag flew beside the US flag.

There were a lot of people involved in the Broyhill corporate family; there was a lot of organization; there was a lot of pride. From Mr. J.E. and Paul, I learned the importance of a personal touch. All through my working years I made a point at least once a week to go by an individual and touch him on the shoulder. After being around for fifty years, I saw the company's history as the history of its people, not just us managers; it was about everyone who worked at Broyhill.

35

Tom Broyhill

Customer Service, Purchasing, Sales Manager, Gallery Program Manager, Key Account Manager, Grandson of Tom Broyhill

OVER THE YEARS that I was a part of the Broyhill team, I was involved in numerous aspects of the business from data processing and customer service, to purchasing, sales management, and national/international account sales.

After Paul left the company, I also left the company and worked for him and Hunt at Custom Sofa Gallery. When the Custom Sofa venture didn't work out, Brent Kincaid, then the CEO at Broyhill Furniture, brought me back as National Accounts Vice President. I handled Sears, J. C. Penney, and Haverty's. I handled those accounts for approximately six years and then went into international sales, contract sales, and the gallery program, where I ended my career in 2009. Representing Broyhill, I attended gallery openings all over the world.

During Paul's regime I participated in the ongoing training program for our sales representatives to develop professional sales skills. We sent the new reps into the factories to learn about production, then into the credit department, and then into customer service to learn some of the inner workings of the company.

We maintained sales cadres of new trainees consisting of five to seven people. While they waited for a territory to open, they worked in the various departments. At times, the trainees temporarily helped

TOM BROYHILL

out in a territory where a salesman was sick or incapacitated and needed someone to service his accounts. When there was a vacancy, we pulled from the cadre to fill it. We kept a trained sales force of over 300. Because of their unparalleled sales training, they were in great demand in the industry itself. So, our competitors frequently raided us. Although we did lose a few good ones, we also lost some bad ones. The ones we kept were the ones that were both good *and* loyal.

Award trips for those who achieved the sales quotas were significant incentives for our sales team. We went on cruises and on trips to Miami Beach, the Poconos, the Lake of the Ozarks in Missouri, even Mexico and pre-Castro Havana.

One of our management practices was to have quarterly and year-end meetings. Paul involved department management in the regular sales and profit reports and the managers felt part of the direction of the company. The year-end meeting was always on January 1, because we had to gear up for the Chicago market soon after.

The gallery concept was one of Broyhill's most innovative ideas. A gallery was almost a store within a store. Everything in the gallery from the furniture to the wallpaper to the paint was for sale. Quite often the customer would purchase an entire room just as it appeared in the gallery.

We hired the absolute best designers we could find to showcase our product in dealers' stores. Our gallery program grew rapidly from its start in 1982, and not long after, we had 250 operating galleries each with a 6,000 square-foot requirement minimum. The galleries boosted growth of the company.

Our biggest year came in 1984. With 11 gallery designers and the support of the sales force, we opened from scratch 53 galleries during that year. That record still stands. Paul Broyhill handled some of the openings and some we handled together. I recall that we were on the road or in the air 47 weeks out of 52.

PAUL AND TOM AT A GALLERY OPENING WITH KEN FLETCHER

ONE OF THE NUMEROUS GALLERY RIBBON CUTTING CEREMONIES

Accessories were a vital part of a gallery. Lamps, chandeliers, wall art, rugs, plants, and other items helped to create the look of a fully furnished home. We required that the gallery be kept clean and presentable at all times and that the dealer stock back-up furniture and accessories in his warehouse so that he did not have to disturb the display. A disheveled or sparse looking gallery undermined the whole marketing concept. That policy was still in force when I retired.

In the heyday of the gallery program, the early to mid '80s, we had incentive gallery retreats and invited all qualified gallery dealers to attend a resort such as the Doral in Miami or the Greenbriar in West Virginia. Our wives were a great help in entertaining the wives of the dealers.

Broyhill Industries has always taken care of customers. J. E. and Paul befriended their customers and that treatment created loyalty, even in the face of adversity. At the time of the Marion fire, I was National Accounts Sales Manager and had made a sale of 700 suites of New Bedford to Sears Canada in Toronto. Their order was coming down the line and all of it burned in the fire. Management called and asked me to see if I could save the order and satisfy the customer. I called Don Clune, the bedroom buyer at Sears Canada, who asked, "Well, Tom, when do you think you can get it?"

"You'll receive it about six weeks later than you normally would have had it," I told him.

"How are you going to produce it?" he questioned.

"We plan to make it at Pacemaker, and we'll get you your product," I promised. Switching production to the Pacemaker plant was an outstanding feat, but we did it.

We were always big on awarding plaques to dealers for meeting their quotas. We gave out hundreds of them. At the markets Paul spent a lot of time having pictures made with customers receiving their plaques. Oftentimes when I went into a dealer's store, I would see those pictures proudly displayed.

For many years our factory showrooms were located at the main office. We entertained our customers at the Green Park, the Blowing Rock hotel owned by Broyhill. Prior to serving a large buffet dinner, we had a cocktail hour and served jumbo Gulf shrimp as an appetizer in the lounge. We were famous for our Gulf shrimp. We topped off the evening with live music and dancing.

In all those years it was amazing that there was no major wreck or catastrophe by sales or management people coming down the mountain to Lenoir after one of those nights. One of our accounts from Virginia complained that going up and down the mountain to the Green Park Inn bothered his ears. Paul told him he would send his pressurized limo to take him back and forth. The man was impressed and told everybody at the market that he rode up in Paul's pressurized limo. There was no such thing as a pressurized limo, but he never knew it.

At one point Paul Broyhill bought a 70-foot Chris-Craft Roamer, which we used for entertaining customers. That craft really enhanced our relationship with many of them. At pre-markets, we entertained at Paul's house at Hound Ears Club. We charcoaled steaks and made salads. Everybody from Broyhill that attended had some part in preparing the meals.

During Brent Kincaid's presidential tenure, Broyhill experienced the most outstanding growth in the history of the company. We exceeded $700 million in sales. Brent followed the same pattern that had been laid out before him, what he had been trained by the Broyhills to do. In 1995, our best year, we did $53 million with J. C. Penney, $53 million with Haverty, and $32 million with Sears, all accounts that I handled.

A climate change came to the company after Paul Broyhill and Brent Kincaid left. Loyalty changed dramatically. Broyhill was operated in an entirely different manner. It wasn't the same company or the same environment. It was no surprise when some of the old guard began to leave.

When Paul was there, Broyhill was a family-run company. All the people enjoyed the family atmosphere of the business, and even today people say, "Tom, can you talk Paul into buying this company back? Let's do it again!"

An incident I will always remember occurred when I was moved from sales rep in Western North Carolina to Sales Manager of Upholstery. I walked over to Paul's office to say thank you. He looked at me and asked, "Well, what do you think about your new job?"

"I'm scared to death," I replied honestly.

"That's alright," he said without missing a beat. "I'm scared every day."

And that's the way he managed. He faced things head on; he took risks; he challenged the status quo, then he made decisions and moved on. He was a businessman with a conscience who knew that the livelihood of thousands of people depended on him.

I retired from Broyhill in 2009, the last Broyhill to leave the company. Looking back over its history I am amazed at the growth of the company my grandfather, Tom Broyhill, and his brother, J.E., started from a small lumber operation. Paul took the ball he was passed and ran with it, but we all played on the same team with the same goal in mind. With Paul as coach, we played a darn good game.

Epilogue

A LOT OF my memories of things from the past are getting a bit dim. It's hard to believe that I left Broyhill Furniture nearly 25 years ago. Everyone considers me a furniture man, but I've had an entire separate career since that time. Those were great days because I was building and building. I've said that I want the word "Builder" put on

PAUL HUNT BROYHILL

my tombstone. I loved to "build" furniture, factories, balance sheets, and people.

Because I have a lot of wonderful memories of the furniture business, for a long time I found it difficult to give up. Even now, I still think about it occasionally, but with all the factory closings and all the merchandise being made overseas, the industry has changed so much that it no longer holds an appeal to me. I enjoyed building those plants. I enjoyed hiring those people. I enjoyed both designing and selling the furniture. Of course, I enjoyed making the money, which is literally a way of keeping score. I did a great job in our basic business. Every time I got away from the basic business, I didn't do very well. I have a lot of "woulda, coulda, shouldas," but few regrets.

During my furniture career we hired and trained thousands of people, and most of them enjoyed successful careers. We built facilities and an organization that produced more than $700 million in sales in the middle '90s during Brent Kincaid's administration. At that time a national survey found that Broyhill was the most recognized brand name in the furniture industry. We created a profit-sharing program whereby rank and file employees were able to supplement their social security with extra retirement income. We grew a charitable foundation that has contributed to countless worthy causes.

I've had a great life with multiple careers, and I have been truly blessed. I've worked hard, but I credit my success to my supportive family, friends, and coworkers. It's sad to see so many of them passing away.

I heard a sermon by Dr. Ron Patterson, my minister in Naples, Florida. His topic was "The Empty Pew." The story goes that a dear lady wanted to be remembered by something other than an empty pew, so she willed a substantial fund to educate young people of the church. As a young man, Dr. Patterson became a recipient of that lady's education scholarship, so that through him and others, she left a lasting legacy. When I was building the parks in Blowing Rock and Lenoir, Faye made the comment that I might be remembered more for building parks than for building factories. At the time I didn't give her statement much credence, as so much of my life had been spent in building the factories. I never dreamed that they would be shuttered and the people gone. Faye was right. My legacy is probably more related to the many worthwhile causes we have been able to support and to the opportunities we created for so many people.

Recently when I was at the Cleveland Clinic, I was reminded of how far reaching our influence has been. I noticed a large, impressive building housing the Lerner Research Institute. Al Lerner was a successful Cleveland banker who endowed a substantial amount of money for medical research. I gave Al Lerner one of his very first jobs out of college. He went through the Broyhill sales training program at an initial salary of $50 per week.

Since 1983, Willard Scott, veteran weatherman on *The Today Show*, has recognized the birthdays of centenarians. As a promotion, Smucker's features the pictures of those people on the backs of their jelly jars. Karen insists that I live long enough to be recognized by Willard Scott, to be on TV, and to appear on the Smucker's jar. Who knows what may happen in the next 14 years? I may have to write a sequel.

APPENDICES

A ◆ Broyhill Plants

B ◆ Broyhill Furniture Sales and Rentals

C ◆ BMC, Inc. Board of Directors

D ◆ Boats and Planes

E ◆ Accomplishments, Awards, Boards, Scholarships and Endowments

F ◆ Career Fields of Paul Broyhill

Appendix A
Broyhill Plants

Bedroom

Newton (a.k.a. Lenoir Chair #2)
Pacemaker
Marion
Harper

Bedroom and Dining Room

Rutherford
Lenoir Furniture Corporation

Dining Room Chairs

Conover

Occasional and Wall Units

Occasional #1 (a.k.a. Lenoir Chair #4)
Wall Unit Plant
Occasional #2

Upholstery

Whitnel (a.k.a. Lenoir Chair #3)
Whitnel (a.k.a. Lenoir Chair #6)
Taylorsville (a.k.a. Lenoir Chair #5)
Central Fabric

Upholstery Frame

Marion (after the fire)
Summerville

Veneer

National Veneer
Lenoir Veneer
United Veneer

Particleboard Plant

Trucking

Appendix B

Broyhill Furniture Sales and Rentals

Alabama
Birmingham

Florida
Clearwater
St. Petersburg
Tampa
Miami (2)
Ft. Lauderdale
Jacksonville
West Palm Beach

Tennessee
Nashville
Knoxville

Texas
Houston

Georgia
Savannah
Atlanta (2)
Augusta
Athens

Illinois
Chicago (2)

Kentucky
Louisville
Lexington

Ohio
Cleveland
Akron
Toledo

North Carolina
Charlotte
Raleigh

South Carolina
Greenville
Columbia

Virginia
Hampton

Appendix C

Broyhill Executives and Related

BMC, INC. Board Members (past and present)

Broyhill Related

J. E. Broyhill	Founder, Former Chairman and President of Broyhill Furniture Industries
*Paul Broyhill	Former Chairman and President of Broyhill Furniture Industries; Chairman of BMC, Inc.
*James Broyhill	Former United States Congressman and Senator
*Hunt Broyhill	President BMC, Inc. and President of various other enterprises
W. E. Stevens, Jr.	Former Executive Vice President of Broyhill Furniture Industries
*Allene Broyhill Stevens	Daughter of J. E. Broyhill; Sister of Paul and James Broyhill
Willard Gortner	Former Sales Executive with Smith-Barney and husband of Bettie Broyhill Gortner
*Jan Gordon	Daughter of Will and Bettie Broyhill Gortner
Ed Beach	Former Vice President of Finance and Accounting at Broyhill Furniture Industries
Clarence Beach	Former Vice President of Manufacturing at Broyhill Furniture Industries
Clarence Holden	Former Vice President of Purchasing at Broyhill Furniture Industries
*Brent Kincaid	Former Chairman and President of Broyhill Furniture Industries
Gene Gunter	Former Chairman and President of Broyhill Furniture Industries

Non-related Members

Bill Cooper	Former President of Dallas Furniture Market
Larry Crockett	Real Estate Developer
Harry Helzer	Former Chairman of 3-M
Dolph Von Arx	Former President of Planters Life Savers

*Michael Landry	Former President of McKenzie Financial-USA
*Gene Hoots	Founder and Former President of CornerCap Financial
*John Little	Former President of Associated Octel, London
*Robert Fox	Former President of New Dominion Bank
*Don Farmer	President of Don Farmer Seminars
*Glenn Orr	Chairman of The Orr Group Financial Consultants and Former President of Southern National Bank
Ron Sorenson	President of W. H. Reaves and Company

*Designates current members

Appendix D

Boats and Planes

Boats

Kept at Lake James

24' Cuddy Cabin Cruiser
18' Chris Craft Runabout

Kept at Ocean Reef and Hilton Head

70' Chris Craft Roamer
18' Dixie Runabout
24' Sailboat

Kept at Naples

24' Formula
33' Sea Ray Sundowner

Planes and Aircraft Experience

	Single	Twin
Cessna	140	310 *
	150	320 *
	170	340 (3)*
	180	411 *
	172	
	182	
Beech	Bonanza *	Twin Beech E-18S *
		Duke*
Piper	Cub	Cheyenne II *
		Cheyenne II XL *
North American	SNJ Trainer *	
Douglas		DC-3 *
Lear		LR 23 *
Brantley		305 Helicopter *

* Owned Aircraft

Appendix E
Accomplishments, Awards, and Boards

Accomplishments of Paul Broyhill

Bachelor of Science Degree in Commerce—the Universtiy of North Carolina at Chapel Hill, 1948
Member Phi Delta Theta—a social fraternity
Member Beta Gamma Sigma—a business honors fraternity
Member Phi Beta Kappa
Trustee Emeritus Wake Forest University
Trustee Emeritus Gardner-Webb University
Trustee Emeritus Baptist Children's Homes of North Carolina
Past President and Chairman of Broyhill Furniture Industries,
Current Chairman BMC Fund, Inc., Broyhill Investments, Inc., Broyhill Realty, and Broyhill Family Foundation, Inc.,
Served on Boards of Directors of Dallas Market Center, Atlanta Market Center, and High Point Market Center,
Served on Board of Directors of American Furniture Manufacturers Association
Lifetime Deacon First Baptist Church of Lenoir
Pilot's License—Single Engine Land/Sea; Multi Engine Land; Instrument; Glider/Lear Jet
President Furniture Rental Association, 1988–89
Honorary Doctor of Humane Letters from Lenoir Rhyne College, 1995
Honorary Doctor of Humanities from Gardner-Webb University, 2002
Doctor of Letters, *Honoris Causa* from Appalachian State University

Awards of Paul Broyhill

,Johnson Wax Centennial Award , for Leadership, 1988
Association for Private Enterprise Education's Herman Lay Award, 1990
Boy Scouts of America Gold Eagle Award
Honorary Commander of North Carolina Naval Militia, 1992
State of North Carolina Order of the Long Leaf Pine, 1992
American Furniture Manufacturer's Distinguished Service Award, 1996
North Carolina Baptist Philantropist of the Year, 1996
Caldwell County Chamber of Commerce L. A. Dysart Award—for Community Service, 1997
Caldwell County Chamber of Commerce Visionary Leadership Award, 2002

Caldwell County Medallion of Honor, 2003
American Furniture Hall of Fame, 2004
North Carolina Citizens for Business and Industry Hall of Fame, 2004
Lenoir-Rhyne College Business Council Business Leader of the Year, 2005
Masonic Veteran's Master Mason Award (60-Year Service), 2009
Treaty of Paris Award from the United States Department of State Diplomatic Reception Rooms
Numerous Citations, Commendations, and Namings

Awards and Recognitions of Faye Arnold Broyhill

Miss North Carolina, 1955
Miss America 3rd Runner Up, 1956
Faye A. Broyhill Building on the campus of Caldwell Community College and Technical Institute
Faye Arnold Broyhill Memorial Highway

Boards

North Carolina School of Science and Math
Baptist Children's Homes
Housing Task Fordce of Caldwell County
Caldwell County Retirement Alliance
Caldwell County Economic Development Commission
Co-Chair North Carolina Governor's Mansion Renovation Committee
Appalachian State University Board of Trustees—First Female Chairwoman
Meredith College Board of Trustees
J. E. Broyhill Civic Center Advisory Council

Scholarships and Endowments

Faye A. Broyhill Talent Award for North Carolina Miss America Pageant
Faye A. Broyhill Leading With Integrity Endowment at Meredith College
Faye Arnold Broyhill Education Scholarship through the Wig Bank of Caldwell County
Faye Broyhill Brain Tumor Center of Excellence Endowment at Wake Forest University Baptist Hospital

Appendix F

Career Fields of Paul Broyhill

Furniture Manufacturing

Bedroom
Dining Room
Upholstery
Occasional

Styles
Contemporary
Traditional English
Traditional French
Traditional Spanish
American Colonial
Early American

Furniture Retail

Retail Stores
Rental Stores

Pre-fabricated Homes Manufacturing

Real Estate

Raw Land
Timber
Christmas Trees
Ornamental Trees
Residential Development
Commercial Development
Industrial Development Lessee/Lessor

Plastics

Molding/Extrusion/Film

Finance

Stocks
Bonds
Options
Leases

Philanthropy